# A Modern Migration Theory

**Comparative Political Economy**
Series Editor: Erik Jones

A major new series exploring contemporary issues in comparative political economy. Pluralistic in approach, the books offer original, theoretically informed analyses of the interaction between politics and economics, and explore the implications for policy at the regional, national and supranational levels.

*Published*

*Central Bank Independence and the Future of the Euro*
Panicos Demetriades

*Europe and Northern Ireland's Future*
Mary C. Murphy

*A Modern Migration Theory*
Peo Hansen

*The New Politics of Trade*
Alasdair R. Young

*The Political Economy of Housing Financialization*
Gregory W. Fuller

*Populocracy*
Catherine Fieschi

*Whatever It Takes*
George Papaconstantinou

# A Modern Migration Theory

An Alternative Economic Approach to
Failed EU Policy

Peo Hansen

**agenda**
publishing

To Hakeem and Mira

First published in 2021 by Agenda Publishing

Agenda Publishing Limited
The Core
Bath Lane
Newcastle Helix
Newcastle upon Tyne
NE4 5TF
www.agendapub.com

ISBN 978-1-78821-054-6 (hardcover)
ISBN 978-1-78821-055-3 (paperback)

**British Library Cataloguing-in-Publication Data**
A catalogue record for this book is available from the British Library

Typeset by Newgen Publishing UK
Printed and bound in the UK by TJ Books

There is no recorded case of a country which suffered by the assimilation of a refugee immigrant population.

John Hope Simpson, *The Refugee Question* (1939)


The illusion of "sound finance" is perhaps the most dangerous illusions of the Right Wing, for it is not only influential in high places but it also forms part of the thinking of the ordinary man. It arises because of a failure to understand the fundamental difference between private and public finance. The failure is understandable, particularly in view of the fact that professional economists themselves have only recently come to appreciate the distinction. Nevertheless, one of the principal tasks of education in citizenship should be to increase human understanding in this regard. The untrained mind works principally by analogy, and though this method is useful in many cases it is dangerous, and nowhere more dangerous than in thinking about economic and monetary matters.

Kenneth E. Boulding, *The Economics of Peace* (1946)

# Contents

*Preface and acknowledgements*                                                 ix
*Foreword by Erik Jones*                                                        xv

1   Migration: the "mother of all problems"                                      1

2   The fiscal impact of migration                                              23

3   A modern migration theory                                                   49

4   Demography, security and the shifting conjunctures of the
    European Union's external labour migration policy                          73

5   Labour migration in a sound finance policy logic                           95

6   Why EU asylum policy cannot afford to pay
    demographic dividends                                                      115

7   "We need these people": refugee spending, fiscal impact
    and refugees' *real* bearing on Sweden's society and economy              139

8   Conclusion                                                                 171

    *Bibliography*                                                            201
    *Index*                                                                   233

# Preface and acknowledgements

Over a few days this past summer, as I was putting the finishing touches to this book, my daughter developed a pain in her left foot after having twisted her ankle. As the pain persisted we went to see a doctor. In the waiting room at the local clinic I took note of the fact that seven of the ten doctors in the corridor had foreign names, three of which were Muslim. I have seen doctors from both Iraq and Romania at this clinic, which was no coincidence given that Iraqi and Romanian doctors make up two of the largest groups within the cohort of foreign-born doctors in Sweden. More than 30 per cent of all doctors in Sweden are born abroad, and in the case of Iraqi doctors most of them arrived as refugees in the noughties. My daughter was examined by a doctor from Germany – another major sending country – who swiftly referred her to the main hospital for an X-ray.

We took a taxi to the hospital, and here as well the person servicing us was foreign-born, maybe from Syria. Around a half of Sweden's taxi drivers are foreign-born and the great majority have come as refugees. The driver dropped us off at the emergency room entrance, and from there we had to ask for directions to the X-ray department. We were helped by a doctor and nurse who came walking our way. Judging from their ID badges it seemed as if the doctor was from an African country and the nurse from a Middle Eastern country. In all likelihood, the nurse who took care of my daughter in the X-ray department was also from a country in the Middle East.

Luckily, the X-ray indicated no fracture (a couple of days later the pain was gone), and so we headed for the bus stop to go home. There was a bus sitting at the kerb, but the driver told us that it would take a while before it would depart. With my daughter in some pain we decided to take a taxi again. This time our driver might have been from Somalia; the same probably applied to the bus driver. Over a half of those working as bus and tram drivers in Sweden are born in another country, and, needless to say, almost all of them have come as refugees. I think I have made my point. But I should mention too that we also passed by a team of cleaners in the hospital. The pattern repeated itself, and no coincidence in this case either. Sixty per cent of the cleaners in Sweden are foreign-born, and, yes, the overwhelming majority have refugee background. They clean Sweden for very low pay, and they continued to fulfil this absolutely essential public function during the Covid-19 pandemic.

My daughter and I had an excursion into the Swedish reality. In this reality people who have come as refugees carry out absolutely vital work without which the Swedish society and economy would cease to function. The dry statistics I was going over for this book as we left for the local clinic came to life. I was already well aware of this reality, and I am not alone; the numbers are out there for everybody to see. Yet this reality persistently fails to register in national and European debates on asylum and migration. The seriousness of this problem cannot be overemphasized, and it is one of the main reasons why I have written this book.

Instead of broadcasting the real benefits that refugees and labour migrants bring to EU countries and, from there, enact policy to improve migrants' often precarious situation, the political establishment, which now includes the extreme right, has done the opposite. It has made sure to soak and trap the European Union in a toxic debate over an alleged plethora of negative effects of migration – although "highly skilled" migration is sometimes spared. A more or less open blaming of non-white migrants for all sorts of societal ills has become ordinary fare, and it speaks to the increasing mainstreaming of the extreme right's position. This is a reality of the European Union, in which mainstream politicians throw cake parties to celebrate the passing of punitive asylum laws; warn about Muslim population replacement; openly state "We're a Judeo-Christian country … of white race" when also asserting that "I don't feel like seeing France becoming Muslim"; and smile contentedly when addressing the press with these words: "Of all things on my 69th birthday – and I didn't order this – 69 people were sent back to Afghanistan" (*New York Times* 2017; Reuters 2015a; BBC 2018).

Fortunately, there are still voices, movements, organizations, researchers and even some political parties working against the growing racism in the European Union. Clearly, however, these are not keeping pace with their adversaries, and the increasingly draconian policies on asylum and migrants' residence and welfare rights are ample testimony to this.

Another hugely powerful shield against Europe's migration reality is made up by what we may call the cost perspective of migration. This perspective, or narrative, is the main focus of this book. As I will describe in great detail ahead, researchers and policy-makers today agree that refugees admitted to the European Union constitute a net cost and fiscal burden for the receiving societies. Whereas researchers draw this conclusion from a seemingly neutral accounting exercise – refugees contribute less in taxes than they receive in welfare assistance – politicians and the media eagerly use this economic science to justify and explain restrictive asylum policies. To be sure, politicians and researchers may judge low-earning and low-skilled labour migrants to be both necessary and affordable, but *only* on the condition that their access to welfare provisions is restricted. This does not apply to refugees, however. Since refugees cannot work and pay taxes from day one and since they may have children, refugees will initially always depend on welfare assistance. By definition, therefore, they are deemed fiscal burdens.

From the perspective of research this is just a scientific fact, and so research cannot be held accountable for being complicit in stoking the sentiment that refugee reception jeopardizes the welfare state and that, consequently, refugee prevention constitutes a prerequisite for the fiscal viability of the welfare state. But, as I will show in this book, research is indeed complicit. It is so for the simple reason that the economic science it is basing itself on is fundamentally flawed. This orthodox "sound finance" economics and its household accounting not only mistakes state spending for being precisely that: analogous to household spending; it also fails to distinguish between real resources, such as labour, and financial resources. Reflecting this failure, researchers cannot grasp the value and indispensability of the labour performed by those 60 per cent of cleaners in Sweden who are born abroad. Instead, they conceive of these workers as fiscal burdens. Their tax contributions fall below average and so they are said to receive more in government welfare spending than they pay in. By always being in the red, so to speak, these workers will neither be able to redeem the costs for their initial stay in the country during which they did not work and pay taxes at all. Of course, if refugees work as doctors they will be able to offset such alleged costs, and they may also be able to offset additional costs, such as their children's schooling. But, if they work as cleaners, they remain perpetual net costs. According to this logic, then, Sweden would have been better off without the cleaners who came as refugees.

When politicians sound the alarm over refugee costs, claiming that these threaten the fiscal sustainability of the welfare state, they do so from the comfortable place of being able to cite research. No accusations of populist fakery here. But most of the time they do not have to cite research. The notion that there is a trade-off between refugee migration and the welfare state is simply common sense in the public debate. The debate is not whether this is actually accurate; everybody agrees that refugees involve costs for taxpayers. The debate is, rather, whether these *costs* are affordable or not. It is clear who is winning this debate in terms of policy outcomes; asylum policy is becoming increasingly restrictive and the residence and social rights for those refugees who still manage to enter the European Union are being curtailed. No EU member state wants to share the "refugee burden".

But it is a strange debate, because the losing side, or those defending refugee rights, almost always contend that human rights never should be allowed to be subjected to cost–benefit analyses. Given that no one is questioning the assumption that refugee reception indeed constitutes a cost, this position is understandable. Under these circumstances, human rights proponents will always lose a cost–benefit debate over refugee reception. But what if the assumption is inaccurate? This is another important reason for writing this book: to show that it is the other way round. As I will explain, refugee reception in the EU is not *costly* from a financial perspective. Rather, it amounts to a beneficial addition of real resources, as illustrated in the snapshot of the Swedish reality above. The government spending on refugees, for its part, will do what government spending always does: it will end up as income in other sectors of the economy – that is, as income for municipalities, businesses and others involved and employed in the management of refugee reception and integration. Those advocating human rights, therefore, do not have to concede the mistaken orthodox assumption that refugees are costly. Nor do they have to think of "the economy" as the enemy. As I will argue, then, receiving refugees in the EU is not an economic or fiscal sacrifice. The book aims to correct this prevailing misunderstanding.

In order to have "the economy" and human rights mend fences, however, and to make this book's case for a "modern migration theory", I soon discovered that I had to find a new and alternative macroeconomic framework – one that would be able to break the orthodox impasse that currently besets academic, political, policy and public debates on migration and asylum in the European Union. I found this in modern monetary theory (MMT), which I stumbled across thanks to a YouTube lecture series given by Randall Wray, one of the chief architects behind the MMT approach to macroeconomics. This happened one January evening in 2016 – and I have never looked back. I thus wish to acknowledge at the outset that it would not have been possible to write this book without access to the stellar work carried out by MMT scholars. One of them, Dirk Ehnts, deserves special mention for his careful reading of Chapters 2 and 3 and for the many helpful comments and suggestions. Dirk should also be thanked for letting me use one of his figures.

I am grateful to Anna Bredström, Ragnar Haake, Stefan Jonsson, Karin Krifors, Jonathon Moses, Donald Pitschel and the two anonymous referees, all of whom contributed valuable feedback on parts or the whole of the book in draft. Erik Jones, Agenda's series editor, made key suggestions on one of the last complete drafts that improved the final version and for which I am very grateful. I am equally indebted to Regine Paul for her helpful feedback in the early stages of the project. Further, I wish to express my appreciation to Agenda's publishers, Steven Gerrard and Alison Howson, for giving me this fantastic opportunity. Alison Howson has carefully read several drafts of this manuscript and she has offered a number of insightful comments and suggestions at each stage of the drafting process. I also wish to thank Alison for her encouragement and patience. Responsibility for shortcomings and errors that remain is, of course, mine alone.

The work on the book has greatly benefitted from a fellowship awarded by the Max Planck Sciences Po Center in Paris on Coping with Instability in Market Societies. I am deeply indebted to Jenny Andersson and Olivier Godechot for giving me this fantastic opportunity, and to Allison Rovny and Marina Abelskaïa-Graziani for all the help and assistance during my stay in Paris. The Osaka School of International Public Policy, Osaka University, and the EU Institute in Japan kindly invited me to give a series of lectures and seminars on my research. Special thanks go to Akihisa Matsuno and Noriko Higashimura for the invitation and for their generosity and hospitality during my stay. The University of Lille also welcomed me for a short and very fruitful lecturing visit. Warm thanks go to Olivier Esteves for making this possible and for all the inspiring discussions. Gurminder Bhambra deserves special acknowledgement; she has given me several opportunities to present and discuss the arguments and topics of this book – in different settings and in different countries. I am very grateful for this support and encouragement.

In the course of writing I have had the good fortune to be invited to present drafts and speak about my book on numerous occasions. These talks and seminars have provided me with much valuable feedback, critique and inspiration. I am particularly indebted to Saleem Badat, Andrew W. Mellon Foundation; Linda Berg, Umeå University; Peter Berggren, Linköping University; Tuba Bircan, Catholic University of Leuven; Elizabeth Buettner, University of Amsterdam; Maria Carbin, Umeå University; Emma Carmel, University of Bath; Olga Demetriou, Durham University; John Holmwood, University of Nottingham; Engin Isin, Queen Mary University of London; Eleni Karageorgiou, Lund University; Gero Kellermann, Akademi für Politische Bildung, Tutzing; Suvi Keskinen, University of Turku; Jürgen Mackert, University of Potsdam; Branka Likic-Brboric, Linköping University; Heidi Mirza, Goldsmiths College; Andrea Monti, Stockholm University; Gregor Noll, University of Gothenburg; Daniele Saracino, University of Bonn; Moa Tunström, KTH Royal Institute of Technology, Stockholm; and Chenchen Zhang, Queen's University Belfast.

I am likewise indebted to a number of non-academic organizations, institutions and individuals who have invited me to speak and exchange ideas and experiences. Here, I would like to thank the Asylum Group in Norrköping; Susanna Löfgren and the Church of Sweden; Maria Lind and Tensta konsthall; Anette Ekström and Älmhults bibliotek; Alexandra Segenstedt and the Red Cross; Göran Dahlberg and Glänta; AnnaTora Huss and Save the Children; the Museum of Work in Norrköping; Bildningsförbundet Östergötland; Senioruniversitetet in Linköping and Stockholm; Rotary Linköping; Stockholm City Mission; Ett Norrköping för Alla; Utrikespolitiska föreningen in Linköping; Niklas Åkerberg and Architects Without Borders; and Britta Stafstedt and Hagagymansiet.

I am grateful for the encouragement from my colleagues at the Institute for Research on Migration, Ethnicity and Society (REMESO) and from the fantastic students in REMESO's MA programme in ethnic and migration studies. Special thanks also go to Erik Berggren, Karl Dahlquist, Sandy Hager, Kai Koddenbrock, Henrik Nordvall and Robin Svensson. I would like to express my gratitude for all the help I have received from the library staff at Linköping University and the Campus Norrköping branch. I am also grateful for the permission to reproduce maps and figures whose copyright belong to Zentrum für Militärgeschichte und Sozialwissenschaften der Bundeswehr and the Swedish Association of Local Authorities and Regions (SKR). Thanks as well to Mike Richardson for his excellent copy-editing. Last but not least, warm thanks go to Anna, Hakeem and Mira.

The research for this book has been backed in part by a grant from the Centre for Local Government Studies (CKS) at Linköping University. I am very grateful for the Centre's generous support.

*Peo Hansen*
Norrköping, September 2020

# Foreword

Erik Jones

The novel coronavirus pandemic taught the world three things: money invested in public healthcare pays huge dividends in terms of social and economic resilience; government deficit spending to support economic performance is better than seeing the destruction of human and physical capital; and some of the least attractive and least well-remunerated jobs are nevertheless "essential" for the functioning of society. Europe's political leaders were quick to recognize these "truths" as manifest. The first major European lending programme targeted national health systems; the second targeted national employment protection schemes; and all the while European leaders celebrated their societies' "frontline workers". Now everyone in Europe is looking ahead to the double challenge of planning for recovery and resilience because meeting that challenge is critical for Europe's next generation. Where European integration looked to be stumbling in the aftermath of the last crisis, particularly following the British referendum, now the European project has a powerful narrative behind it.

The question Peo Hansen asks is whether that new narrative is powerful enough to overturn deeply rooted misconceptions shared among Europeans about the financial cost of refugees and asylum seekers. These are people who come to Europe by necessity rather than out of choice. When they arrive, they are usually prevented from seeking employment until their applications for asylum can be processed. By implication, they receive "benefits" in the form of food, lodging, healthcare and education long before they are able to pay taxes. Once those applications are processed, those who are accepted enter the workforce wherever they can find a job – which often means doing unskilled or semi-skilled labour in the public or private sector. Because those jobs tend not to pay high wages, these refugees tend not to pay high taxes even as they continue to access social benefits. Hence, the conventional wisdom in Europe is that refugees impose a cost that the rest of society must bear.

For Hansen, however, that financial reckoning is wrong because it focuses too much on the refugee as "benefit recipient" and on the rest of society as a sort of aggregate "taxpayer". But the money spent providing food, housing, healthcare and education does not disappear once it touches the refugee or asylum seeker. Instead that money travels from one part of the government to another, providing revenues for those agencies that provide essential services. In turn, the public servants who direct those agencies use at least part of that revenue to invest in maintaining, upgrading and expanding those public services. The rest of society gains from this investment because the rest of society also includes people who need healthcare, education, housing and other benefits.

The question is whether this investment needs to be financed immediately or whether it will pay dividends in terms of economic performance and therefore future tax revenues. The answer can be found by widening the circle of benefit to include the salaries of those public servants who provide essential services, and the payments made to the firms that contract to provide food, materials, utilities and construction. Supporting refugees is an activity that not only justifies investment in public services but also ripples across the rest of the economy. Moreover, these ripples are geographically concentrated, which means they reinforce local economies. Imagine an alternative, more austere reality where spending on such services is reduced instead of being expanded. The withdrawal of public services would cause economic activity to contract and so make the local economy less resilient.

None of this is to deny that refugees do benefit. Rather it is to emphasize that those refugees are people who can provide a resource as well as a cost. Hansen shows that these refugees are disproportionately represented in those parts of public sector services provision that are least attractive even if no less vital. They clean, give care, cook, drive, build and repair. In pandemic parlance, they are frontline workers. But they are also an essential reason that public services remain available and affordable in societies that are well advanced in terms of population ageing. And when they bring their families or have children, these individuals provide additional essential human resources from a societal perspective. It is not necessary to project on how "successful" these younger generations will be economically to recognize that their youth is its own contribution.

Hansen's argument is not limited to refugees. Instead, it is part of a much larger conversation about the way Europeans think about immigration, about the political rhetoric that has overtaken the debate, and about how the academic research community is complicit in reinforcing unhelpful frames or narratives. But Hansen's claim about refugees is worth emphasizing in light of the pandemic. Societies that took care of their refugees were better prepared for this crisis because of those efforts; the broader economic impact of those efforts was positive and not negative; and when the pandemic hit, those refugees took care of them.

Erik Jones
Bologna
December 2020

# 1

# Migration: the "mother of all problems"

In a European survey conducted by the French think tank Fondapol in 2017, respondents were asked to consider the following statement: "It is our duty to welcome in our country refugees fleeing war and poverty." Sixty-four per cent of those surveyed "agreed with or strongly agreed with" this statement. Given the anti-immigration climate following in the wake of the 2015 Syrian refugee crisis, this should strike the reader as surprisingly high. But the survey also included another statement: "We cannot let in more refugees because that would harm the country's economy." Curiously, 61 per cent of the survey respondents also "agreed with or strongly agreed with" this statement (Fondapol 2017).

In this book, I argue that we must come to terms with this contradiction if we are to gain a proper understanding of the so-called refugee crisis in 2015–16 and the persistence of the migration issue's political explosiveness in Europe. For one, it seems safe to say that the future existence of international protection in the European Union will come to hinge on the resolution of what we may call a *clash of moral and fiscal imperatives*. That is to say, although many people still think that we have a moral duty to protect "refugees fleeing war and poverty", the majority are also convinced that society cannot afford to realize this duty. Were we to leave out the part about refugees "*harm[ing]* the country's economy" and instead simply ask people whether they agree or disagree with a statement such as "Refugees and refugee reception constitute a net cost, at least in the short term", then I am certain that close to 100 per cent of respondents would agree.

The reason I feel confident of such an outcome is that practically all politicians, news media outlets *and* scholars subscribe to the view that refugees constitute a net cost or a fiscal burden. This does not mean that they necessarily have anything against refugees or migration in general. It just means that they are all convinced that certain types of migrants weigh on the public purse, at least initially. As one scholar put it in a recent publication:

> The refugees represent a fiscal burden for the host countries at least short and medium term. Under these conditions refugee migration is unable to help to alleviate the aging related fiscal burden of the host societies, on the contrary, it contributes to its worsening. Thus, when the majority thinks that refugees represent a fiscal burden (they "take out more from the public purse than they pay in"), they are not wrong this time. It is not possible to argue against this with solid empirical evidence. Naturally, the moral (and legal) obligation argument for accepting the refugees is still valid but it couldn't be underpinned with further economic reasoning. The moral obligations and the economic benefit are in conflict here. (Gál 2019: 352)

If refugees and low-skilled migrants – i.e. those who are said to contribute less in taxes than they receive in welfare assistance – are singled out as a net fiscal cost for the receiving society, this clearly makes for a poor starting point for their integration. If people believe that refugees constitute a fiscal burden, integration is synonymous with a loss on the part of the host population – a loss many are not ready to take, particularly those who are struggling financially. In response to this, the proponents of the cost perspective simply say that to mask or hide the truth about refugee migration – or any other migration deemed costly – makes for an even worse place to begin integration. Many would add that tampering with the truth will only aid the anti-immigration populists (a particularly common retort from mainstream political parties, pundits and scholars). Since so few challenge the basic principles and maths of the cost perspective, it has gained an air of unassailable truth. But those who claim that they side with accuracy in order to avoid playing into the hands of the anti-immigration right do something even worse than allowing the cost assumption to stand unchallenged. They give it new life and credibility by insisting it be acknowledged *in advance*. It is like starting a discussion about equal pay by insisting that we acknowledge that women are a fiscal burden on men because they pay less in taxes – and that trying to diminish or hide this "fact" only plays into the hands of the sexists.

This book is not just an argument to debunk the cost perspective's detrimental impact on integration and inclusion. It will also, and more importantly, demonstrate that the cost perspective builds on a flawed economic conception. Much of this is attributable to the heavy imprint of the orthodox "sound finance" doctrine on migration policy and research – the assumption that governments face a budget constraint much in the same way as households, municipalities and businesses. Money spent is money lost, so to speak, and if the state does not "live within its means" it will sooner or later face a solvency crisis in a principally similar way to a household that fails to pay its bills (for more on this fallacious analogy, see Ehnts 2017; Mitchell & Fazi 2017; Wray 2015). As a consequence, when refugees, low-earning migrants and their families arrive in a country and receive social assistance, this means that the country also incurs a net cost or a fiscal burden. Another way of putting this is to say that there is an inherent trade-off between migration and the welfare state, also expressed as the "numbers versus rights trade-off" (Ruhs & Martin 2008). Put simply, we either have high levels of immigration or we have a sustainable welfare state, but we cannot have both. Or, in a different scenario, we either admit many migrants whose access to the welfare state is restricted, or we admit very few migrants who all receive equal treatment in terms of welfare state access. Of course, given the household budget accounting involved, if a country admits many high-skilled, high-earning migrants, these will not impact negatively on the public purse, although their non-working spouses and children may.

The notion of a migration–welfare trade-off makes up an important baseline and consensual position within much research on migration. As one of the world's foremost inequality scholars, migration experts and former World Bank lead economist Branko Milanovic (2016a: 152) has it: "We can debate the sharpness of the trade-off, but we cannot deny its existence." This book will demonstrate why this assumption and outlook is both conceptually and empirically mistaken.

An intriguing aspect of the cost perspective is that it cuts across political, theoretical and ideological divides. This is what lends it its seemingly incontrovertible status. Whether pro- or anti-immigration in the political world, whether advocating less or more immigration control in the academic policy world or whether endorsing a mainstream or Marxist theoretical perspective, the fiscal cost and trade-off assumptions remain constant.

Milanovic is a case in point. He wants to see more migration from poor countries to rich countries, he likes to pay homage to Karl Marx and he despises the Davos class (Milanovic 2019). But he also claims to be acutely aware of the fiscal constraints in the real world. "The arrival of migrants," Milanovic stresses (2016b), "threatens to diminish or dilute the premium enjoyed by citizens of rich countries, which includes not only financial aspects, but also good health and education services." In his attempt to "make greater migration acceptable to the native population of the rich countries", therefore, Milanovic makes a case for the second trade-off scenario mentioned above. He thus proposes that rich countries admit more migrants but make sure to restrict their social and residence rights, affirming that "[r]estricting the citizenship rights of migrants in this way would assuage the concerns of the native population", to which he adds: "The more we insist on full rights for all residents, the less longstanding residents will be willing to accept more migrants" (2016b). If only "longstanding residents" are made aware, in other words, that policies are going to be enacted that make low-skilled, low-earning migrants worse off, this will soon soften the edges of the migration debate and facilitate harmonious relations between natives and immigrants. It is a bit like arguing that white people's awareness of black people's inferior rights portfolios in Jim Crow America or apartheid-era South Africa made white people more welcoming and hospitable towards black people. Today, many EU citizens are already aware of the disproportionate precariousness faced by low-skilled labour migrants toiling in, for instance, agriculture, the service or care sectors across the European Union, with little or no access to social and labour rights. But who would seriously argue that such awareness has made EU citizens more tolerant or accepting towards migrants? In Milanovic's quest to figure out ways to "pay for increased migration" (2016a: 152), such policy proposals – or "discriminatory treatment", as he terms it – are both necessary and beneficial to all (2016b). Migrants, Milanovic (2016b) suggests, "could also be made to pay higher taxes since they are the largest net beneficiaries of migration".

Although they are far apart on the utility of Karl Marx's ideas, Milanovic's tiered or discriminatory approach to migration is almost identical to the one adopted by Deutsche Bank's global head of research, David Folkerts-Landau. As Folkerts-Landau (2016: 34) outlines his blueprint:

> For example, why not ask migrants, but not refugees, to pay a higher rate of tax until they naturalise as citizens? Or compel migrants to contribute to social service for a certain period in order to earn their citizenship? The general principle is to loosen physical borders and at the same time build stronger ties of obligation – fiscal and other-wise. A new settlement along these lines would allow the current wave of migration to become a political and economic opportunity, far outweighing the fiscal costs, discomforts and political risks. A tiered welfare system is the most effective tool to reduce the integration strains from immigration – and an equitable solution to the legit-imate objections by nativists to unfettered welfare access for those yet to make their contributions to society.

A third case in point would be the real Marxist and former head of Cambridge's sociology department, Göran Therborn. He is a solid anti-racist and he shares none of the anti-egalitarian and pro-discrimination approaches of

Milanovic and Folkerts-Landau (e.g. Therborn 2018a). This notwithstanding, Therborn's perspective fails to steer clear of the orthodox cost perspective. In a recent book on class in Sweden, Therborn (2018b) brings up the issue of migration and how it is being manipulated by liberals and the right to hide class conflict, systemic problems and exploitation. But, instead of showing how the claims about migration's net costs *also* are part and parcel of this manipulation, Therborn (2018b: 34) writes: "If we are to believe the Moderate party [conservative/neoliberal right], the net cost of migration amounted to 40 billion crowns in 2018. That is 0.9 per cent of Sweden's national income. The wealth hidden abroad by the Swedish upper class is estimated at 500 billion crowns by leading researchers, or around 10 per cent of national income."

This discrepancy is then graphically illustrated by placing a migration bar next to a tax haven bar. When seen in such comparative light, the tax haven bar of 10 per cent greatly dwarfs the migration bar of 0.9 per cent. The message is clear: migration costs are small in comparison to the huge amount of unpaid taxes stored in tax havens. By the same token, the exercise serves to illustrate politicians and the media's disproportionate alarm around migration costs.

There is of course nothing new about Therborn's maths, this being a time-honoured way of drawing attention to skewed and class-biased perspectives on what various things really cost. Needless to say, this is also a very common strategy among individuals and organizations advocating refugee and migrant rights. On the face of it, it is hard to disagree with this approach. Yes, the argument goes, hosting and integrating refugee incurs a cost, but it is a small one in comparison to so many other things in the budget. The bottom line is this: we can afford it. "Britain has the sixth largest economy in the world," says the co-leader of the British Green Party, Jonathan Bartley; "we can afford to look after refugees and asylum seekers if we want to" (*Independent* 2018).

Again, my intention here is not to deride those who do the cost comparisons between refugees and wealthy tax dodgers and who argue the sympathetic case for refugee reception being within our means. It is, rather, to further press my point about the *general* agreement around the mistaken cost perspective – from right to left, from anti- to pro-immigration, from mainstream to Marxism. The dividing line instead runs between those who think we can afford it and those who think we cannot, those who think the *costs* are manageable and those who think they pose a fiscal risk. There is of course a literature that critiques the trade-off theory; yet it stops short of questioning the theory's basic sound finance premise.

What I also wish to emphasize is that not all Europeans are anti-immigration, anti-asylum and racists; far from it. To verify this, we need look no further than to the extensive and long-standing work conducted by refugee movements and related non-governmental organizations (NGOs). We can also consult numerous polls. Even so, all are convinced that refugee reception constitutes an outlay that subtracts from the government budget and its capacity to meet other welfare needs. Of course, those who support refugee admission and human rights may not always express it in such negative terms. Rather, their claim is that *despite* the extra spending we can still afford it. This immediately opens the door for those, on both the right and the left, who hold that the refugee-welcoming people are just a bunch of well-to-do do-gooders, all living at a safe distance from those deserving nationals, or, if on the left, the "left-behind" working class who, allegedly, foot the bill for the refugee party. Of course, *they* can afford it, but the poor cannot. This, by the way, was the precise platform on which the leftist Aufstehen (Stand Up) movement in Germany sought to build its case when it was launched in 2018. As put by Deutsche Welle (2018), this was "the movement" that "could present a leftist case for limiting immigration" – or, more accurately, the movement that obliviously sold sound finance orthodoxy as a friend of the working class.

Given this, the cost conception may be crowned the common denominator among all the actors, organizations and institutions that in one form or another try to influence the course and content of migration and asylum policy – be they from the governmental, EU-supranational, non-governmental, Church, think tank, activist or academic worlds. It is the one thing that no one can ignore. Again, governments and pro-asylum NGOs draw radically different conclusions from the conception of migration costs, the former saying we cannot afford it, the latter saying we can, although the latter will concede, when pressed, that, of course, there are outer financial limits.

As everybody is aware, however, in terms of policy influence, there is no equilibrium between these two positions. Hence, in today's migration debate and policy-making there is no room for the "yes, we can afford it" perspective. Instead, it is the "no, we cannot afford it" perspective that has the upper hand. Accordingly, this book will attend closely to the consequences of the latter's dominance and, from there, point to ways in which this dominance can be challenged. I will do this by examining the cost and trade-off perspective's impact on two central migration policy fields and crisis spots in the European Union: (1) labour migration; and (2) refugee migration, or asylum. By introducing the alternative macroeconomic framework provided by modern monetary theory, I will also show why our current cost perspective within both scholarship and policy-making is deeply flawed. From there, finally, I bring this to bear empirically on the economic and societal impact of the 2015 refugee crisis, looking specifically at the consequences of the increased government spending on refugee reception and integration in Sweden. Sweden is the country that, proportionally speaking, has admitted the most refugees in the European Union, and it is also the EU country that has spent the most on refugees as a percentage of gross domestic product (GDP) (EC [European Commission] 2016a: 12, 17).

Before outlining my study any further, I need to situate what I have said so far in a broader context, taking in the historical circumstances but, more importantly, pointing to the contradictory and politically fraught climate of the present.

## "Do not come to Europe"

Judging from the current political conjuncture, there seem to be both too many migrants present in EU Europe and too many migrants and refugees wanting to enter. As expressed in 2018 by the German interior minister, Horst Seehofer, migration is the "mother of all problems" (quoted in Maurice 2018). Hence, in a European Union failing to agree on most matters, there is at least one sure and solidifying consensus. This consensus holds that immigration into the EU needs to be curbed; that migration since the 2015 refugee crisis continues to pose one of the greatest threats to the European Union, even an "existential crisis", to use then Commission president Jean-Claude Juncker's phrase (2016: 16). More specifically, refugee migration and the "refugee burden" are said to jeopardize both the fiscal and political stability of the Union as well as risking the future viability of an already dented Schengen system of free movement. The fact that there are too many poor migrants and asylum seekers entering the Union, or aspiring to do so, has intensified the calls for stronger border enforcements and binding buffer state and return agreements with governments in Africa and elsewhere – as demonstrated by the "EU–Turkey Statement" and the EU's migration cooperation with Libya. As put by the president of the European Council, Donald Tusk, in 2016: "I want to appeal to all potential illegal economic migrants. Wherever you are from, do not come to Europe!" (quoted in Euronews 2016).

This message was taken to the next level when the refugee emergency around the Turkish–Greek border flared up again in February 2020, with the European Commission president Ursula von der Leyen commending Athens for its staunch action to defend "our border", which, in effect, was a violent crack-down on mainly Syrian refugees: "I want to thank the Greek border guards and the coast guards … I thank Greece for being our European ασπίδα [English: shield] in these times" (Leyen 2020). As the *Financial Times*

(2020a) reported the day before von der Leyen's praising of the Greek government, "Greek authorities have fired tear gas and staged military exercises using live ammunition along the country's eastern borders in an effort to prevent thousands of migrants including young children crossing from Turkey". Besides the human rights abuses in the form of directly violent acts – allegations of killings by the Greek border guards were also made – scores of legal experts, scholars and NGOs also pointed to Greece's official and highly publicised suspension of asylum law as being unlawful. EU law professor Alberto Alemanno, for instance, spoke of Athens' move as "a manifest breach of both European asylum law and international humanitarian law" (Euronews 2020).

Brussels' deliberate contempt for human rights and EU law – in the full glare of publicity – may strike many as a novel move. Foremost, however, it needs to be studied as the latest intensification of a steady development in and by the European Union, dating back to the mid-1980s (Hansen & Hager 2012). For more than three decades the trend has been one of a perpetual escalation of both anti-immigration rhetoric and policies to repel asylum seekers. Election campaigns in practically all EU countries have turned into veritable slugfests not between anti- and pro-migration positions but between a variety of anti-immigration and anti-refugee positions. Meetings, summits and statements at the EU level speak a similar language. Remember, for instance, the then home affairs commissioner and vice-president of the European Commission, Franco Frattini, and his warning at the Lisbon High-Level Conference on Legal Immigration in 2007:

> The dark side of the "old" migration strategy includes the fact of integration problems, often taking the form of the deliberate denial of Europe's founding values and principles. Until a few years ago, our chosen multicultural approach allowed some cultural and religious groups to pursue an aggressive strategy against our values. The targets of this ill-conceived "attack" were individual rights, equality of gender, respect for women and monogamy. We have to combat this dangerous attitude, which can destroy the fabric of our societies, and we have to work hard to build up and pursue a positive integration approach. All too often we neglect to strengthen our fundamental roots, the principles we inherited from our Founding Fathers.
>
> (Frattini 2007: 5)

Prior to this, when discussing the integration of Muslims, Frattini had spitefully remarked: "We are not governed by sharia, after all" (quoted in Kubosova 2006).

Long before that – in 1991, to be precise – Jacques Chirac, when serving as mayor of Paris, spoke of France as suffering from an "overdose" of immigrants (quoted in Riding 1991), to which he attached the following explanation:

> That there were more foreigners before the war is probably true, but they were not the same type and it makes a difference. Having Spaniards, Poles and Portuguese working in our country certainly poses less problems than having Muslims and blacks. [...] Imagine the average French worker who, with his wife, earns around 15,000 francs a month, and who sees across the landing of their council flat, all piled up, a family with a father, three or four wives and twenty children, who earns 50,000 francs of social benefit without lifting a finger. Add to that the noise and smell and, well, the French worker will go crazy. And it's not being racist to say that.
>
> (quoted in Lévy-Vroelant 2016: 220)

While I am on this subject we might as well refresh our memory about the British government's response to the upsurge in support for the extreme right Republicaner party in Germany, in 1992, a party led by the former Waffen SS officer Franz Schönhuber. According to the then home secretary, the rise of the Republicaner party could be traced to one singular cause, namely "the flood of migrants and would-be asylum seekers whose continuing numbers have aroused public concern" (cited in Collinson 1993: 11).

It is crucial to bear in mind that these and countless similar statements by member state governments and Brussels officials were made a long time ago, long before the terms "refugee crisis" or "migration crisis" were on everyone's lips. Equally important to keep in mind, then, is that these anti-immigrant and racist statements were commonplace and part of the EU establishment's vocabulary long before Hungary, Poland, Slovakia or other central and eastern EU members had started to vent their aversion towards Muslims and refugees, and long before these countries became EU member states.

For many liberal, and "pro-European", commentators and scholars who lack the historical background, it has been convenient to differentiate between an eastern and western approach to migration in the European Union, with, needless to say, the former said to be the less tolerant of the two. But, for this highly presentist distinction to be sustainable, geography has to be rearranged, with several of the western members being relocated to the east. When looking at the development in recent years one has to ask: where do we find the clear-cut tolerance distinction between countries such as Austria, Denmark and Italy, on the one side, and Hungary, Slovakia and Poland, on the other? "Denmark wants to seize jewelry and cash from refugees" and "Denmark plans to send some migrants to an island once reserved for experiments on animals" are two headlines in the *Washington Post* (2015, 2018) that underline this point. Said Italy's home secretary in 2008, after a mob had firebombed and assaulted a Roma settlement in Naples, forcing some 800 Roma to flee: "That is what happens when Gypsies steal babies" – to which another minister added: "The people do what the political class isn't able to do" (Milne 2008). In 2019 Austria's vice-chancellor affirmed that "[w]e are consistently following the path for our Austrian homeland, the fight against population exchange, as people expect of us" (Euractiv 2019). In 2020 Austria's chancellor, Sebastian Kurz, contended that in the absence of migration control "we will not be able to keep our identity" (*Financial Times* 2020c). Suffice it to say too that the German interior minister, Horst Seehofer, and his government party, the Christian Social Union, openly praise Viktor Orbán. And what are we to make of the rise of the Alternative für Deutschland (AfD), or the fact that many analysts do not think it unrealistic any more that Marine Le Pen becomes the next president of France ("polls suggest she has a strong chance of taking her comeback all the way to the Elysée Palace": *Financial Times* 2020b)? Is this attributable to the successful spread of some ideas particular to eastern Europe, or could it have a source in western Europe too?

## Polish surprise

In saying this, I am not denying the existence of differences between member states. Numerous surveys detect significant differences between EU members in popular attitudes towards migration and where an east–west pattern can be detected (e.g. Organisation for Economic Co-operation and Development [OECD] 2018a: 132). Yet this should not blind us to the many similarities across the Union, not the least between political establishments, similarities that do not align with simplistic east–west patterns. And the same applies to differences between EU member states with regard to migration, such as the different historical experiences with migration, which vary greatly across the EU – its scope, in general, and the type of migration (e.g. refugee, labour, irregular, family) in particular. There are also notable differences as to the structural function performed by migration in the different member states' economies and labour markets (e.g. Schierup, Hansen & Castles 2006).

Again, although a portion of these differences may align according to some rough east–west pattern, others do not. For instance, we are often led to believe that there is significantly less migration to the new central and eastern

European members than to the old western ones. "None of central Europe's countries," an article in *Politico* assures us, "has seen much migration in recent decades, and the idea of allowing in large numbers of culturally dissimilar Muslims is deeply unpopular" (Cienski 2016b). According to *The Guardian* (2015a), Poland "accepts vanishingly small numbers of migrants" – a claim that fits well with the abrasive anti-immigration rhetoric by the country's government, led by the Law and Justice party. Similarly, three years later an article in *The Guardian* (2018a) summed up the developments since 2015:

> Everyone agrees Europe needs to urgently overhaul its asylum and immigration rules. […] However, no one can agree on what to do: some countries want tougher external border controls, or fairer distribution of new arrivals. Any solution will have to balance the concerns of "frontline" southern states with those of wealthier northern "destination" states, while dealing with the refusal of hardline central and eastern ones (such as Hungary and Poland) to accept any migrants at all.

But is this an accurate depiction of Polish migration policy? No, it is not. A few years ago Poland emerged as the EU country that admits the most migrants of all. Starting in 2014 it is estimated that as many as 2 million Ukrainians have arrived in Poland. As one *Financial Times* (2018a) headline tellingly had it: "Polish companies target Ukrainian workers as consumers: telecoms, banking and property groups take advantage of growing number of immigrants." Drawing on statistics from the Polish Ministry of Family, Labour and Civic Policies, the report in the *Financial Times* (2018a) noted that, whereas the short-term work registrations granted to Ukrainians grew from 400,000 in 2014 to 750,000 in 2015, they numbered as many as 1.7 million in 2017. Despite the fact that the numbers reported by the OECD are lower, Poland still led the OECD area in temporary labour migrant admittances in 2016, counting some 670,000 migrants. It was an increase of more than 61 per cent from the year before. The United States came in second (660,000) and Germany finished a distant third, with around 470,000 temporary labour permits issued that year (OECD 2018a: 25–6).

Knowing this, it should be obvious to anyone that Poland's Law and Justice government cannot be characterized as anti-immigration in practice. Yet the consensus view holds that it is one of the most virulently anti-immigration governments in the European Union. Racist, yes, and virulently anti-Muslim, yes indeed. But not anti-immigration. True, the Polish government has not been too keen on talking domestically about the fact that it has opened the country for large-scale immigration (Lindsay 2018), but it *has* used it as a pawn against the EU's attempt to oblige Poland to receive Syrian refugees and participate in the EU's (now defunct) refugee relocation scheme (or the Emergency Relocation Mechanism). While hardly ever granting refugee status to the Ukrainian migrants, the Polish government has nevertheless claimed that it has done far more than its share when it comes to admitting refugees into the Union. In a debate in the European Parliament as early as January 2016, for instance, the then prime minster, Beata Szydło, claimed: "Poland has accepted around a million refugees from Ukraine, people whom nobody wanted to help." The Ukrainian ambassador to Poland immediately denied this claim, saying that the correct term was not "refugees" but "economic migrants" (Reuters 2016a). Subsequently, Szydło's successor, Mateusz Morawiecki, trimmed the refugee figure, saying that "[w]e are accommodating hundreds of thousands of refugees from Ukraine" (Deutsche Welle 2017), a number that is in blatant disagreement with the official asylum statistics. According to Eurostat (2018), Poland received a total of 3,005 first-time asylum applicants in 2017, 300 of whom came from Ukraine.

Refugees or not, the arrival of large numbers of Ukrainians in a very short time has been appreciated by the Law and Justice government. Consequently, the ubiquitous practice of labelling the Polish government "anti-immigration" needs to be rethought.

Most importantly for our purposes here, however, is to relate this conclusion to my initial depiction of the current EU/European mood. There, I pointed to a seeming consensus that holds that there are too many migrants in the Union and that this unsustainable surplus of migrants is eating away at the EU's welfare and political stability. Yet what the Polish case proves is that the reverse is true too: Poland has simply suffered from the plight of having too few migrants, something that the roughly 2 million Ukrainians are starting to redress. But, apparently, even 2 million Ukrainians will not be enough, and the recent growth of labour migrants from Bangladesh, India, Nepal and Pakistan seems to confirm this. As one executive for a Polish staffing company was quoted saying to the *Financial Times* (2018b), Poland's labour demand "will not be fulfilled by Ukrainians only".

Some prominent members of the Law and Justice party are of course carefully observing this development, and they are not happy with what they are seeing. One of them, Krystyna Pawłowicz, addressed this in a letter to the prime minister in June 2018, arguing that the party's vocal anti-immigration message was being compromised by its practical conduct. "Voters observing Poland's streets," she wrote, "feel cheated, uninformed and irritated" (*Financial Times* 2018c). In a parliamentary debate in June 2018, moreover, the leader of

Poland's National Movement party, Robert Winnicki, accused the Law and Justice government of having silently initiated a policy of population replacement, letting in "hundreds of thousands of Ukrainians and dozens of thousands of Asians" in just a couple of years' time. "You have lied to the Poles," Winnicki contended in parliament, "breaking the promises thanks to which you have won the elections in 2015" (Bault 2018).

Clearly, then, the Polish government has not crafted a pro-immigration rhetoric (yet) that matches up with its actual conduct and the realities on the ground; or one that could compete with the disingenuous anti-immigration rhetoric on which so much of Law and Justice's political credibility, appeal and identity are supposedly built. But things may be changing. In the summer of 2018 the Polish prime minister, Mateusz Morawiecki, let it be known that labour immigration had become an absolute economic necessity for Poland. Failing to attract enough foreign labour, he claimed, would pose a direct threat to economic growth and sustainability. As put by Morawiecki: "We have 350,000 people entering the labour market every year, but we also have 500,000 leaving it. The ranks of the retired are being swelled by the generation from the post-war demographic boom" (Poland In 2018).

Given the deeply fraught relations between Warsaw and Brussels, not least over migration, Morawiecki's pro-immigration statement is deeply ironic in that it tallies so neatly with Brussels' position on labour migration. As the then home affairs commissioner, Cecilia Malmström (2010), put it some years ago: "We need migrants to ensure our economic survival." I will come back to the fact that the European Commission rarely misses an opportunity to address the Union's so-called *demographic deficit* and the increase in labour immigration that it calls for. According to the Commission, the European Union as a whole, then, suffers from too little labour immigration, and this is costing it dearly in terms of growth and competitiveness.

## Europe's emigration crisis

In contrast to Brussels' main inducement to persuade the member states to adopt its stance on labour migration, which is prompted by the EU's dismal demographic ageing, the Polish government also has another and perhaps even more dismal circumstance to reckon with: the country's chronic haemorrhage of working-age people who emigrate to mainly the north-western EU members. Today around 2.5 million Poles reside in another member state, mainly Britain (no longer a member) and Germany (OECD 2018a). This is a problem common to practically all the member states from central and eastern

Europe that joined the European Union in 2004, 2007 and 2013 respectively. Bulgaria, Croatia, Latvia, Lithuania, Poland and Romania are the hardest hit – and, according to the United Nations (2017: 13), these countries' populations are on course to decline by more than 15 per cent by 2050. As put by the Polish prime minister in 2018:

> From every corner of Poland, I hear pleas for more hands and heads to do the work available. We have estimates that already there is a shortage of 150,000 of workers in Poland. I wish that at least a part of the people who left Poland in the early noughties would return. Many already have, but we need more. Without labour, we won't be able to attract investments. (Poland In 2018)

Since the financial and eurozone crisis took hold in 2009, Greece, Ireland, Italy, Portugal and Spain have also suffered from large-scale emigration.

In November 2018 Romania's finance minister, Eugen Teodorovici, spoke his mind and proposed that Romanian citizens' right to work in other EU countries be limited to a maximum of five years. This, he explained, was a measure to stop the massive loss of working-age people and the "brain drain" that have plagued the country during the past decade. Since gaining EU membership, in 2007, around 3.6 million people have left Romania, or about 16 per cent of the population (*Financial Times* 2018c). As noted by the United Nations (2016: 19): "Between 2000 and 2015, some countries have experienced a rapid growth in the size of their diaspora populations. Among the countries and areas with the fastest average annual growth rate during this period were the Syrian Arab Republic (13.1% per annum), Romania (7.3% per annum), Poland (5.1% per annum) and India (4.5% per annum)." Romania and Poland are "contending" with Syria for probably the least wanted recognition a country can receive. But instead of being hit by a long and harrowing war – the plight of Syria – Romania and Poland have become members of the European Union, the most affluent club in the world. But this club's affluence is far from equally shared, and neither are its members equally functional when it comes to citizens' welfare and employment. One thing all members share, however, is ageing populations. And in the race to attract labour internally, from the Union's shrinking labour pool, Germany and the EU's richer members win. British and German labour has not been flocking to Poland and Romania, but Poles and Romanians have been flocking to Britain and Germany.

Although this development is hurting Poland and Romania and benefiting Britain and Germany, it was nonetheless the latter's governments that started to claim they got the worst of it, asserting that "EU migration" made up a fiscal burden and so posed a threat to their welfare systems. In Britain, as we all know, this political game would go so far as to have a decisive impact on the country's vote to leave the Union. "EU migrants" coming to Britain, the claim went, were hurting the country's welfare state and labour market, hence the call for a taking back of control over immigration.

We need to remember, however, that it was not Britain that started this toxic trend. Rather, it was Austria, Germany, the Netherlands and other supposedly "pro-European" countries that initiated the assault during the first eastern enlargement in 2004, and, with it, governments in the richer parts of the EU soon replaced the positive-sounding term "free movement" with "EU migration" and "benefit tourism". In 2013 Britain joined forces with Austria, Germany and the Netherlands in launching a frontal attack on free movement, demanding, in a joint letter to the Irish presidency, the European Commission and the other member states, that the system be overhauled, emphasizing that "the right of EU citizens to freedom of movement is not unconditional". Referring to "certain immigrants from other member states", the letter claimed that "[t]hese immigrants avail themselves of the opportunities that freedom of movement provides, without, however, fulfilling the requirements for exercising this right". Consequently, "[t]his type of immigration burdens the host societies with considerable additional costs, in particular caused by the provision of schooling, health care and adequate accommodation". It was also asserted that "a significant number of new immigrants draw social assistance in the host countries, frequently without a genuine entitlement, burdening the host countries' social welfare systems". The letter called for stronger and more efficient expulsion measures and re-entry bans applicable to EU citizens and requested that "[a]ll necessary measures need to be taken to deal with the consequences of this type of immigration and to fight its causes", including "legal as well as financial measures" (Mikl-Leitner *et al.* 2013).

For some 15 years, then, rich north-western members have been complaining about an allegedly unsustainable welfare debt incurred by too much uncontrolled EU migration. But it is only recently that the real losers have been starting to raise their voices: the poor members' concern over too much EU *emigration*. As Romania's finance minister put it when motivating his proposal to limit Romanian emigration: "Maybe this is a restrictive measure. But there has to be some sort of social cohesion, you cannot keep strengthening the West, and leaving the rest of Europe behind" (*Financial Times* 2018c). Subsequently this issue has drawn more and more attention. In January 2019 Croatia – among the five countries in the world hardest hit by population reduction – put demographic decline atop the agenda for its EU presidency (*Financial Times* 2019a).

## Three migration crises … and no babies

Where does this leave us? It leaves us with a set of interrelated EU migration crises that simultaneously involve too much immigration (asylum seeking), too little immigration (labour migration) and too much emigration ("EU migration"). To complete the picture, there are also too few babies; and, as a result, too much ageing and a "demographic crisis". At the same time, practically all EU governments peddle an anti-immigration message in some shape or form, which helps foment and legitimize racist sentiments. It also helps strengthen the perception that migration, particularly with regard to refugee and low-skilled migration, is fiscally detrimental and so a burden on the receiving state's welfare system. Furthermore, it is a message that contradicts some of the same governments' rhetoric about the importance of migrant "integration", and it also helps explain why migration is being framed as a curse, steeped, as it is, in a myriad of negative connotations. In many places, moreover, we are past the fomenting or dog-whistling stage, with some governments and high-ranking politicians having developed an explicitly and consistently racist and anti-Muslim stance. Not only does Seehofer say that migration is the "mother of all problems", he also says that "Islam does not belong to Germany", to which the AfD leader in Saxony could reply: "Horst Seehofer has taken this message from our manifesto word for word" (Martin 2018).

Meanwhile, these same governments are scrambling to recruit more migrants to their ageing and understaffed labour markets, the problem the European Commission has been requesting the member states to tackle for the past 20 years. We may have been led to believe that countries in central and eastern Europe are having none of this, but even Viktor Orbán feels he cannot afford to shut the door completely. Not only that, Orbán is doing some of this – wait for it! – with the aid of EU migration directives. "In Hungary," the OECD (2018a: 54) notes in its *International Migration Outlook for 2018*, "the employment of third-country nationals from neighbouring countries – at any skill level – was facilitated; the deadline of the single application procedure[1] was reduced from 21 to eight days, and temporary employment relationships were allowed."

---

1. EU directive to facilitate third-country labour migration.

To add further to the Polish case above, the government there has steadily been increasing labour migration from Asian countries; as many as 13,000 work permits were issued to Bangladeshis, Indians and Nepalese in 2017 (Tilles 2018). In 2017, moreover, Poland and Bangladesh signed a cooperation agreement aimed at increasing and facilitating skilled migration from Bangladesh to Poland (bdnews24.com 2017). The Law and Justice party may portray Muslims in the most demeaning way – for example, they "carry all sorts of parasites" and will use churches as "toilets" (Cienski 2016a) – but, in a situation of severe labour shortage and severe emigration, temporary Muslim labour migration is obviously just a symbolic price worth paying.

Similarly, Seehofer might be thinking he is strengthening his position by flashing his anti-Muslim racism. In his homeland of Bavaria, however, the small and medium-sized companies have been eager to hire those same Muslim refugees their interior minister says should not have been there in the first place. As reported in the *Financial Times* (2019b), "Mittelstand feels strain from ageing workforce", and this predicament is driving "SMEs to increase training, flexible working and hiring of refugees". German Labour Office figures showed refugees from the eight most common source countries landed more than 100,000 jobs between May 2017 and May 2018 (Reuters 2018). Little surprise, then, that the head of the German employers' federation, Ingo Kramer, could be quoted in a *Der Spiegel* headline in December 2018 saying: "The integration of refugees goes better than expected." With more than 400,000 refugees either in work, education or training since 2015, Kramer said he "was surprised at how fast this has happened", while also taking the opportunity to dust off German chancellor Angela Merkel's saying "*Wir schaffen das*", claiming she had been right on the money (Spiegel Online 2018). Job vacancies in Germany stood at over 1.2 million at the beginning of 2018 (OECD 2018b).

## What the book is about

What we have before us is the big picture of EU migration policy and EU migration crises. Outlined as such, we are able to spot a tension, contradiction or puzzle that fundamentally permeates this picture and that this book will try to resolve. This revolves around the seemingly contradictory objectives of *less* migration, which is the current approach to refugee reception, and *more* migration, which is the current approach to the demographic crisis. Consequently, our examination and analysis cannot rest with migration prevention and the building of "Fortress Europe"; the Polish example alone should make this apparent. On the contrary, we must also attend to Brussels' and member states' anxious quest to admit the millions of labour migrants said to be needed to avoid a default on the ageing Union's dire demographic deficit.

This means that I will focus both on asylum policy and labour migration policy. Given all the measures currently in place to prevent asylum seekers from arriving in the European Union, the logic driving EU asylum policy is quite straightforward and thus corresponds well with the epithet "Fortress Europe". The system or regime within which Brussels' anticipated large-scale labour migration is to be managed is much more complex since it is set to attract the right type of migrants, keep strict control on how many are admitted and make sure that stratified rules for migrants' length of stay and welfare access are followed. (Much of this also applies to the various national labour migration policies in the EU.) Accordingly, this nascent EU system's most conspicuous component consists of a plethora of control and security measures designed for the purpose of selection, control and prevention. As will be shown, for instance, EU labour migration policy puts its emphasis on limiting low-skilled labour's access to welfare rights and permanent residence, thus, presumably, ensuring the fiscal sustainability of an increase in labour migration. The high-earning and highly skilled strata of labour migrants, such as those qualifying for the EU's Blue Card, are of course given very different treatment, but, as will be shown, even here the path to permanent residence is no cakewalk. I will then go on to juxtapose this external labour migration policy with the workings of asylum policy, seeking to explain their incompatibility and why refugee migration sits so particularly ill with a labour migration regime dictated by sound finance principles.

Subsequently, the book devotes its attention to Sweden's response to the refugee crisis in 2015 and its societal and economic consequences, particularly as these played out at the local level. Having established sound finance's strong bearing on policy and the legitimacy this receives from research, the Swedish case will put all of this to empirical test. From the perspective of policy-makers' warnings about the fiscal unsustainability of large numbers of refugees and the scholarly assurances concerning refugees' negative fiscal impact, the Swedish situation in 2015 should provide the ultimate worst-case scenario. Sweden, one of the EU's most comprehensive welfare states, admitted 163,000 asylum seekers in one year, the majority of whom were given permission to stay and thus incorporation into what orthodox economics already takes to be a bloated welfare state. In other words, all the conditions for a perfect storm were in place. By the same token, so were all the conditions for a perfect natural experiment to test the literature's assertions about fiscal burdens and trade-offs. Likewise, the Swedish situation provides a natural experiment to also test the advantages of the alternative macroeconomic framework offered by modern monetary theory (MMT).

The Swedish case becomes even more ideal for these empirical tests once we consider the country's long-standing experience of receiving the most refugees in the EU, proportionally speaking, while also having one of the EU's most comprehensive welfare states. Up until the post-2015 era, moreover, Sweden had few welfare restrictions for refugees and their families, and also had permanent residence, family reunification and short paths to formal citizenship as a rule. Again, this makes Sweden the ultimate testing ground for the fiscal burden and trade-off assumption. How did the Swedish welfare state weather the refugee crisis and the unprecedented increase in government spending that accompanied it? And, vice versa, how has the cost perception and trade-off theory weathered the outcomes of Sweden's large refugee admission and refugee spending?

## The structure of the study

In what follows I will start out in Chapter 2 by examining the hugely influential complex of literatures studying the fiscal impact of migration and the trade-off between migration and the welfare state. I will show how orthodoxy and sound finance fundamentally govern the ways in which this research approaches migration and the profound implications thereof. I will also evince that, whereas sound finance's reign is made explicit by research on migration within the field of economics, its influence operates in much more implicit ways for those working in political economy, political science, sociology, and so on. The power of sound finance thus manifests itself most clearly in the fact that, although so much migration research is premised on sound finance logic, there is, save for the economists, limited awareness of this fact among many of those conducting this research. In fact, not even all economists seem aware of this.

In Chapter 3 I continue this critique by presenting an alternative macroeconomic framework, namely modern monetary theory. Although MMT scholarship so far has not focused on migration I will show its usefulness for coming to terms with the sound-finance-induced errors and misconceptions that permeate much of the migration literature. I also demonstrate how the adoption of an MMT framework helps us understand the devastating impact that sound finance has on migration policy and its instrumental role in stoking the toxic debate on migration in the EU. But MMT does more than offer tools for critique. Most importantly, it also offers the tools with which we can modernize both migration research and migration policy and so establish a realistic approach to migration, one that perceives of refugees and low-earning migrants not as fiscal burdens but as the real resources they actually are.

For the reasons explained above, Chapters 4 and 5 then take a close look at the EU's external labour migration policy. Whereas Chapter 4 examines the general development and logic, Chapter 5 zeroes in on the actual labour migration policies and legislation that have been enacted at the EU level. The latter are the results of protracted and arduous negotiations between EU institutions and the member states and so helps us get a clear picture of the lowest-common-denominator agreements that have enabled existing policy. As I will show, the most instrumental common denominator can be spotted in the policy's relentless hedging against migrants' access to residence and welfare rights.

Chapters 4 and 5 set the scene for Chapter 6. Here, I begin by briefly mapping the 2015 refugee crisis. Next, I go on to locate the crisis in the context of the historical trajectory of EU asylum policy, a trajectory that was set in motion in the mid-1980s. As part of this, I explain the logic and consequences of the EU's preventive and hence security-oriented approach to asylum and the alleged "refugee burden". The remainder of Chapter 6 then deliberates on the EU policy incompatibility between labour migration policy and asylum policy. As noted above, I reveal how the EU's sound finance consensus helps to partly explain why asylum policy and refugee reception have come under such fierce attack in recent decades. It also helps explain why refugees are not conceived as helping to mitigate demographic ageing in the EU but are, rather, seen as fiscal burdens that subtract from government welfare spending. Subsequently, Chapter 7 takes a closer look at the Swedish case, as already outlined above.

The concluding Chapter 8 summarizes and synthesizes the arguments and empirical evidence into a comprehensive analysis. In addition, the chapter shows how my analysis also can be brought to bear on the crisis of EU free movement and EU citizenship. Finally, I situate the knowledge and lessons garnered from Sweden's refugee management in the wider EU context. To be sure, the Swedish government soon shut the door to both asylum seekers and to its own way of handling the refugee situation from 2015 to 2017. But, from the perspective of the government and all the researchers, economic policy experts and pundits subscribing to sound finance, the damage had already been done, so to speak. Since so much money had already been spent on reception and integration, the reasoning went, the negative economic consequences could not be undone. Moreover, with welfare spending to the newly arrived set to continue into the future, this would also prolong the fiscal problems.

As I will show, however, these supposedly foregone conclusions would all come to naught. Not only did the large refugee spending in Sweden prove fiscally risk-free; by supplying the depopulating and financially deprived municipalities that received the refugees with considerable extra funding in

2015/17, the central government's refugee spending also helped stimulate economic growth and brought about a significant investment in the Swedish welfare state. The impossible thus turned out to be possible, after all. That which, as Gál (2019: 352) claims above, we cannot "argue against […] with solid empirical evidence" actually proved possible to refute. What I will show, then, is the emergence of a short-lived, yet very real and sustainable, refugee model. This Swedish model became visible in a natural experiment environment in which – from the sound finance perspective – two allegedly inauspicious developments occurred simultaneously, namely the reception of a large number of refugees and a sizeable increase in government spending. As will become apparent, however, for many of the ageing and cash-strapped municipalities that received refugees, this coincidence proved a winner. Given that this model has since been both discarded and slandered, I take it to be all the more important to reconstruct it and reveal its effects and local political reception to a wider European and international audience.

## 2

# The fiscal impact of migration

No one can have failed to take note of the public debate and political man-oeuvring over the fiscal impact of migration, in general, and of refugee migration, in particular. As one author puts it, "Fiscal impacts of immigration are one of the hottest and most controversial topics in recent debate on migration" (Kaczmarczyk 2015). "Objections to the perceived burden placed by immigrants on public finances," another author observes, "seem to motivate much popular opposition to immigration" (Preston 2014: 569). "Is migration good for the economy?" is the title of an OECD paper that goes on to ask: "Benefit or burden – what's the reality" (OECD 2014: 1). Under the title "Are migrants good for the host country's economy?" yet another scholar observes: "Indeed, the impact of migration on the host country's economy is possibly the most crucial question that policy-makers have to answer. Furthermore, it is a question that can drive changes in immigration policies as well as ignite fervent debates in the media and other forms of public discourse" (Ratna 2016: 75; see also Vargas-Silva 2015).

According to Dustmann and Frattini (2014: 593), moreover, the public concern over "whether immigrants contribute their fair share to the tax and welfare systems [...] is more important for individuals' assessment of immigration policies than concerns about wages or employment". As already noted, numerous surveys confirm this, with public attitudes heavily in favour of the notion that migrants burden the public purse and that they receive more welfare benefits than they help to finance (Dustmann & Frattini 2014: 593–4; Preston 2014). In the Fondapol (2017) survey that I referred to in the previous chapter, an overwhelming majority of the respondents were not only of the opinion that refugees harm the economy; almost 90 per cent also said they were "worried" or "very worried" about "funding for social programs". In addition, 77 per cent expressed these same sentiments over "government debt and deficits".

In the news media and media punditry, the message concerning migration's ostensibly negative fiscal impact is also commonplace, and during the 2015/16 refugee crisis it was amplified even further. In September 2015 the *International Business Times* fretted: "EU refugee crisis: how will European countries pay for the influx of thousands of people?" (Tomkiw 2015). In an equally rhetorical style, a headline in *The Atlantic* queried: "Can the welfare state survive the refugee crisis?" (Horn 2016). Already, in January 2016, *The Economist* (2016) was fairly certain about the outcome, claiming that "Europe's new arrivals will probably dent public finances". As for Germany, one headline warned that "Ballooning refugee costs threaten Germany's cherished budget goals" (Reuters 2015c), while another claimed that the "[r]efugee crisis could cost nearly one trillion euros" (*Die Welt* 2015). In a commentary on the situation in Sweden in late 2018, *The Economist* (2018: 26) knew exactly where the shoe pinched:

> Between 2013 and 2017 Sweden let in 353,000 refugees, equivalent to 3.5% of its population. It has failed woefully to integrate them. Red tape makes it hard for them to find jobs. […] Combined with large handouts, this means that refugees tend to drain the public purse. And this avoidable policy error has helped to poison Swedish politics. The Sweden Democrats (SD), an anti-immigrant party, warns that newcomers will bankrupt Sweden's welfare state.

*The Economist*'s depiction of what may best be described as "failing Sweden" first makes the erroneous claim that refugees have received "large handouts" when, in fact, these are extremely meagre and have been getting ever more meagre with each policy change since 2015. (It was municipalities, businesses and households that received "large handouts", but more on that in a chapter ahead.) It also asserts that these handouts "drain the public purse", a claim that then goes on to lend credibility to the Sweden Democrats' claim that refugees "will bankrupt Sweden's welfare state". Subsequently, the article informs the reader that the party being lent credibility has "neo-Nazi roots".

Similarly, a post-election analysis in *The Guardian* (2018b) claims that the "163,000 migrants" that arrived in Sweden in 2015 had been "magnifying popular concern about a welfare system many felt was already under strain". In particular, the article goes on, Sweden suffers from "[l]ong waits for operations, shortages of doctors and teachers and a police force that has had difficulties dealing with a spate of gangland shootings and grenade attacks – often in deprived areas with high concentrations of immigrants". These problems, the article concludes, "have all shaken faith in Sweden's prized model of generous welfare and inclusiveness".

*The Guardian* establishes a connection between a shortage of doctors and "gangland shootings and grenade attacks" and the magic connector is "migration". Ironically, however, what the British newspaper fails to see is the fact that, had it not been for migration, the queues for surgeries would have been much longer and the shortage of doctors much more acute. As an in-depth OECD (2019: 18) study on the matter found, the share of foreign-born medical doctors in Sweden stood at 30.5 per cent in 2015/16, up from 23 per cent in 2000/2001. That is one of the largest proportions in the world. Foreign-born nurses in Sweden constitute over 13 per cent of the current staff. Within Swedish elderly care, moreover, around 28 per cent of the personnel are foreign-born, and in some of the bigger cities the foreign-born are in the majority (Socialstyrelsen 2019: 47). Refugee migration constitutes the biggest factor in this development (Giertz & Jönsson 2018: 2). As one Swedish regional newspaper heading puts it: "Without immigration elderly care falls apart" (*Östgöta Correspondenten* 2015). Although it never tries to make any point about this fact in the public debate, in a report from 2018 even the Swedish government (2018b: 16) concedes as much: "Without the foreign-born women and men, the elderly care would face significant problems in fulfilling its task." As another regional Swedish newspaper headlines it: "Without the immigrants, healthcare collapses" (*Södermanlands Nyheter* 2015). The article points out that the region's healthcare organization employed some 7,900 people in 2014, of whom 1,340 were either foreign-born or children born to two foreign-born parents.

Staff shortages in the care and healthcare sectors are of course not unique to Sweden but predominate in the European Union as a whole. Italy, for instance, has for many years relied on migrants (both regular and irregular) to make up for severe staff shortages in its healthcare and elderly care system (e.g. Coda Moscarola 2013). Moreover, some 1.5 million migrants are working in Italian households to care for the elderly or children (Lutz 2018). In 2018 Italy recorded the fewest births in a year since 1861, while at the same time experiencing the worst emigration trend in decades. As the *Financial Times* (2019c) reports, more than 1 million people (a conservative estimate) have left the population registry since 2011, making Italy the only major EU economy to see a population decline between 2015 and 2020. Italy now has the highest proportion of elderly in the EU and it is second only to Japan globally. The situation is hardly helped by other ageing EU countries recruiting Italian medical and care personnel to compensate for their growing shortages; or, as one headline has it, "Germans turn to Italy to fill 'catastrophic' medical staff shortage" (Armellini 2019). Nonetheless, for the then deputy premier, Matteo Salvini, what is ailing Italy is the influx of too many migrants: "With five million poor Italians

I cannot possibly admit hundreds of thousands from the rest of the world. Not because I'm mean but because if you visit the suburbs of the big cities you'll find many Italians with problems. Hence, we have introduced stricter rules, more controls, we have cut costs, and thanks to that we are employing more police" (quoted in Swedenmark 2019; my translation from Swedish). Instead of admitting refugees and migrants, many of whom would help stop the decline in Italy's health and elderly care, Italy's former government proudly employed more police to prevent them from coming into the country.

The prevailing outlook, as expressed in politics and media, can be broken down into three interrelated components or claims. (1) Refugee and low-skilled migration are a fiscal burden on the host state. Hence (2) there is a trade-off between this type of migration and the sustainability of the welfare state. As echoed in *The Economist*'s verdict on Sweden, moreover, the parties and pundits who do not belong to the extreme right also have a third claim at their disposal, which holds that (3) too much migration and the accommodation of refugees have "poisoned" European politics and thus explain the rise of the populist extreme right. In other words, in being too "soft" on asylum seekers, traditional parties have lost votes to the extreme right. In order to counter the trend, there-fore, mainstream parties have taken to adopting some of the extreme right's positions on migration. They have done so sometimes because it is deemed the smart thing to do, at other times because it is deemed the honest thing to do, given that mainstream parties and media pundits increasingly acknowledge the "migration problem" as real. This is not a new development, of course, but dates back to the late 1980s and the emergence of what was to become today's extreme right. Already, back then, there were scholars warning about the tri-angulation strategy and the attempts to beat the extreme right at its own game. Gerald Neuman (1993: 513) was one of them; in 1993 he noted the following about the political strife in Germany over asylum policy: "The conservative parties are thus under particular pressure to reabsorb right-wing voters. One method is to display toughness toward asylum-seekers."

Before exploring the role of research in all this, let us take a quick yet very instructive look at how these three components played out in the Swedish election campaign of 2018. Being the first general election to be held after the refugee crisis and Sweden's reception of some 163,000 asylum seekers in 2015 alone, the refugee and migration issues overshadowed much of the campaign. The incumbent Social Democrats were particularly eager to convince voters of their commitment to a "realistic" and "responsible" migration agenda, and much of the focus was invested in the economic-fiscal realm. Refugee recep-tion and integration, according to the Social Democrats, had become a hugely costly affair for the public purse and so every new campaign week became tantamount to a new measure or proposal to rein in spending on migration and to new disciplinary stick-and-carrot measures related to work, education, language training, housing and benefits. This was done despite the fact that a battery of restrictions already had been implemented during the period from 2015 to 2017, including new laws and preventive measures to abolish permanent residence, increase returns, restrict family reunification and cut welfare benefits for refugees and asylum seekers (see, e.g., Skodo 2018).

During the campaign the Social Democrats thus continued their work to depict the newly arrived as not being keen enough on learning the language, joining education and training programmes, finding work and thus contributing to the welfare of their new country. Whereas the prime minister, Stefan Löfven, spoke about refugees' "duty" to make themselves "employable" in the same breath as he promised to show organized crime the door, the finance minister, Magdalena Andersson, said asylum seekers had better go somewhere else. Andersson, who took the most hawkish position, repeatedly declared migrant integration a failure and went as far as claiming that a restrictive asylum policy was a fiscal prerequisite for fighting child poverty in Sweden (*Dagens Nyheter* 2018). Around the same time the minster for justice and home affairs, Morgan Johansson, asserted that a government summer programme to subsidise bus fares for high school students had been made possible and affordable only thanks to spending cuts on migration: "If we had not tightened up our migration policy in 2015 there would have been no fiscal space left" (*Fokus* 2018).

It is worth mentioning that in the 2014 election campaign it was the centre-right governing coalition that had warned about a "substantial increase" in refugee costs and that "more refugees will affect the budget". After the press conference at which these warnings had been issued, just a few weeks before the election, the Social Democrats retorted that such warnings about cost increases would only play into the hands of the anti-immigrant Sweden Democrats. Magdalena Andersson said she was surprised by the focus on costs and downplayed the whole thing by saying that "we are talking about a billion kronor in extra costs, which is a normal fluctuation with a budget of 800 billion kronor". The party leader, Stefan Löfven, also criticized the government: "We have many costs in Sweden that go up and down, like the sick leave which is going up with ten billion every year now. To just emphasise this [refugee] cost as particularly difficult, that goes against the grain for me" (Swedish Radio 2014).

Four years later the Social Democrats' election campaign sought to convince voters that Sweden's spending on refugee reception had been in excess of what its welfare system could sustain, but that, thanks to the government's incessant work to reduce spending on refugee-related matters, it had succeeded in turning things around. *Because* the government had reined in spending on refugees, its sound finance framework had been brought back from the brink and there was now some fiscal space to spend on a limited set of welfare items. The outcome? The Social Democrats ended up with the worst democratic election result in the party's history. Meanwhile, the Sweden Democrats, the party with "neo-Nazi roots" and the party whose anti-refugee message the Social Democrats sought to exploit to its own advantage, achieved the best result in its 30-year history.

Given this deceitful and menacing political "state of the art", the need for sound science becomes all the more pressing. It is needed to correct and respond to the false political and media refrains concerning the "fiscal burden" posed by low-earning or non-earning migrants and refugees. But, as we shall see below, such scholarly work on migration is very hard to find. At best, we find research that bases itself on the same sound finance premises as the one arriving at the trade-off conclusion, but that, instead of costs, finds fiscal benefits from migration. This conclusion rarely applies to low-earning migrants, however, and – basically – never to (the initially) non-earning refugee migrants. This is a serious omission, to say the least. When it comes to the growing problems of racism and fascism in the EU we can at least spot a growing scholarly literature that cautions, confronts and seeks empirically and theoretically to explain the phenomena. But the fact that the political establishment in the EU takes refugee reception and welfare state sustainability to be incompatible – that a Social Democratic finance minister in Sweden can say, with a straight face, that refugees pose an impediment to the fight against child poverty – has failed to attract much research at all – that is, research into whether the question of a migration–welfare trade-off is a valid starting point to begin with. Instead, we have seen the trade-off literature grow even further.

The research into migration's fiscal impact is voluminous. Consequently, it is not possible to conduct a comprehensive review and critique of this literature within the space allocated here. Instead, I will survey and critique a representative part of the literature. I will pay particular attention to sound finance's strong imprint and the consequences thereof.

## The general fiscal impact of migration

There is much scholarly literature on the fiscal impact of migration, in general, and a growing one on refugee migration, in particular. The literature can be divided roughly into two main streams, although they frequently flow into one another. The first focuses on migration's fiscal impact, broadly speaking, and thus has a strong focus on whether migrants, in general, fiscally burden or benefit major public functions (e.g. social welfare, pension systems and other services) and so potentially undermine or aid the fiscal sustainability of the welfare state (e.g. Betts *et al.* 2014; Burgoon 2014; Camarota & Zeigler 2015; Dustmann & Frattini 2014; Evans & Fitzgerald 2017; Facchini & Mayda 2009; Gál 2019; Holler & Schuster 2018; Kancs & Lecca 2017; Manthei & Raffelhüschen 2018; Münz *et al.* 2006; National Research Council 1997; OECD 2013, 2014; Rowthorn 2008; Ruist 2015, 2018; Soroka *et al.* 2016; Storesletten 2000, 2003; Vargas-Silva & Sumption 2019; for overviews, see Liebig & Mo 2013; Vargas-Silva 2015).

Building on the general results from the first, and economics-dominated, stream, the second is more directly concerned with what is found to be a negative fiscal impact of low-skilled and refugee migration and what this does to welfare policy. This is where we find research on the alleged trade-off between migration and welfare – or trade-off between numbers and welfare rights – as well as the related debate on how the migration-induced ethnic and racial diversity impacts on social cohesion and welfare sustainability in mainly (north-) western European societies (e.g. Alesina & Glaeser 2004; Alesina, Miano & Stantcheva 2018; Bell & Piper 2005; Boeri 2010; Borjas 1999; Burgoon 2014; Cappelen & Midtbø 2016; Cummins & Rodriguez 2010a, 2010b; Emmeneggar & Klemmensen 2013; Finseraas 2008; Freeman 1986, 2011; Garand, Xu & Davis 2015; Hanson 2010; Kolbe & Kayran 2019; Koopmans 2010; Milanovic 2016a; Nannestad 2007; Nauman & Stoetzer 2018; Nyman & Ahlskog 2018; Putman 2007; Ruhs 2013, 2016; Ruhs & Martin 2008; Stichnoth & Van der Straeten 2013; Thielemann & Hobolth 2016; for an overview, see Afonso & Devitt 2016).

Starting with the literature that deals with migration's more general fiscal impact, it should be remembered that this is mainly the preserve of economists. The fundamental axioms, assumptions and groundwork, whether acknowledged or not, come from economics – or, to be more specific, orthodox economics. It is on this foundation that the work of most political economists, political scientists, sociologists and others rest. Below, therefore, I will start by accounting for the economics research and then, in the next sections, I shall turn to the input from other disciplines and what I refer to as the *trade-off theory*, which, again, derives many of its assumptions from the orthodox economics literature.

Given the dominance of orthodox perspectives, whether explicit or implicit, this means that most studies conducted by economists on the fiscal impact of migration are replete with claims to scientific rigour and extensive mathematical equations and formulae. Behind the scientific façade, however, this research involves very little real-world complexity, empirical substance or concrete policy context. Instead, it is very simple – or, more precisely, simplistic. Basically, it is about accounting for money in and money out, in that order. How much taxes do migrants pay in (public revenue) and how much government expenditure do they attract (public costs)? The scholarly literature's assumption is that all governments, in order to spend, *first* have to tax (or borrow). Consequently, the accounting starts on the revenue side, and then moves to the expenditure side and the question concerning migration's fiscal costs and benefits. Out of this accounting exercise we get migration's fiscal position. Burden or boon? Do they pay in *more* or *less* tax than they receive from public expenditure?

For those unfamiliar with the research in question, this may sound too simple (or simplistic) to be true. But, in large part, this is actually the way it is being done. But why, some would ask, does this research often come across as so convoluted; where does the need for all the elaborate mathematical equations come from? Of course, there are ways of making this basic accounting more complicated and attentive to complexity. There are thus two main approaches within this field. Whereas the first one consists of the simple "static" or "cross-sectional" accounting, the second adopts a much more intricate or "dynamic" accounting model. As Robert Rowthorn (2008: 566) explains – and note the sequence of spending and taxation – a static method "takes a particular group of people who are classified as 'immigrants' (or 'migrants') and calculates the taxes they pay and the amount of government expenditure they absorb in a given period of time, typically a year. The difference between [again, note the sequence] taxes and expenditure is their net fiscal contribution." In contrast, the dynamic approach projects migrants' fiscal position into the future, and this exercise also accounts for migrants' future family situations.

Although Rowthorn (2008: 566) points to several advantages with the latter approach – such as its usefulness for policy-making – the enterprise of projecting several decades into the future also entails numerous caveats. These stem from the fact that the dynamic approach must factor in a number of assumptions about future developments that – unsurprisingly – cannot be known today. Among such unknowns Rowthorn mentions government spending, fertility, productivity and employment, but to these we could also add financial crises, wars, sudden large-scale refugee admissions, changes in monetary policy, and so on. Such caveats lead Rowthorn to the conclusion that "the static approach may still be useful". In contrast, Ian Preston (2014: 582) asserts that it "is widely accepted" within the literature that the dynamic approach is the superior of the two.

However this may be, for our purposes here we shall attend chiefly to the dynamic approach, since it offers the advantage of revealing more clearly the fundamental assumptions that buttress the scholarship in question.

## Spending like a household

From what has been said so far, we can already infer that studies into migration's fiscal impact are intensely preoccupied with the government's fiscal position, which, for the most part, should be kept in balance or in surplus in order to be sustainable over time. This stems from the fundamental assumption within orthodox economics that all governments face a so-called budget constraint. "To discuss fiscal policy," University of California – Berkeley economist David Romer (2012: 586) asserts, "we need to know what the government can and cannot do."

> Thus we need to understand the government's budget constraint. A household's budget constraint is that the present value of its consumption must be less than or equal to its initial wealth plus the present value of its labor income. The government's budget constraint is analogous: the present value of its purchases of goods and services must be less or equal to its initial wealth plus the present value of its tax receipts.

Similarly, in a paper on Sweden's public debt and fiscal policy, Huixin Bi and Eric Leeper (2010: 13) state that, "like the household, the government must satisfy a budget constraint each period." In the *Oxford Dictionary of Economics*, moreover, the "budget constraint" is described as "[t]he limit to expenditure. For any economic agent, whether an individual, a firm, or a government, expenditure must stay within limits set by the ability to finance it" (Hashimzade, Myles & Black 2017). Accordingly, the existence of a budget constraint means that governments – that is, *all* governments and under *all* circumstances – face a solvency risk. If governments are not careful to abide by the budget constraint and "live within their means", the story goes, they will pile up an unsustainable amount of debt that, eventually, may force them to default. Such a conviction about the real risk of the ultimate catastrophe – state bankruptcy – conveys a sense that the growing research interests into migration's fiscal impact, or risk, is self-explanatory.

Examining the dynamic approach to migration's fiscal impact, we thus encounter study after study that locates its points of departure in a taken-for-granted budget constraint, based on an equally taken-for-granted solvency risk. When acted on in practical policy, this is what policy-makers and fiscal frameworks at both EU and member state levels refer to as *sound finance*.

Following the household analogy, the central government, or the state, is always assumed to have a spending logic akin to that of a household, not only in the sense of being financially constrained as a household, in general, but also in the particular sense of having to collect before it can spend – again, following the sequence of taxing/borrowing first and spending second. Hence, Preston (2014: 570) begins his study – "The effect of immigration on public finances" – by defining "the state of the public finances" as resulting from "the rates of taxation at which government can fund different levels of spending, or, in other words, the factors determining the government budget constraint" (see also, e.g., Fehr, Jokisch & Kotlikoff 2004; Holler & Schuster 2018; Manthei & Raffelhüschen 2018). Similarly, Storesletten (2000: 313) sets out to test whether migration policy change "can be used as an instrument for satisfying the government's long-run budget constraint, given that current tax and spending policies remain unchanged". As explained by Rowthorn (2008: 568), moreover, in studies using the dynamic method "it is normally assumed that taxes and expenditure will eventually be adjusted so as to ensure that the appropriate solvency condition is satisfied". The extent to which migrants are appraised as replenishing or burdening the public purse will then determine the type of measures suggested to ensure solvency – e.g. tax increases, transfers between budget areas, spending cuts or borrowing.

From here we then get a multitude of different scenario inputs for projecting the future fiscal impact of immigration. Just as in the static approach, the bottom line is the difference between how much migrants contribute in taxes and how much they absorb in government spending. But, in contrast to the static approach's focus on accounting for this difference in a single year in the past, the dynamic approach projects and simulates the difference into a distant future, accounting for migrants' lifetimes of tax payments and spending receipts. Since the future is unknown, however, the scenarios that can be projected are practically infinite in number. According to the logic of the dynamic approach, for instance, the budget constraint will vary with net additions of people – i.e. migrants – which means that we have a new scenario to play with every time there is an increase or decrease in migration. Studies can create a baseline scenario (and budget constraint) in which there is no migration and then, from there, seek to project the fiscal impact of various migration scenarios and new budget constraints (e.g. Preston 2014).

A similar infinitude problem applies to issues concerning the age at which migrants arrive and their levels of skill and education. Do they, for instance, come as newborns, as 43- or 57-year-olds, as retirees or as highly educated and skilled young adults? Do they arrive with few skills, and so with few opportunities but to enter the low end of the labour market, or with little prospect of gaining employment at all? Or are they asylum seekers granted protection, but not legally entitled to work until after a specified period of time? Furthermore, do migrants bring spouses and children? Do they have children once they have arrived in the country, and, if so, how long does it take before they have children, and how many children do they have?

The list can be made to go on and on, of course; what I have listed so far concerns factors only directly related to the migrants arriving and their future offspring in the new country. In fact, I have not seen any scenarios in the literature that seek to account for sudden refugee emergencies such as those in relation to the wars in Bosnia and Syria. Neither have I encountered a scenario in which financial and economic crises are considered. Wars? Climate change? Epidemics? These are all phenomena with enormous fiscal implications that are not factored into the dynamic approach's long-term projections. Instead, it singles out some migration scenarios, measures their respective fiscal impact and then omits from consideration the zillions of other possible scenarios. It simply settles for scenarios with varying characteristics related to migrants themselves (e.g. skills, education, age, number of children, etc.); but, as noted above, even so it can incorporate only a very limited number of scenarios. And that is, of course, the only realistic option; but it is a realism that just serves to further underline the utter unrealism of the research enterprise.

Above, Rowthorn (2008: 568) explains that within the dynamic paradigm "it is normally assumed that taxes and expenditure will eventually be adjusted so as to ensure that the appropriate solvency condition is satisfied". This is truly intriguing. The *raison d'être* for this field of research is precisely to provide policy-makers with knowledge and understanding of migration's long-term impact. Specifically, it is to make sure that governments have the optimal policy tools with which to abide by the budget constraint and hence safeguard the "solvency condition". But, if it is already assumed that governments will follow orthodoxy's prescriptions for sound finance regardless, then much of the research appears superfluous.

## Begging the question

A related problem can be spotted when we turn to this research's major findings. Before delving into this, however, we need to say something about what the major findings are. Rowthorn (2008: 568) provides a concise summary:

> [E]stimates of the fiscal contribution of the immigrant population as a whole are typically quite small. The positive contribution of some migrants is largely or wholly offset by the negative contribution of others. This finding holds across a variety of countries and methodologies. Estimates of the net fiscal contribution of past immigration [as produced by the static approach] normally lie within the range ± 1 per cent of GDP. This is also the conclusion of most, but not all, forward-looking estimates [as put forward by the dynamic approach] of the potential contribution of future immigration.

As Rowthorn (2008: 576; see too 2015: ch. 4) also notes, therefore, "The most striking feature of this literature is the degree of consensus" – a claim that is echoed in many accounts (e.g. Kerr & Kerr 2011; Preston 2014). Nevertheless, and as Rowthorn *does* indicate, there are also studies that present migrants as a considerable fiscal burden. And, as far as low-earning migrants and refugees go, here the consensus is very close to total: they always constitute fiscal burdens, and this predicament can change only if, over time, the migrants in question move up the wage ladder and start to contribute more than they take out. Even though refugees may be high-skilled, they are thus best placed within the low-skilled category – not because they are necessarily predominantly low-skilled but because their said negative fiscal position best resembles that of the low-skilled (OECD 2013; Kaczmarczyk 2015).

Refugees, therefore, make up the category of migrants demonstrating the trade-off most clearly. That is to say, from the trade-off perspective, refugees' low and laggard labour market participation, their welfare dependence and low tax contribution signify a strong incompatibility with the fiscal sustainability of the welfare state. As put by Fehr, Jokisch and Kotlikoff (2004: 26), "If the expansion of immigration is concentrated among the low-skilled, the developed world's fiscal finances will deteriorate significantly" (see also, e.g., Razin & Sadka 2005). Asylum seekers and refugees thus present the ultimate trade-off case. To be sure, refugees who are highly skilled may move up the wage and tax ladder quite rapidly. But compensating for the initial deficit can still take a long time, and it will also be contingent on spouses' tax contributions and whether or not refugees have children. Should refugees and low-earning migrants leave the country once they are about to retire and receive pensions (and, most likely, more healthcare), however, then this will be fiscally beneficial for the host state and so might offset previous outlays. Again, as indicated above, the scenarios are practically endless.

Needless to say, there is also close to total consensus about the fiscal benefits – or, at least, not fiscal losses – of hosting high-earning migrants who pay in more than they receive and who carry no other "liabilities" that can reverse this condition.

Yet, in reality, what all this amounts to is a massive exercise in begging the question. All studies within this field (both static and dynamic approaches) assume as starting point and as *fact* that high-earning, high-skilled migrants are net fiscal contributors whereas low-earning, low-skilled migrants and refugees are net fiscal burdens. As per definition, then, the latter category is in conflict with sound finance principles; these migrants compromise the budget constraint and so jeopardize the long-term solvency requirements. Consequently, for orthodox economics – and derivatives thereof – to *prove* these relationships is not proving anything. Rather, it is simply that: begging the question. Thousands upon thousands of article pages later, then, what has already been presupposed as an incontrovertible fact can be confirmed: "In the case of immigration, our results suggest a double-edged sword. [...] [I]f immigration is expanded primarily among the low skilled, fiscal conditions will significantly deteriorate. The opposite is true in the case of expanding immigration among the high skilled" (Fehr, Jokisch & Kotlikoff 2004: 3).

"There certainly exist large differences across migrant groups in the costs and benefits they cause for a host country," another study summarizes: "the net impact depends heavily on the migrant's age, education, and duration of stay" (Kerr & Kerr 2011: 25). Similarly, Rowthorn (2008: 577; see also 2015: 47–8) notes that "most studies find that highly skilled migrants normally make a large fiscal contribution, whereas unskilled migrants are likely to impose a cost on native taxpayers". As one study on Austria claims to find, the latter applies even more so to refugees:

> [R]efugee migration shows certain peculiarities that substantially influence its impact on public finances. First, in contrast to regular migration, initial basic welfare support, handling and management and integration of refugees that apply for asylum cause substantial short-run costs that play an important role in the overall determination of net fiscal impacts. Second, the productivity and skill levels of refugees are in general considerably lower than those of regular migrants. Third, even if one corrects for skill differences, the labor market integration of refugees follows a slower pattern compared to regular migration. [...] The government's primary balance is strongly negatively affected in the short run. [...] The public debt level is substantially and robustly higher during the simulation horizon 2015 to 2060 compared to the baseline. (Holler & Schuster 2018: 32–3)

(See also, e.g., Dustman & Frattini 2014; Ekberg 2009; Aldén & Hammarstedt 2016.)

According to yet another study: "Achieving higher levels of refugee integration is more costly for the public budget" (Kanks & Lecca 2017: 17). As Camarota and Zeigler (2015: 1) assert for the US case: "Very heavy use of welfare programs by Middle Eastern refugees, and the fact that they have only 10.5 years of education on average, makes it likely that it will be many years, if ever, before this population will cease to be a net fiscal drain on public coffers – using more in public services than they pay in taxes." This means that the stronger the efforts to integrate refugees into labour markets and have them start paying taxes, the heavier the initial budget burden. Other studies, however, project that the medium- to long-term effects of such initially costly integration measures may turn out to be fiscally beneficial (Kanks & Lecca 2017; Evans & Fitzgerald 2017).

## The realism concerning "fiscal burdens"

As the reader may recall, in the previous chapter I tried to elucidate the absurdity of the fiscal cost perspective on migration by applying the same fiscal cost–benefit logic to the relationship between men and women. We know that men have higher incomes than women and so contribute more in taxes; hence, we may speak of the category of women as a fiscal burden on men and on society in the aggregate. Think of the high proportion of women in the low-paying sectors and in part-time employment, and think of their frequently lower employment rates and the fact that women spend much more unpaid time caring for children than men. However strange this may seem to those unfamiliar with the research under scrutiny, it is this logic and perception of society and economy that underwrites it. It means that all people who are not grouped into the net contributor category are defined and modelled as fiscal burdens, as expenses for society and economy. Preston (2014: 583) refers to this relationship as "reality", and as such it defines the "government budget constraint". Preston (2014: 583) outlines the rudiments of the whole thing as follows, quoting from the British Office of Budget Responsibility:

> From birth until leaving full-time education, an individual will be a net fiscal cost, due to the costs of providing education and other services. But once an individual enters the labour market they are likely to make a net fiscal contribution, as taxes paid will usually exceed the cost of services consumed. This will depend on the employment

rate, level of earnings and amount of services consumed. Finally, upon retirement an individual is likely to be a net burden again, as they are receiving pensions and often require greater use of medical services.

In accordance with this logic, Holler and Schuster (2018: 33) want us to believe that "higher fertility has a negative fiscal effect in the short and long run but a positive effect in the very long run (after 2060)". If this is true, it should be excellent fiscal news for all the EU countries with declining fertility, at least from now until some 40 years down the road. Taking this absurd logic further, the fiscal boon from low fertility should also make a case for the EU's fiscal rules being adjusted to also include an upper limit on fertility. If we are to believe the literature, then, there might actually be one category ranking below low-skilled migrants and refugees in terms of fiscal burdensomeness: children. Asking "whether increased native fertility could serve as an alternative to immigration and as a remedy for the future fiscal strain associated with an aging population", Storesletten (2003: 504) "find[s] the answer to be 'no', since newborn children actually represent a net liability".

Harvard's George Borjas argues along similar lines: "The more unskilled the immigrant, the more likely the immigrant will be a fiscal burden. It's the same thing in terms of a native" (quoted in Horn 2016). What Borjas is saying, in other words, is that anyone – whether migrant or native – who fails to be above average in terms of income and tax payment will be a fiscal burden. This is silly, since not everyone can be above average. But it is also absurd, since this means that not only children and retirees are relegated to the status of "fiscal burdens". Huge swathes of a country's working people are also consigned to this status: for example, workers in the healthcare sector, public transportation, education, child-care, cleaning, the service sector, agriculture, food processing, criminal justice, as well as scores of workers in other sectors and industries. Needless to say, without people doing these and other types of jobs there is no society.

Another piece of research in this genre goes even further. It claims that "the second-generation non-Western immigrants [in Denmark] make a negative contribution of almost twice the level of natives" and then claims too that natives "also make a negative net contribution" (Frank Hansen, Schultz-Nielsen & Tranæs 2017: 949). This means that the great majority of people in Denmark, and probably elsewhere too, should be approached as fiscal burdens, their net contribution being negative. This says something fundamental about the sort of reality and sense of realism within which the research in question operates. Studies into the fiscal impact of migration are, as already noted, exercises in question begging. But they are also exercises in plain silliness and absurdity.

## The fiscal impact as trade-offs between migration and the welfare state

As should be obvious by now, it is orthodox economics that underwrites what I referred to earlier as the "trade-off theory", or "numbers versus rights trade-off". Many orthodox economists are of course also part of developing these latter perspectives and research fields, but so are scholars from political economy, political science, sociology and the wider social sciences. The proponents of the trade-off or "cost" perspectives on migration are often unaware of their basis in orthodox and sound finance assumptions, although many, of course, are very aware of these and actively espouse them. What we have, then, and contrary to the field described above, is a rather mixed field of both openly orthodox economists (e.g. George Borjas and Alberto Alesina) and ostensibly progressive political economists, political scientists and sociologists (e.g. Branko Milanovic and Martin Ruhs). As I noted too, most migration scholars and other scholars within the social sciences, including those on the left, who do not share the trade-off literature's fiscal concern nevertheless agree with the basic "cost" perspective. While saying that "we can afford it", they thus admit that refugee admission and integration indisputably generate "costs" that are borne by taxpayers.

Again, this goes to show orthodoxy's and sound finance's powerful influence on contemporary migration research within the broader social sciences. Consequently, much research espousing the trade-off perspective derives – knowingly or unknowingly – its assumptions and principles from orthodox economics.

Yet, in contrast to the research described in the previous sections, much of the trade-off literature does not make these assumptions and principles explicit. Instead, they are just postulated as self-evident starting points, or economic laws or truths. As Ruhs (2013: 46) can aver, then, "The lower the skills and earnings of migrants in the host country, the greater will be the strictly economic case for restricting some of their welfare rights in order to minimize the fiscal costs for existing residents." Hence, we learn that there is a "strictly economic case" that legitimizes limits on those migrants who generate "fiscal costs", the latter also taken to be an incontrovertible fact. Milanovic (2016a: 152), as shown in Chapter 1, similarly postulates that "a more open migration policy" for low-earning migrants "requires withholding some civic rights. We can debate the sharpness of the trade-off, but cannot deny its existence."

Besides seeing how the trade-off theory employs some of the question-begging "findings" from orthodox economics, as surveyed above, we also see something else, something we see less of in the orthodox economics literature.

This concerns the trade-off literature's stronger engagement with explaining and prescribing both current and future policy. Why, they ask, do we observe a trade-off between numbers of low-skilled migrants and the rights they are afforded, and why does this make sense from a government perspective? In Ruhs and Martin (2008: 255), we learn that there are "interests and policies of the state" that help to "generate a negative relationship between the number of low-skilled migrants and their rights". The answer to what it is that generates such a negative relationship, according to Ruhs and Martin (2008: 255, emphasis added), is self-evident: "the fiscal effects of immigration":

> The public finance impact of migrants, the balance between the taxes they pay and the cost of tax-supported services they receive, depends largely on their age, wages, and eligibility for and take-up of govern-ment benefits and public services. Migrants with *lower than average incomes*, i.e., those in low-skilled and low-wage jobs, tend to pay less in taxes and, because of their lower incomes, may be eligible for more government-funded services, especially if their families are with them. In order to minimize the fiscal costs of low-skilled migrants, high-income countries may be expected to limit migrant numbers or their access to welfare benefits.

"To be sure", they go on to concede, there may be other interests driving government policy, such as egalitarian concerns. At the end of the day, however, egalitarian concerns will have to adapt to inevitable constraints. Ruhs and Martin (2008: 255), therefore, spell out a big "nevertheless", as in: "Nevertheless, policies that lead to sustained fiscal losses are often pol-itically unpopular and may be unsustainable in the long term, so it is rea-sonable to expect fiscal considerations to play an important and perhaps dominant role in the 'politics' of migrant rights." The key takeaway here, then, is that, ultimately, the " 'politics' of migrant rights" is neither grounded nor decided within the realm of the political and political choice. Rather, economic laws of fiscal sustainability constrain what is politically feasible. In this research context, however, there is much less explicit reference made to the government's budget and solvency constraint; the same goes for the frequency of mathematical equations.

One of the ironies of the research into migration's general fiscal impact is that, whereas most economics studies detect a rather small impact in the aggregate (i.e. ±1 per cent of GDP), the trade-off research turns most of its attention to the low-skilled migrants and to refugees and consequently always identifies a significant and negative fiscal impact. The trade-off in this con-text, therefore, is specifically one between numbers and rights: the number of low skilled migrants who are let in, on the one side, and the welfare rights they become entitled to, on the other. In taking this road, trade-off research can lay claim to a high degree of policy relevance. They can both explain why governments may try to limit refugee and low-skilled migration and point to fiscally sustainable solutions for those governments who already do or want to admit large numbers of low-skilled labour migrants. Apparently, there is no case to be made for a large-scale intake of refugees. Refugees' labour market participation is delayed and low and their welfare dependence is, by definition, high. Unless all public spending on refugees is terminated during the initial phase, during which refugees are not working and paying taxes, there will always be an absolute trade-off between refugee integration and the welfare state.

The reasoning around the trade-off between migrant numbers and welfare involves two steps. First, as Ruhs (2016: 5) explains, "empirical research suggests that the tension between immigration and migrants' access to national welfare states is not only a theoretical possibility but is in fact reflected in policy-making in practice". Ruhs thus finds that migration policies in rich countries "that are more open to admitting migrant workers are also more restrictive with regard to specific rights, and *vice versa*".[1] Most of these rights restrictions concern access to the social rights of the welfare state. In the second step, Ruhs (2016: 5) maintains (see also Ruhs 2013)

> that these empirical findings are consistent with a cost–benefits approach to regulating labour immigration aimed at maximising the net-benefits of employing migrant workers for the national interest (however defined) of host countries. Where rights create net costs for the receiving country, openness to labour immigration can be expected to critically depend on the extent to which costly rights can be restricted and hence the trade-off between openness and rights.

Once again, we see that the core of the policy in question relies not on political choice but on economic laws and inescapable fiscal constraints. Anyone failing to comprehend this fact, or "avoiding an explicit discussion of the numbers-vs-rights trade-off altogether", "simply confuses the issue and can obscure an important policy choice" (Ruhs & Martin 2008: 261).

There are at least two problems with Ruhs and Martin's assertion. If, as they have already postulated, welfare access for low-skilled migrants is not fiscally

---

1. Whether this is actually the case has been convincingly rebutted by, for example, Bearce and Hart (2019) and Cummins and Rodriguez (2010a, 2010b); see also Boräng (2018).

sustainable, then the "policy choice" they refer to is not really a choice but an imperative. Second, and as noted above, they call for "an explicit discussion" yet fail themselves to explicate the fact that the fiscal imperative of their trade-off between numbers and rights is based in orthodox economics.

## A trade-off between research and realism?

As noted, exponents of the trade-off school are less interested in orthodox economics' general "finding" about migration's small fiscal impact in the aggregate (i.e. ± 1 per cent of GDP). Instead, they zoom in on the certain negative impact of the low-skilled, and from there they tell a trade-off story in which low-skilled migration can become fiscally sustainable only if it is combined with a devaluation of these migrants' access to the welfare state. If governments fail to put in place such an offsetting measure, low-skilled migration will either have to be curbed or the welfare state will become fiscally unsustainable.

As I have already highlighted, this prescription goes hand in glove with the message that Europe's politicians and media are peddling. The staff shortage crisis in the EU's healthcare sector that I cited in the introduction to this chapter, which a regional Swedish newspaper summed up with the following headline: "Without the immigrants, healthcare collapses", suggests an alternative view, however. At present the Swedish food and nutrition branch organization is sounding the alarm over an acute shortage of trained kitchen personnel. Practically all of Sweden's 290 municipalities are reporting a severe shortage that is affecting daycare centres, schools and elderly care facilities in particular. Since the mid-1990s the upper secondary school's restaurant programmes have seen their applicants drop from 8,000 to 2,000 per annum. In an interview on Swedish Radio (2019a), the director of administration in the mid-sized municipality of Hässleholm (with around 52,000 inhabitants) explained that the only reason the municipality's kitchens were still in service, albeit just barely, was because migrants, after having completed adult education, were plugging the shortage. As the director put it, migrants "show a greater interest in training for this sector, and that is what saves us right now".

The migrants plugging the shortage in Hässleholm and the rest of Sweden are usually not the low-skilled labour migrants that the trade-off theory has in mind. Instead, they are refugees with permanent residence and full access to the welfare state. This, combined with their initial non-working status, should make them an even greater net cost than low-skilled labour migrants who can work immediately. Employment, of course, improves refugees' fiscal position, but since kitchen work is not high-paying it does not transform them into net contributors. So, what to do, if we were to reason from the trade-off perspective? How do we make net contributors out of these kitchen workers, and/or how do we jettison the net costs incurred by them? Do we strip them of their social rights? Remove their access to healthcare, daycare, schooling, upper-secondary education and training and higher education – unless they can pay for it in full? Or do we do as Milanovic (2016b) suggests, and slap additional taxes on them, in order to "pay for increased migration" (Milanovic 2016a: 152). Given the already low incomes of these workers, such measures would be tantamount to pauperization. Without daycare and schooling, moreover, those with children would have to quit their jobs and end up paying even less in tax. Would deportation be an option – as a last fiscal resort – provided that these people's permanent residence status could be revoked? Or should we just leave them alone and focus instead on changing policy so as to not repeat the mistake of admitting refugees in the future? This "solution" actually tallies very well with what the European Union and most EU governments have been working to implement since 2015, and with considerable success at that.

But, just as in the healthcare and elderly care examples above, we need to ask: who will replace the refugees in performing the vital societal task of preparing meals for children and the elderly? Equally important, we need to ask how it can be that scholars categorize people who fulfil such vital social functions as fiscal costs and burdens. Earlier, I quoted Ruhs and Martin when they state that "[m]igrants with *lower than average incomes*, i.e., those in low-skilled and low-wage jobs, tend to pay less in taxes and, because of their lower incomes, may be eligible for more government-funded services, especially if their families are with them". These migrants are defined as net costs. We already know as much, and, consequently, this is not the reason for putting my own emphasis on "*lower than average incomes*". Rather, it is to point out what everyone should know: not everyone can earn above-average incomes, as, by definition, some will be above whereas some will be below. Except for the fictional country where everyone earns the same income, this is the situation in all countries today. What purpose does it serve to consign those who earn below "average" to the status of costs and burdens when, as everyone should know too, society is impossible without them?

Not only migrants but also citizens whose incomes fall below average make up fiscal burdens, however, as seen in Borjas' reasoning above. Ruhs' (2015: 5, emphasis added) approach is the same: "The net fiscal impacts of migrants (*and citizens*) – i.e. the taxes they pay minus the value of the services and welfare benefits they receive – critically depend on their skill levels and earnings." Every individual, then, can be assigned a positive or negative fiscal position. But who wants to be a burden, and what should the alchemical message to

THE FISCAL IMPACT OF MIGRATION

society's huge cohort of "burdens" be, those toiling in the low-paying sectors? Get above average!

Again, the absence of reality is obvious in this research. It fails to understand the meaning of real resources, as in labour, and instead promotes a financial incentive structure, in which governments are directly or indirectly encouraged to stockpile the highly skilled, strip the unskilled of benefits and curb the admission of asylum seekers and would-be refugees. Anything else runs the risk of being fiscally unsustainable, and is also the reason why one of the world's leading scholars on inequality, Branko Milanovic, thinks it is necessary to increase the inequality between low-skilled, low-earning migrants and the citizens of the hosting state, since, as he puts it, "[t]he arrival of migrants threatens to diminish or dilute the premium enjoyed by citizens of rich countries, which includes not only financial aspects, but also good health and education services" (2016b). But what if healthcare for the citizens hinges on these same migrants' labour? In order to avoid such an embarrassing question, it is important to be able to distinguish between *real* and *financial* resources and the fact that the real constraints lie with the former – a thread I will pick up again in Chapter 3.

## The ethno-racial trade-off or the trade-off between recognition and redistribution

Before I present the alternative approach to all this, as offered by modern monetary theory, I need to say something about the related trade-off debate that concerns itself with how the growing and migration-induced ethnic and racial diversity impacts on welfare sustainability in mainly (north-)western European societies. Many scholars argue that an increasing ethno-racial diversity, together with the multicultural policies that have followed in its wake, have impacted negatively on the cohesion and trust that are said to underwrite a redistributive welfare state. Part of this literature argues that low-earning migrants and refugees, perceived as ethnically different newcomers, lay claim to a disproportionately large part of the welfare state's fiscal space and that this works to undermine the majority population's readiness to finance the welfare state.

Accordingly, there is also a trade-off between the cultural difference and recognition that results from migration, on the one hand, and the social solidarity and trust that create and fiscally sustain socio-economic redistribution, on the other. In this line of reasoning, "social solidarity" and "trust" are often simple proxies for ethno-cultural or ethno-racial homogeneity and unity. According to Robert Putnam (2007: 142), "it is fair to say" that the overwhelming majority of research finds that "diversity fosters out-group distrust and in-group solidarity". The reason for this is mainly "contention over limited resources" – or, put differently, over limited fiscal space. Hence, Putman (2007: 142) argues that "the more we are brought into physical proximity with people of another race or ethnic background, the more we stick to 'our own' and the less we trust the 'other'".

Similarly, welfare dependence on the part of refugees and minorities with a migrant background is said to alienate majority populations, thus working to delegitimize high and progressive tax levels and overall fiscal solidarity – something that leads to welfare state retrenchment. As summed up by Gary Freeman (2011: 1554), one of the proponents of this perspective: "Ethnic heterogeneity is likely to be associated with less enthusiasm for programs that are redistributive or are targeted at minority groups. Immigration seems to erode support for redistributive programs both because it increases social heterogeneity and because newcomers, whatever their ethnicity, may be seen as exploiting social protection schemes" (see also, e.g., Freeman 1986; Alesina & Glaeser 2004; Borjas 1999; Burgoon 2014; Garand *et al.* 2015; Koopmans 2010; Milanovic 2016a; Nannestad 2007).

A crucial aspect of this is also referred to as the "progressive's dilemma". It refers to an alleged irreconcilability between the objectives of openness to immigration and cultural diversity, on the one side, and a strong, universal welfare state and socio-economic redistribution, on the other (Pearce 2004; Goodhart 2004; Koopmans 2010; Kulin, Eger & Hjerm 2016; see also Putnam 2007). The reason for the "dilemma" is the fact that progressives are inclined to embrace both of these two sets of (presumably incompatible) objectives. Given the incompatibility of the two objectives, the argument goes, a polarized confrontation emerges between those prioritizing the benefits and value of migration and diversity over socio-economic redistribution and those giving precedence to social cohesion over refugee protection and policies promoting ethnic diversity and inclusion. Scholars and policy-makers who claim that the trade-off between diversity and welfare solidarity is an accurate description, yet see migration as beneficial for ageing societies and something that should be allowed to continue, may thus see a solution in imposing limits on migrants' access to welfare provisions – along the same lines as Milanovic and others. Those who do not see such benefits, or see them as more than offset by migration's corrosive impact on social cohesion, will advocate various limits and restrictions on migration.

In sharp contrast to these descriptions and theoretical perspectives, other scholars argue that there is very little empirical evidence supporting the incompatibility between diversity and social cohesion, or between migration and redistribution. On the contrary, strong, comprehensive welfare states may be those best equipped to harbour and reconcile whatever conflicts that may stem from growing migration and diversity (Banting 2010; Banting & Kymlicka 2006; Kymlicka 2015; Bloemraad 2015; Crepaz & Damron 2009; Gesthuizen, van der Meer & Scheepers 2009; van Oorschot & Uunk 2007; Spies 2018; Taylor-Gooby 2005; Uslander 2012). As Will Kymlicka (2015: 1) argues, for instance, no one so far has been able to empirically demonstrate that there exists an "inherent or inexorable universal tendency" whereby ethnic diversity erodes support for redistribution.

There is also a historical complication, in that it is difficult to speak of the postwar evolution of the western European welfare state and mass migration as two separate or distinct phenomena. This is for the simple reason that western European welfare states (i.e. from 1950 to 1970) were built in tandem with a large-scale intake of migrants, citizens from colonies and former colonies (Bhambra 2017), and an unprecedented number of refugees. In the most universal and advanced welfare state, namely the Swedish one, labour migrants (recruited for manual work in manufacturing) and refugees gained full and immediate access to most welfare provisions, and they were also afforded permanent residence and short waiting periods for full formal citizenship (Schierup, Hansen & Castles 2006; Sainsbury 2012).

Although they are critical of the trade-off theory, Rainer Bauböck and Peter Scholten (2016: 6) suggest that we approach the progressive's dilemma less "as empirically grounded in social facts" and more as something to be "taken seriously as a political reality". Even though "empirical research shows that levels of redistribution, immigration and cultural diversity seem to vary rather independently from each other", the current political climate takes no notice of this research and so continues to present the trade-off as a reality (Bauböck & Scholten 2016: 6). When seen in this light, scholars making the case for the scientific plausibility of the trade-off are sometimes hard to distinguish from those making the political case for the trade-off. Acknowledging that the political climate favours the trade-off thesis is not, then, tantamount to a scientific confirmation of migration or diversity's negative causal effects on the performance and viability of the welfare state. Nevertheless, Bauböck and Scholten seem to hold the door open for a compromise with regard to the scientific merits of the trade-off perspective, and they do this through the perspective's massive political salience: "A realist approach will consider the politicized trade-offs as facts that are just as hard as if they were grounded in general social laws." Another way of putting this would be to say that the perspective championing the trade-off thesis holds a hegemonic status. As an alternative to a "realist approach", Bauböck and Scholten put forward Kymlicka's normative approach, which contests the trade-off "by invoking a conception of solidarity and political community that defies the dilemma", or trade-off (Bauböck & Scholten 2016: 6). They end, however, on a very discouraging note: "Comprehensive alternative visions how to resolve the progressive's political dilemma have yet to be developed."

Indeed, for one of Europe's most crucial and explosive issues – migration – there is no "comprehensive alternative vision" for how to break the trade-off impasse. And this is unsurprising, given that researchers fail to identify the main obstacle to an alternative vision, namely sound finance, as conceived within orthodox economics. We must also remember that, in many of the debates over the possible trade-offs between numbers and rights and recognition and redistribution, the economics research and its notions of *solvency requirements* and *budget constraints* are not really part of the picture. This means that the very concepts that set the parameters of the debate are hidden from view. For the most part, they are just perfunctorily assumed. Liberal and progressive scholars are either groping in the dark, appealing to a topsy-turvy host-population solidarity (that is, solidarity with those who end up benefiting rich EU countries by performing vital tasks such as caring for the sick and elderly) or simply treating the trade-off as a self-evident fact that justifies rights restrictions on migrants.

Political theorist Joseph Carens, who is a leading scholar on the ethics of migration, is a case in point. As one of the foremost academic advocates of migrants' rights, Ruhs and Martin (2008: 261) refer to Carens as contending that, "even if there is a trade-off between migrant numbers and rights, restricting the rights of migrants is always morally problematic". And, since Carens *does* acknowledge the trade-off as a reality (Carens 2008a: 438–9), this also forces him into an intricate exposition concerning those instances when morality actually (albeit problematically) takes a back seat to the presumed trade-off reality. As an example of when it is morally justifiable to exclude migrants from welfare, Carens (2008a: 430) argues that

> the programs from which temporary workers are most likely to be excluded and the ones where the normative justification of the exclusion seems to me most plausible are programs that are financed by some general tax and that have as their primary goal the transfer of resources from better off members of the community to worse off ones. I have in mind things like income support programs (often called welfare in the United States) and perhaps other programs aimed at poorer members of society such as social housing.

Correspondingly, Carens (2008b: 169–71) mentions schooling for children of irregular migrants as an example of when it is *not* morally legitimate to exclude. It is important to mention, however, that this is prefaced with an acknowledgement that "granting irregular migrant children a right to a free public education imposes a substantial financial cost on the receiving society against its expressed will". He admits that this and other arguments against such free public education "have some force"; but he also believes "that ultimately they are outweighed by the moral reasons for granting irregular migrant children a free public education".

Carens walks us through a number of other instances when it may or may not be morally permissible to exclude migrants from social rights. The point, however, is that this entire exercise is undertaken solely because Carens accepts the trade-off notion at face value. He is adapting his own theory to a trade-off thesis he takes to be so self-evident it needs no scrutiny. Had he done the opposite, he would rapidly have discovered, as I will soon show, that social rights to this or that migrant group do not pose a financial cost or danger to the host country.

Here, then, we can spot the problem also with much of the normative political theory around migration, citizenship and migrants' rights. It fails to examine what are presented as economic constraints – the trade-off, the costs – and hence feels compelled to adapt and adjust to what are really political constraints dressed up as economic ones. As I have already pointed out, there is of course also the option of acknowledging the reality of the constraints but then saying that, in practice, we can still afford it because economic losses sometimes have to be accepted in exchange for moral gains. In essence, this is what Carens does when he reasons around irregular migrants' right to education. As one representative voice has it: "There may well be a trade-off between numbers and rights, but refusing to grant immigrants a path to residency and citizenship has been argued to be fundamentally unjust and indeed inconsistent with liberal democratic ideals" (Neo 2015: 157).

## Conclusion

What happens when the state spends money on refugee reception and integration? The answer from the literature on the fiscal impact of migration – in all its different genres – is unequivocal: such spending burdens the public purse as a net cost. The same applies to all government spending on migrants who do not "beat the average" and contribute more in taxes than they withdraw in welfare benefits. Because of assumptions regarding intrinsic fiscal constraints and solvency risks that apply universally – no notice being taken of real-world varieties of monetary policy – the literature is thus keen to establish the various circumstances under which migration may or may not be fiscally sustainable, over the short to long term. As I noted too, the economics literature is the more easy-going when it comes to the fiscal impact and sustainability, mostly showing migration, as a whole, to have a small impact (± 1 per cent of GDP). Yet, when disaggregating the whole, this literature also feeds the more general social science literature on migration (e.g. political economy, political science and sociology) with crucial notions and findings with regard to categories of migrants whose fiscal position is deemed to be significantly negative – i.e. refugees, low-skilled labour migrants, low-earning migrants with children, etc. From here, as I show, we then get a growing body of research that focuses on the negative fiscal impact of these latter categories of migrants and how this "fiscal burden" problem should be tackled by policy-makers.

In critiquing the literature on migration's fiscal impact, I began with an immanent critique, showing that many of the "findings" in fact beg the question and thus rest on what are already unquestioned assumptions and premises underwriting the research enterprise in the first place. In other words, the research sets out to prove what it already has postulated as indisputable truths – i.e. that refugees and low-skilled migrants are fiscal burdens whereas high-skilled ones are fiscal contributors.

I have also pointed to the many absurdities that permeate this research, broadly speaking. For instance, it fails to take note of the fact that those categories of migrants, but also certain categories of citizens, who are referred to as fiscal burdens correspond to the same people who, for society at large, perform absolutely vital work in the low-wage sector. The research's tacit message and driver is that we are better off without fiscal burdens. But this is foolish thinking, since it also means that we are better off without, let us say, healthcare, elderly care, public transportation and daycare facilities. Another way of putting this would be to say that the literature on migration's fiscal impact fails the test of realism.

It is hard to overstate the seriousness of this failure. The research on the fiscal impact of migration has a tremendous impact on current policy-making in the European Union, and beyond. It permeates the bodies of experts advising governments, and its "findings" are echoed daily by politicians and the news media. To say that refugees and low skilled migrants are a fiscal burden on the welfare state is thus about as uncontroversial a statement as one can get in today's Europe. The only challenge heard is from voices who claim "We can afford it". But, as I have argued above, although the intention is to go against anti-immigration tendencies, this stance does not fundamentally challenge the trade-off thesis and cost perspective. In order to do that, we need a fundamentally different macroeconomic framework, one that can help us gain a realistic understanding of migration. This is the task of the next chapter.

# 3

# A modern migration theory

In the previous chapter I discussed Rainer Bauböck and Peter Scholten's (2016: 6) "realist approach", whereby they "consider the politicized trade-offs as facts that are just as hard as if they were grounded in general social laws". Listening to EU governments, researchers and the news media, this might indeed seem like a realist approach, at least at first glance. But, as the reader may have noted, in the preceding chapter I have already begun to display, and thus cultivate, an alternative type of realism. It comes to the fore in the scattered quotes in Chapter 2, such as when the Swedish government (2018b) concedes in a report on the future of elderly care that, "[w]ithout the foreign-born women and men, elderly care would face significant problems in fulfilling its task". Tucked away in this report we also find this phenomenal piece of information from the Swedish government, one it made sure not to reveal during the election campaign in 2018: "The number of persons in the population belonging to the most labour active age is expected to increase from 5.7 million in 2015 to 6.3 million in 2035. It is those who are foreign-born who are expected to make up the entire increase of working-age persons" (Swedish government 2018b: 13–14). This is refugee migration's *real* impact on Sweden; it has blessed it with a unique boost in the working-age population, one that puts Sweden in a uniquely fortunate position when dealing with the increase of the elderly population.

In the previous chapter, I also pointed to the severe staff shortages within Swedish and European healthcare and care sectors and how migrants and refugees increasingly are becoming the mainstay of these and other public services. Various versions of the message "Without the immigrants, healthcare collapses" are thus becoming commonplace across the European Union. As seen, many depopulating areas in Sweden and across the EU realize that welfare services are unsustainable if labour is unavailable, and this goes for welfare functions and services in urban areas too, of course. This is a realistic perspective that is grounded in *real* resource constraints, meaning, in this case, labour constraints. As opposed to Bauböck and Scholten's "realist approach", then, the realism we are dealing with here helps us spot the unrealism of the trade-off conception. Instead of having to wish for host-society solidarity coming from the sky to save progressive scholars from having to fret over the migration–welfare trade-off, what we are seeing are migrants and refugees literally coming to save the welfare state and rural communities.

With the aid of modern monetary theory, it is now high time to enter upon a more detailed critique of the basic assumptions that underpin the economics research into migration's fiscal impact and that, as shown in Chapter 2, seamlessly and often inadvertently trickle down all the way to the political and moral theory of migration and citizenship. But I will not use MMT just to critique the dominant fiscal impact approaches; my intention is also to describe MMT as an alternative macroeconomic framework in its own right. In doing so, as I will demonstrate, it becomes possible to break sound finance's stranglehold on migration research and outline a new and realistic theoretical approach to migration's impact on the economy and the welfare state.

## Real versus financial resources

Above, I have already pointed to a few irreparable flaws in the literature surveyed; for example, the major results are question-begging, and the reasoning around how people fall above or below "average" incomes and tax contributions is both unrealistic and illogical. By spelling out the absurd consequences of the latter flaw – the fact that those who perform much of the work without which there would be no society are categorized as fiscal burdens – we also unearth another fatal flaw. This, then, has to do with the literature's failure to distinguish between *financial* resources and *real* resources, which also happens to be one of the starting points of MMT. Again, I have already shown some of the absurd consequences of this failure above. For instance, I pointed to cases in which migrants and refugees are performing absolutely vital tasks for society's functioning, yet in the trade-off literature these same people, should they have equal access to the provisions of the welfare state, are described as fiscal burdens. Hence, their presence would also be deemed unsustainable, unless restrictions on their access to social rights were to be imposed.

From an MMT perspective, real resources always take precedence and, universally speaking, in the area of real resources there are always real constraints.[1] Consecutive Swedish governments, for instance, have been hard at work trying to provision the school system with more teachers to cover a severe staff shortage, which is expected to number 45,000 in 2033 (Skolverket 2019). For years on end, therefore, governments have been providing universities with additional financial resources to increase the places on teacher-training programmes. This has done little to educate more teachers and stem the shortage, however. The autumn semester in 2019 saw teacher student enrolment drop yet again in Sweden, and as a direct consequence two whole university programmes had to be closed (Swedish Radio 2019b). So, although the financial resources have been forthcoming, the real resources – or the teacher students – have failed to show up.

To illustrate this further, let me reuse an exchange that several MMT scholars (e.g. Kelton 2018) have employed to highlight the relationship between real and financial resources. During a hearing in the House Budget Committee in 2005, US House representative Paul Ryan and the chairman of the Federal Reserve, Alan Greenspan, had an instructive exchange. Ryan's mission was for Greenspan to back his plan for social security privatization, on the grounds that this would stave off insolvency and make the system secure. Ryan thus asks: "Do you believe that personal retirement accounts can help us achieve solvency for the system and make those future retiree benefits more secure?" To this Greenspan, who was under oath, responds:

> I wouldn't say the pay-as-you-go benefits are insecure in the sense that there is nothing to prevent the Federal Government from creating as much money as it wants and paying it to somebody. The question is, how do you set up a system which assures that the real assets are created which those benefits are employed to purchase? So, it is not a question of security. It is a question of the structure of a financial system which assures that the real resources are created for retirement as distinct from the cash. The cash itself is nice to have, but it has got to be in the context of the real resources being created at the time those benefits are paid and so that you can purchase real resources with the benefits, which of course are cash. (Kelton 2018)

---

1. Although the MMT literature is growing, it is still small. Instead of burdening the text with references to all the authors within this literature for every description based on MMT, I will mostly limit direct referencing to those instances where I quote. The works that I draw from in this section are as follows: Connors and Mitchell (2017); Ehnts (2017); Kelton (2020); Mitchell and Fazi (2017); Mosler (2010); Wray (2015); Mitchell, Wray and Watts (2019).

As seen, Greenspan refers to "real resources" no fewer than three times and to "real assets" once, and basically says that, although "cash itself is nice to have", it has little purchase if the real resources are not available. In the literature surveyed in Chapter 2, the perspective is the opposite. Here, migrants and citizens in general are exclusively covered as financial liabilities (those contributing taxes below average) or financial assets (those contributing taxes above average). Their reasoning falls within the same paradigm as Paul Ryan's: their aim is financial resources, but they fail to realize that, in their quest, they may end up sacrificing what these financial resources are supposed to enable society to afford, namely the real goods and services produced by real people.

### Why solvency requirements and budget constraints are mistaken

Even more importantly, perhaps, the quote by Greenspan pinpoints another of MMT's most basic descriptive starting points. This comes to the fore when Greenspan allays Ryan's insolvency worries, stating – again, under oath – that the benefits are not "insecure in the sense that there is nothing to prevent the Federal Government from creating as much money as it wants and paying it to somebody". In an address at the Catholic University Leuven in Belgium, Greenspan (1997) elaborates on the government's ability to create money:

> Central banks can issue currency, a non-interest-bearing claim on the government, effectively without limit. They can discount loans and other assets of banks or other private depository institutions, thereby converting potentially illiquid private assets into riskless claims on the government in the form of deposits at the central bank. That all of these claims on government are readily accepted reflects the fact that a government cannot become insolvent with respect to obligations in its own currency. A fiat money system, like the ones we have today, can produce such claims without limit.

One of the reasons why MMT scholars like to quote people and institutions that are on the opposite side when it comes to MMT's policy prescription – such as the free marketeer and Ayn Rand admirer Alan Greenspan – is precisely to make the point that what we are talking about here, at this stage, is not policy prescription but a pure description of how monetary and fiscal policy works: how the central government spends. Greenspan may have been ignorant about many things, but as the head of the Federal Reserve he surely knew something about how the US government spends, and something too about its (in principle unlimited) capacity to spend.

Greenspan's successor, Ben Bernanke, knew this too, of course, and during the financial crisis he would use the Fed's money-creating capacity in an unprecedented way. When interviewed on CBS's prime-time *60 Minutes*, the host, Scott Pelley, asked Bernanke where the money to bail out the banks came from; he asked whether it was tax money that the Fed was spending. "It's not tax money," Bernanke answered. "The banks have accounts with the Fed, much the same way that you have an account in a commercial bank. So, to lend to a bank, we simply use the computer to mark up the size of the account that they have with the Fed. It's much more akin to printing money than it is to borrowing" (CBS 2009).

"[I]t is important to remember that the government differs critically from businesses and individuals," two economists at the Federal Reserve Bank of St Louis write. They explain: "As the sole manufacturer of dollars, whose debt is denominated in dollars, the U.S. government can never become insolvent, i.e., unable to pay its bills. In this sense, the government is not dependent on credit markets to remain operational" (Fawley & Juvenal 2011: 5).

Again, this is mere description: a country whose government is the monopoly issuer of the currency can never face a solvency risk in its own currency, unless, that is, it adopts a fixed exchange rate policy, pegs its currency to a commodity (often gold) or borrows excessively in foreign currency. What is needed to remove any risk of insolvency, then, is an inconvertible, or fiat, currency, with a floating exchange rate. If these requirements are fulfilled, the country will always be able to meet all the financial obligations that are placed on it in the currency it issues. MMTers like to point out that such a monetarily sovereign country could, technically speaking, always buy everything for sale in its own currency. This is not something they think governments *should* do, however, again highlighting the crucial difference between description of actual operations and policy prescription. Neither is MMT saying that there are no limits to spending, for the obvious inflationary risks involved in reckless spending. Too much spending by the central government could, for instance, lead to real resource constraints, such as there not being enough idle labour to hire. "Since the government," as Wray (2019: 7) argues, "'cannot run out of money' it could 'win' a bidding war, taking resources away from other uses (in the private sector, or in use by lower levels of government). [...] The inflationary consequences might also be undesired. And inflation can be sparked before full employment (bottlenecks in some sectors) so it matters where the government's spending is directed."

What MMT does prescribe, however, and what follows from the monetarily sovereign country's ability to buy things for sale in its own currency, is that governments should guarantee full employment and thus hire the unemployed labour not hired by the private sector and the regular public sector. Springing from Hyman Minsky's proposal to have the central government taking on the responsibility as an employer of last resort, the "job guarantee" constitutes MMT's signature policy plan (e.g. Tcherveva 2020, 2018; Wray 2007, 2016).

A job guarantee for full employment would hardly be realistic in cases when governments adopt a fixed exchange rate or a foreign currency, as is the case with dollarization in countries such as Ecuador or with the eurozone, where the member states do not issue their own currencies or set the interest rate. A country that, for instance, promises to convert its currency into another currency, such as the US dollar, or to a commodity, such as gold, may lose a significant amount of domestic policy space because it constantly has to worry about having access to a currency that someone else is issuing, or to a scarce commodity. In such cases, it would be accurate to speak of solvency risks and budget constraints. But, again, even here the constraints are ultimately political, not inescapable economic laws, since they stem from a monetary policy that is instituted by people. As we also know, it is quite common for fixed exchange rates to be converted into floating ones, often on account of the former being unsustainable and crash-sensitive.

The problem with the literature examined in the previous chapter, however, is that, when it explicates or assumes solvency risks and budget constraints, it does not explain that these constraints apply only under the specific circumstance of the currency being pegged or foreign. It fails to grasp that it is assuming constraints to apply universally, to all countries under all circumstances, and hence it also assumes that all countries operate under the same monetary system – or, perhaps more accurately, it fails to see that this, as by definition, needs to be the assumption. Clearly, this is not the case. Some countries have currencies pegged to other currencies; some have adopted the US dollar as their official currency; some countries are part of currency unions, such as the eurozone or the CFA franc; and some issue their own currencies. In addition, it is ironic that much of the economics literature dealing with migration's fiscal impact that I attended to in Chapter 2 has its basis in the United States and Britain, two countries that issue their own sovereign currencies and so do not face any solvency or budget constraint in their own currencies. What this testifies to is an acute ignorance or unawareness of the absolutely decisive role played by money and monetary systems for fiscal policy and domestic policy choices. In fact, the literature on migration's fiscal impact, the numbers versus welfare rights trade-off and the trade-off between recognition and redistribution does not deal at all with money or monetary policy. It fails to do so despite the fact that the ultimate driving force for the research stems from money worries: the concern that there may not be enough fiscal space to pay for migrants and refugees who fail to beat the average.

The main reason for this huge error has less to do with the literature scrutinized here per se, and everything to do with the fact that it forms part of or derives – knowingly or unknowingly – its assumption from the general field of mainstream orthodox economics. Within orthodoxy, as Wray (2002: 24, emphasis in original) has it, "money plays no *essential* role"; here, rather, "money is essentially a commodity that functions primarily as a medium of exchange, invented to reduce transactions costs" (2002: 27). Money, then, is the invention of barterers in the market, not of the state, and it is there to minimize the transaction costs of bartering. Accordingly, in the delusional world of orthodox economics, Wray (2002: 24) notes, "modern technology should allow barter-based markets to function without many transactions costs of the sort that money's creation was supposed to have eliminated – so money's continued existence is even called into question".

As Dirk Ehnts (2017: 11) underlines, such a misleading conception of money adds to the more well-known errors within orthodoxy, foremost the idea that actors in the economy are alike in their rationality and that they come equipped with complete information about the economy. Orthodox models thus "ignore the functioning of real monetary systems, working instead on the assumption that money is a commodity, something like a heap of gold coins" (Ehnts 2017: 12). Provided that this antiquated "gold standard logic" still pervades mainstream macroeconomics (Mitchell, Wray & Watts 2019: 14), we should not be surprised that the household analogy and sound finance are pervasive too, since they all belong to the same orthodox paradigm.

## Issuing, taxing and borrowing

In failing to account for the monetary system's crucial importance, it follows that orthodoxy also fails to distinguish between money issuers and money users – another of MMT's basic starting points. Since orthodoxy's sound finance basically models the central government in accordance with the household analogy, the central government is, by definition, always forced to collect money before it can spend. Hence, it appears to be a mere currency user, on a par with other users, such as constituent states of federations, municipalities, businesses and households. As I pointed out above, this explains the literature's sequential logic. When studying the fiscal impact of migration, researchers thus *first* account for how much taxes migrants pay in (public revenue) and then, *second*, how much government expenditure migrants attract (public costs). If the former fails to offset the latter, the budget constraint is being tested and the government will have to make sure to find the money to cover for the shortfall. The options would be to raise taxes, borrow, transfer money from other budget areas or, as suggested by scholars within the trade-off school, restrict migrants' access to welfare benefits and/or hit them with additional taxes.

For countries that issue their own currencies, however, none of this applies. Rather, the sequence runs in the opposite direction. Since the central government is the monopoly issuer of the currency, it follows, both in logical and in concrete terms, that it necessarily has to spend or lend the currency (via the banking system) into existence before it can collect it back in taxes. If this was not the case, there would be no money to pay taxes with. Such governments are thus the exact opposite of municipalities, business and households, all of which have to collect, earn or borrow the money before they can spend it; they are mere users of money, not issuers.

With governments spending first, taxing second, it also follows that there can be no intrinsic budget constraint, as the orthodox literature stipulates. As MMT conveys it, currency-issuing governments are not revenue-constrained. This means that taxes collected by the central government are not used to fund government spending as they are when collected by currency-using bodies such as municipalities or constituent states in federations. Central government taxes thus fulfil other indispensable functions and purposes. According to MMT, taxes are what ultimately "drive the currency", in the sense that tax obligations ensure an unceasing demand for the currency. Moreover, by constantly removing a large chunk of money – and thus spending power – from the private sector, taxes work as a powerful anti-inflationary measure while at the same time moving resources from the private to the public sector. If the private sector, including households, is constantly obliged to pay taxes to the central government, this ensures a great demand to earn the money that is issued by the government, or the sovereign issuer of money. "This means that many will work for the sovereign, or work to produce what the sovereign wants to buy" (Wray 2015: 148). Taxes, furthermore, work as an instrument regulating income and wealth distribution, and thus they have a great impact on the aggregate level of inequality in a country. Taxes, when lowered, are also used to promote and stimulate, let us say, certain industries, professions and behaviours, whereas, when increased, they work to discourage or limit others. For instance, tax cuts may be used to spearhead innovation in green energy and technology, while tax hikes may be used to reprimand industries that drag their feet. And there are, of course, other purposes that central government taxes can be made to fulfil – but revenue for spending and saving for future spending do not form part of them. Again, as the monopoly issuer of the currency, the government can always spend its own currency.

By the same token, such governments do not have to borrow their own currency in order to spend. As MMT scholars demonstrate, the real purpose of bond sales in a sovereign currency is not fiscal (for financing purposes) but monetary. They are carried out in order for the central bank to hit its overnight interest rate target (the interest banks pay when borrowing reserves from each other overnight).[2] When a government runs a deficit – i.e. when it spends more than it taxes – this leads to a net addition of central bank reserves in the banking system, which in turn causes the overnight rate to fall towards zero. In the banking system as a whole, the supply of reserves has increased and demand has not. For the interest rate to remain on target, the central bank therefore sells interest-bearing bonds to *drain reserves*. Conversely, when reserves are drying up and thus putting upward pressure on the central bank's overnight target, the central bank *adds reserves* by, among other things, buying bonds. But, as MMTers are fast to point out, if the government so decides, it may also "leave excess reserves in the banking system, in which case the overnight rate would fall toward zero" (Mitchell, Wray & Watts 2019: 326). While at zero, the finance department can then choose "to sell short-term bonds that pay a few basis points [one basis point = 0.01 per cent] above zero and will find willing buyers because bonds offer a better return than the alternative (zero). This drives home the point that a sovereign government with a floating currency can issue bonds at any rate it desires, normally a few basis points above the overnight interest target it has set" (Mitchell, Wray & Watts 2019: 326).

To be sure, all countries that issue their own currencies still impose unnecessary fiscal frameworks, including balanced or surplus budget rules, debt brakes and spending ceilings, and in some cases (e.g. Germany and the European Union) they form part of the constitution or have a constitutional character, which make them very hard to change. One of the most common rules stipulates that governments must "borrow" and thus sell bonds to the private sector when it lacks the funds or deposits at the central bank to match the spending. But, again, currency-issuing governments do not need to borrow

---

2. Although the targeting of the overnight interest rate defines the so-called independence of central banks (in those cases in which law-makers have chosen to grant it such a repealable status), ensuring that the rate stays on target also reveals the very limited nature of this "independence". As MMT shows, because of the fact that "government spending and taxes both impact bank reserves, the central bank normally offsets undesired impacts" – something that necessitates a close "coordination of central bank and treasury operations" (Mitchell, Wray & Watts 2019: 326–7). This is why MMT always insists that we take the talk about central bank "independence" with more than a grain of salt.

the currency whose issuing it monopolizes. In fact, as William Mitchell and Thomas Fazi (2017: 184, emphasis in original) reveal, such governments "could run fiscal deficits *without issuing debt at all*: the central bank could simply credit the relevant bank accounts to facilitate the spending requirements of the treasury, regardless of whether the fiscal position is deficit or surplus". Another option would be for the finance department to sell debt directly to the central bank, a procedure also prohibited by most countries as part of the big smorgasbord of voluntarily imposed constraints.

MMT does not outright disqualify the selling of government debt to the private sector, however; rather, MMT deems it a policy option that governments may want to use in order to provide the private sector with interest-bearing safe assets. For instance, pension funds' portfolios are often mentioned as being very well served by such safe assets.

But, even when currency-issuing governments sell bonds to the private sector, these bonds can be "sold" only on the premise that the government first provides the reserves with which banks purchase the bonds. Again, a government "must spend (or lend) its currency before it can receive it back either in payment of taxes or in purchase of its debt" (Mitchell, Wray & Watts 2019: 338). MMT is thus careful to explain that, even when currency-issuing countries impose unnecessary and ideologically driven constraints, at the end of the day the currency-issuing reality still trumps gold standard myths. So, when currency-issuing governments create fiscal frameworks that require bond sales to the private sector, or banks – instead of no sales or sales directly to the central bank, as mentioned above – the banks pay for this by using the reserves that they have in their accounts at the central bank. But where do these reserves come from and what happens if banks that want to purchase bonds do not have enough reserves? William Mitchell, Randall Wray and Martin Watts (2019: 322) explain:

> If a bank that wants to buy bonds has no excess reserves to debit, then it will either go to the interbank market to borrow them from banks with extra reserves, or it will borrow them from the central bank … We know that if the banking system has no excess reserves, the central bank will respond to any pressure on overnight interest rates that might be created by banks trying to borrow reserves in order to buy the bonds. It [the central bank] will either lend them at the discount window, or engage in open market purchases, creating reserves by buying bonds from the non-government sector.

Hence, "banks will always be able to get the reserves they need in order to buy bonds" (Mitchell, Wray & Watts 2019: 322).

Again, currency-issuing governments, generally speaking, have rules that prohibit them from doing what they could, namely selling bonds directly to the central bank or simply abstaining from issuing bonds at all. But, as MMT is able to demonstrate, despite this self-imposed restriction, currency issuing is still king. This is so because, even though governments require themselves to sell bonds to the private sector, this procedure ends up being equivalent to the situation whereby the Treasury had sold them directly to the central bank. Save for the fact that the private sector gets to hold interest-bearing safe assets, the only difference is that "the central bank buys the bonds in the secondary markets from the private banks rather than buying them directly from the treasury in the primary market" (Mitchell, Wray & Watts 2019: 339).

## Deficits and surpluses explained

In explaining why sovereign currency issuers cannot be revenue-constrained in their own currencies, MMT also corrects the mistaken sound finance conception regarding fiscal deficits and surpluses at the central government level. As noted above, the entire literature on migration's fiscal impact and the trade-off between migration and welfare is driven by the concern that spending on low-skilled migrants and refugees will generate unsustainable fiscal deficits or undermine welfare systems and redistribution. The same applies to the media and politicians. When, for instance, the Swedish parliament adopted the government's amended extra budget in the late autumn of 2015, prompted by the need for a spending increase to accommodate the large refugee admission, the Finance Ministry made it very clear that this would be fiscally painful for Sweden. As I will deal with in more detail in Chapter 7, the Finance Ministry claimed that the extra refugee spending would increase the deficit, force Sweden to borrow and transfer funds from other budget areas. But, although no one dared to bring it up, what had already been proved was that the Swedish state could spend at will (before it borrowed and before it collected taxes), and that when push came to shove the fiscal framework's spending limits were just that: a self-imposed constraint that could be nullified by a self-imposed sensibility.

But, if a deficit is not the dangerous thing that the literature, governments and the media would like us to believe, what is it? As MMT explains, a government deficit is merely another way of expressing net financial savings (or surpluses) in the non-government sector. What most people take to be a bad thing – i.e. the deficit with the central government – is actually equivalent to what most people take to be a good and prudent thing, namely net saving by, for instance, households and businesses. And this applies to all countries, whether they issue their own fiat currencies or not. In MMT, the method by which we grasp this relationship goes via an understanding of financial stocks and flows (the "flow of funds approach") as applied within a sectoral balance framework.[3]

For one thing, MMT emphasizes the most basic principle of accounting, namely that all financial assets, by definition, will be matched by an equal number of financial liabilities. By the same token, every financial deficit will be offset by a financial surplus. Everyone cannot run a surplus, just as everyone cannot beat the average – although, when listening to politicians and those doing research into migration's fiscal impact, one can get the sense that this indeed might be possible. Hence, a sectoral balance approach "builds on the accounting rule that a government deficit (or surplus) must be exactly offset by a surplus (or deficit) in the non-government sector" (Mitchell, Wray & Watts 2019: 14). Since the non-governmental sector has to be divided into a domestic (encompassing households and firms) and a foreign or external sector (exports and imports with foreign firms, governments and households), we end up with three sectors. In adding the balances of each sector, we get the following accounting identity (Wray 2015: 14):

domestic private balance + domestic government balance + foreign balance = 0

Although the sectors, which represent the economy as a whole, must balance in the aggregate, each sector does not have to balance, but can run deficits or surpluses; in other words, they can spend more or less than their incomes. In keeping with the accounting identity, however, when "one sector spends more that its income, at least one of the others must spend less than its income because for the economy as a whole, total spending must equal total receipt or income" (Mitchell, Wray & Watts 2019: 14).

The reason why research into migration's fiscal impact and the alleged trade-off between migration and welfare is so anxious about central government deficits is precisely because it approaches things from the perspective of sound finance and the household analogy. For a private household, of course, taking on a lot of debt and running a continuous deficit is always risky and, eventually, unsustainable; this is clear. By now, however, it should also be clear that a currency-issuing government does not spend and "borrow" like a private household, and hence the analogy has absolutely no bearing on reality.

Thanks to the sectoral balance approach we are now able to clarify something else too: that a central government deficit equals a non-government surplus. Those who think it unwise for firms and households to deficit-spend and recklessly pile up of debt should thus be aware that a central government deficit will be very helpful in preventing that. In cases when a country imports

---

3. The latter was developed into a proper theory first by the economist Wynne Godley.

more than it exports, such a central government deficit will be a necessity. Again, this is just an accounting identity. If the domestic private sector has a desire to net-save (i.e. to spend less than its income), which is quite normal and often amplified during slumps, high unemployment and uncertainty about the future, then governments most probably (depending on the foreign sector balance) need to run large deficits to cover for such savings desires. Since the financial flows within the private sector always sum to a net wealth of zero – with financial assets always being equal to financial liabilities – the only way the domestic private sector can net-save, or "accumulate a stock of wealth in the form of financial assets", is to secure "financial claims on another sector" (Wray 2015: 11, 10). If the sector should be the government sector (which is very likely), it also means that the government, by definition, must spend more than it taxes; it must run a deficit.

Yet this is not understood in the literature dealing with migration's fiscal impact. To further illuminate this awkward state of affairs, let us look at a working paper published by REMINDER, a large EU-funded research consortium on European mobility, consisting of 14 of Europe's most prominent research institutions. The two authors of the working paper present "the first large cross-country estimation of the fiscal effects of migration of EU citizens within the EEA [European Economic Area]". In accounting for the previous research on migration's fiscal impact, the paper goes through the usual motions, claiming, for instance, that previous studies indicate that "countries with predominantly skilled labour immigration showed markedly more positive fiscal effects". Among the other most important "moderators of fiscal contributions", the authors also point to "the sustainability of the host country's fiscal regime (since long-term systematic deficits make even the average citizen a net liability)" (Nyman & Ahlskog 2018: 2). As the last bit in the parenthesis postulates, a deficit at the central government level, or sector, is interpreted as automatically equalling a net deficit also for households. A few pages later the authors spell out this mistake in full: "A country running a large budget deficit will tend to have inhabitants that are net liabilities on average, while a large budget surplus will yield inhabitants that are net assets" (Nyman & Ahlskog 2018: 14).

The study operates with a mistaken accounting identity that builds on the assumption that central governments are analogous to big households. Again, it fails to understand that governments running deficits do not subtract but, rather, add financial assets and wealth to the private sector, including households. Prior to the financial crisis, for instance, Spain's central government ran a surplus whereas the private sector ran a deficit (meanwhile Spain imported more than it exported and so ran a current account deficit). What took the economy down was an unsustainable amount of private debt, and,

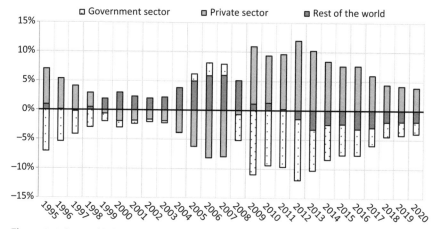

**Figure 3.1** Sectoral balances for Spain, represented as sector's gains/GDP, compared to real GDP annual growth

*Note*: The current account is inverted, meaning that when it is showing a surplus this indicates that the rest of the world is running a current account surplus against Spain, and vice versa.

*Source*: Courtesy of Dirk Ehnts (see, further, http://econintersect.com/pages/contributors/contributor.php?post=201607142330).

contrary to what the authors above want to have us believe, the fact that the Spanish government ran a surplus did not "yield inhabitants" who were "net assets" (see Figure 3.1).[4]

We can also look at the current situation in Sweden, where the government balance has been in surplus from 2015 until the Covid-19 pandemic. Yet Sweden's household sector is one of the most indebted in the OECD area, with household debt standing at about the equivalent of 190 per cent of annual disposable income, some 80 per cent of the debt consisting of mortgages. The households are, in other words, soaked in liabilities (which are the banks' assets). The Swedish central bank's *Financial Stability Report* from May 2019 thus warns, for the umpteenth time, "that Swedish households' high indebtedness remains the greatest risk in the Swedish economy" (Riksbank 2019: 4). The household debt, the Riksbank (2019: 4) states, "has increased for a long time and households are currently highly indebted, both from a historical perspective and in international comparisons. This means that households are sensitive to changes that affect their finances, such as rising interest rates, rising unemployment and falling housing prices." Of course, the households also hold highly valued *real* assets (i.e. the apartments and houses), but the

---

4. For more on Spain and the eurozone crisis, using a sectoral balance approach, see Ehnts (2017).

Riksbank (2019: 13) warns that "the value of real and financial assets can fall in times of economic unease, while the size of debts remains unchanged". In the report, the Riksbank notes that household debt has been swelling in tandem with real estate prices going through the roof. In addition, the bank issues a warning concerning the surge in corporate indebtedness too, pointing particularly to the increased debt taken on by real estate companies.

As for the drivers of household debt in Sweden, the Riksbank cites low property taxes and the fact that interest payments are tax-deductible. Although these create incentives to borrow, the Riksbank (2019: 10) also highlights a driver of a more coercive nature: "Long queues for rental housing, above all in the major cities, may be contributing towards households feeling forced to purchase homes, which almost always requires taking on debt" (see also EC 2019a). Indeed, when buying, rather than renting, constitutes practically the only way of living, then most people have little choice but to go into debt. With credit being easy too, we have gathered all the ingredients for the (next) perfect financial storm. To understand why rented flats are in such short supply in Sweden, we need to go back to the early 1990s, when the fatal decisions were taken to, among other things, eliminate state subsidies to housing construction and also allow for what would become a mass sell-off of the public housing stock. These policies formed part of Sweden's decision to implement a sound finance fiscal framework, with the goal of running continuous central government surpluses.

This is just one among scores of other examples in today's European Union of what happens when the central government is chasing balanced (or surplus) fiscal positions. As seen in the Swedish case, it results in an extremely unbalanced housing market and dangerously indebted households that risk bringing down the entire economy. Even though the latter predicament is acknowledged by the Swedish government, its various economic agencies and its central bank as well as the European Commission, the former problem remains unacknowledged. In every country report on Sweden in recent years the European Commission has issued grave warnings about the dangerously indebted Swedish households. At the same time, it continues to praise Sweden for its "extensive track record of fiscal soundness" (EC 2017a: 17). "Sweden," it keeps repeating, "has been able to preserve a sound fiscal position" (EC 2019a: 13). The Commission also says, moreover: "Sound fiscal management and strong economic performance under the Commission's baseline no-policy change scenario is projected to bring government debt close to 16% of GDP in 2029 from 37.8% of GDP in 2018, well below the 60% of GDP Treaty reference value" (EC 2019a: 23). As Wray (2015: 8) puts it, however:

> The most "unsound" budgetary policy is mindless pursuit of something called a "balanced budget" … If that outcome is achieved, it means that all government's currency supplied through its spending [over a year] will have been "returned" in tax payments so that the nongovernment sector has nothing left – no extra funds to set aside for the proverbial "rainy day".

This can also be explained via the "demand gap" that results from private sector savings, whereby, as Ehnts (2017: 68) shows, it becomes "a macroeconomic requirement to run public deficits". Rather than perceiving of continuous central government deficits as a "pathological symptom", which is the orthodox view, such deficits provide the means by which the non-government sector can fulfil its savings objectives. These are savings flows that accumulate as stocks of financial wealth within the non-government sector, exactly mirroring the accumulated stock of what practically everyone – scholars included – mistakenly thinks of as an unsustainable government debt. If, however, governments run balanced or surplus budgets while segments within the private sector continue to save, it then follows, as Ehnts (2017: 68) explains, that "the quantity of circulating money would gradually decrease – and so would effective demand. Firms would not be able to sell all of their production. Subsequently, output would be reduced or grow less strongly, leading to lower rates of economic activity and higher unemployment." When the crisis hit the eurozone, this is basically what happened, with the difference that most governments could not run balanced budgets because of automatic stabilizers and the fact that private sector spending froze, leading to a dramatic drop in tax revenue. Yet EU and eurozone fiscal rules prevented governments from engaging in countercyclical spending and instead forced them to "save" and cut back in a situation in which the private sector sat tight. This austerity medicine killed the patient, of course, resulting, as it did, in a vicious spiral of collapsing demand, enormous unemployment and overall social crisis.[5]

Unless a country has a very large current account surplus, governments need to run a fiscal deficit pretty much permanently in order to satisfy saving aspirations and plug the demand gap. The latter could of course also be taken care of through a private credit expansion, which has been a frequent substitute for government spending in recent decades. But, as seen above, such an expansion will not be sustainable over time, which, again, serves to highlight the difference between currency issuers and currency users.

---

5. Besides the MMT literature, Mark Blyth's (2015) work offers an excellent and thoroughgoing account of the misguided policy of austerity.

It is important as well to remember that a government deficit never inhibits a currency-issuing government from spending its own currency, and neither does a surplus constitute a saving in the sense of boosting future spending capacity (or the government's "fiscal space"), as is the case with a private household or any other currency user. What also speaks against governments trying to hit some predefined fiscal goal or target has to do with the fact that governments cannot know or control beforehand the spending, investment and saving behaviours and desires of the other sectors for the coming fiscal year. Not knowing this also means that a government cannot know beforehand how much tax will come in. I will come back to this in Chapter 7 when discussing the Swedish government's and the economic expertise's predictions about the fiscal impact of the refugee spending from 2015 and onwards.

This provided, MMT argues that the fiscal position of a country should be considered "in the light of the usefulness of the government's spending pro-gramme in achieving its national socio-economic goals" (Mitchell, Wray & Watts 2019: 15). Here, as I will also discuss further in Chapter 7, MMT draws from Abba Lerner's "functional finance" approach, which was developed in the 1940s, in opposition to sound finance (e.g. Lerner 1946: ch. 24). According to functional finance, a government's spending should be made to match object-ives that answer to a society's welfare and sound functioning. Whatever fiscal balance emerges at the end of the year will form part of the sectoral accounting identity that "tells us *ex post* what the changes in the financial aggregates are as a result of discretionary government policy choices and the state of the economy" (Mitchell, Wray & Watts 2019: 322).

In contrast to sound finance, functional finance is primarily geared towards realizing the public purpose or interest. Traditionally, such a public interest has been defined in terms of full employment and low inflation. In theory, how-ever, there is nothing preventing the public interest from being defined in other terms – such as, for example, first-rate schools, good elderly care, sustainable climate and energy policies, robust refugee reception capacity, and so on. But, again, what is important and truly defining of functional finance is that the fiscal position of a government's budget is a relative creature, fluctuating with the spending levels needed to secure, say, full employment, climate sustain-ability, the welfare and investment needs of municipalities or the savings needs of households and the private sector. This is the opposite of sound finance, whereby a fiscal position in balance or in surplus is deemed an end in itself. A balanced fiscal position thus trumps everything else, imposing constraints on spending and other fiscal tools that might be absolutely necessary to meet important public goods and functions.

## The hard yet unnecessary constraints of the eurozone

As already mentioned, countries that adopt fixed exchange rates or foreign currencies are in many ways a completely different story. In the eurozone, member states do not issue their own currencies, and because of this their central banks neither have the option of creating the amounts of currency needed by the government at any point in time nor set the overnight interest rate for interbank borrowing. It is the European Central Bank (ECB) in Frankfurt that sets the overnight rate, which is the same for all the members. Having adopted what, in essence, amounts to a foreign currency that they do not control, eurozone members should be conceived of as currency *users* rather than currency *issuers*. In this crucial sense, they can be likened to municipalities or constituent states of federations. As Ehnts notes (2017: 181), when countries scrapped their sovereign currencies for the euro, they also became "forced to incur debts in what amounts to a quasi-foreign currency". Consequently, Ehnts (2017: 181) continues, eurozone countries also set themselves up for big trouble down the road, since they, from here on, would "run the risk of becoming illiquid if (expected) tax income" failed to cover the servicing of the debt.[6]

Since members of the eurozone are exposed to bond markets in a real sense – as opposed to currency-issuing countries, which sell debt denominated in their own currencies to private financial institutions – this means that, when markets become hesitant about a country's ability to service its debt, they sell the bonds that they hold in their portfolios, causing the price of old bonds to drop. This increases the yield of the old bonds. In order to issue new bonds that are attractive to financial investors, their yield has to at least equal the yield of the old bonds, thus driving interest rates on new bonds up. This increases the fragility of the whole structure of public debt, leading to a vicious circle. If rates continue to appreciate this will sooner or later lead to the country getting shut out from bond markets altogether, being unable to sell its debt in the primary market. Eurozone countries, such as Greece, thus face the possibility of having to default on their debt for political reasons. Even though, technically, the ECB could easily help out eurozone governments, it is prohibited from doing so by article 123 of the consolidated version of the Treaty on the Functioning of the European Union.

---

6. For an excellent study of the negative political consequences of the European Monetary Union and, consequently, the crucial advantages of monetary policy autonomy, see Jonathon Moses (2017).

Despite the fact that Japan's ratio of debt to GDP is much higher than both Greece's and Italy's, it is the latter two that are perceived as risky by bond markets, not Japan, which has the higher debt ratio. As Wray (2015: 182) highlights, this goes to illustrates the fundamental difference between a currency issuer and a currency user. When Japan manages its debt, Wray explains, "it does so by making 'keystroke' entries onto balance sheets. […] It can never run out of the 'keystrokes' – it can create as many Yen entries as necessary. It can never be forced into involuntary default." In sharp contrast, the Eurozone's separation of monetary (ECB, supranational) and fiscal (national) policy was conceived precisely "to ensure that no member state would be able to use the ECB to run up budget deficits financed by 'keystrokes'. The belief was that by forcing member states to go to the market to obtain funding, market discipline would keep budget deficits in line" (Wray 2015: 182). This explains why it was necessary to institute the so-called "no bail-out" clause in the eurozone's constitution.[7]

The formation of the European Monetary Union (EMU) thus involved the creation of a monetarist policy framework of appropriately high interest rates – supposedly all by themselves leading to low inflation rates – governed by the ECB and a set of restrictive fiscal policies, known as the Stability and Growth Pact (SGP). A synthesis of the EMU's original Maastricht convergence criteria, the SGP was established in 1997 to rein in state spending by limiting annual budget deficits and accumulated debt to the equivalent of 3 per cent and 60 per cent of GDP respectively. In the wake of the financial and eurozone crises, a number of new disciplinary laws and measures were added to the SGP in order to better monitor, consolidate and enforce the fiscal rules. In 2010 the European Semester was launched, with the explicit mandate of "ensuring sound public finances (avoiding excessive government debt)" (EC n.d.–a). This was followed by a new legal package to boost fiscal governance, known as the Six Pack, which was subsequently further reinforced by the Two Pack, the Fiscal Compact and other initiatives, all aiming to ensure "fiscal consolidation" and hence perpetual austerity.

As noted above, these austerity measures were imposed precisely at the time when crisis-hit eurozone countries were in desperate need of the exact opposite medicine, namely a substantial government-led demand stimulus to counter rapidly contracting private investment and consumption. With the counter-cyclical option effectively checked and with tax revenues continuing to plummet in tandem with increasing unemployment, both annual deficits and aggregate debts continued to increase as a percentage of GDP,

---

7. As stipulated by the Lisbon Treaty's article 125.

which, in turn, made bond markets even more jittery. This development conclusively invalidated all the alchemic guarantees to the contrary made by those who were designing and providing "scientific" confirmation to the various fiscal consolidation measures – i.e. the European Commission, the ECB, the International Monetary Fund (IMF) and most governments, as well as numerous economists.

As the situation continued to deteriorate, then ECB president Mario Draghi decided that it was high time to set to work, stating at a meeting in London on 26 July 2012 that the ECB was "ready to do whatever it takes to preserve the eurozone", adding: "And believe me, it will be enough." Understanding this to mean that the ECB was ready to buy government debt on the secondary market, the markets soon calmed, initiating a drop in the interest rates on the debt issued by crisis countries. Such bond buying by the ECB had already been applied to Greece, and subsequently also to Spain and Italy, but the "whatever it takes" policy was different, in that it made plain that the ECB, from now on, would act as a backstop and thus effectively preclude default risks. As part of the intervention in 2012, the ECB launched two programmes: the Outright Monetary Transactions (OMT) programme and the Securities Market Programme. Both programmes authorized the ECB to buy bonds in the secondary market, the former from troubled eurozone countries and the latter from all countries in the eurozone.

The main reason for elaborating on these changes is to show that, even in the eurozone, which for some may seem like a place where budget constraints and solvency risks are truly intrinsic, the constraints in fact result from political decisions and ideological leanings. Hence, the economics literature on migration's fiscal impact does not apply to the eurozone either. But, then again, my point may be redundant, because of the fact that this literature never really discusses monetary policy or spells out to what monetary system it may or may not apply. At the same time, it is still very important to emphasize that the rules and laws of the eurozone are politically determined, and so can be changed. It should also be emphasized that the euro *is* a freely floating fiat currency – it is not convertible to gold or anything else – and this means that the ECB could operate like the Federal Reserve or the Bank of Japan; it too could finance member state deficits via "keystrokes". In fact, when Draghi launched the Outright Monetary Transactions programme in 2012, "the ECB stated that *unlimited* amounts of sovereign bonds could be purchased under the OMT program to reach its objectives" (Acharya & Steffen 2017: 24, emphasis added). As Mitchell (2020) has it, "The only reason the Eurozone survived intact in 2010 and 2012 and subsequently was because the ECB became a quasi-fiscal agent in the absence of a federal capacity and defied the strict rules of the Treaty by funding government deficits to the tune of billions of euros."

But, although the "whatever it takes" initiative demonstrated the fiat quality of the euro as well as the relative flexibility of eurozone rules (the subsequent Covid-19 crisis would demonstrate this even more forcefully), it was still part of a larger initiative that resulted in an even more rigid adherence to sound finance orthodoxy and perpetual austerity. Numerous austerity strings were thus attached should a country ask to be part of the OMT programme. Moreover, the Fiscal Compact – or Treaty on Stability, Coordination and Governance in the Economic and Monetary Union – stated that governments had to "maintain sound and sustainable public finances and to prevent a government deficit becoming excessive" (EC 2012a). The European Commission (2017b) thus emphasized that "[t]he main provision of this Treaty is the requirement to have a balanced budget rule in domestic legal orders (the Fiscal Compact)".

Although the crisis forced the ECB to open for bond buying in the secondary market, it also forced member states, particularly those most severely hit by the crisis, to adopt even grimmer and even more counterproductive austerity measures. Yet again, however, this does not take away from the fact that the eurozone, as Mitchell and Fazi (2017: 189) underline, "is itself a system of voluntary constraints that are reflected in legal statements, all of which could be changed via appropriate legislation". In sharp contrast to the literature on the fiscal impact of migration examined in Chapter 2, MMT thus helps us discover and fully understand "the notion of voluntary versus intrinsic constraints in a fiat currency system" (Mitchell & Fazi 2017: 189).

## Conclusion

As I have demonstrated here, modern monetary theory presents a comprehensive and realistic alternative to the flawed orthodoxy that ultimately underpins all the fiscal impact literature, as well as much migration literature in general. MMT offers the tools with which we can fundamentally grasp the deep flaws and impasses in both contemporary migration scholarship, on the one side, and migration policy and politics, on the other. By the same token, MMT offers a descriptive framework with which both scholars and policymakers can approach the migration problematic in a new and realistic way.

How, then, would MMT answer the question that I asked in the conclusion to the preceding chapter concerning the basic consequence of government spending on the reception and integration of refugees – supposedly the most "costly" category of migrants? From an MMT perspective, the first thing to say would be to point out the very basic yet rarely considered fact that the money spent will, by definition, go *somewhere* rather than nowhere. This contrasts with the orthodox perspective that guides the fiscal impact literature, for which the spending amounts to little more than a cost, in the same way that a household looks at its outlays – i.e. as something that subtracts from the household's income, savings or borrowed money. As a consequence, the money spent on refugees would have to be made up for through tax hikes or risky borrowing or by removing funds from other areas, such as welfare benefits intended for needy citizens. But, as MMT demonstrates, money spent never disappears, which is attributable to the fact that "all spending must be received by someone, somewhere, as income". Again, spending equals income – or, as Wray (2015: 18) puts it: "Aggregate spending creates aggregate income." This means that, when the central government spends on refugee reception and integration, the money shows up as net income in the non-central government sector. In the fiscal impact literature, this fact is never considered, which, when one comes to think about it, is strange indeed. Had it been seriously pondered, I suspect the whole notion of the potential unsustainability of such spending would have had to be reconsidered. In other words, what is so bad or dangerous about households, businesses and municipalities receiving net incomes? These are currency-using, and hence revenue-constrained, instances in the economy; they need to earn, borrow or collect the money before they can spend it. As discussed above, when the revenue-constrained sectors are able to run surpluses and save, instead of having to deficit-spend through credit, this also helps stabilize the economy as a whole. In cases when the government engages in continuous belt-tightening, this undermines such stability, either depressing the economy or pushing households, businesses and municipalities to accumulate a perilous debt burden. As I will discuss further in Chapter 7, the refugee spending that took off in some EU countries in 2015 stimulated aggregate demand and so also created economic growth (e.g. OECD 2015a, 2017a and 2017b). The fact that government spending can create economic growth is another overlooked fact in the fiscal impact literature.

Most important of all, of course, is that spending on the reception and integration of refugees helps refugees get started in the new country while at the same time presenting the receiving country with additional real resources. The distinction, which MMT stresses, between financial and real resources is thus absolutely crucial to make and to understand. Failing to do so produces the absurdities we saw in the preceding chapter, with researchers mistaking real resources for fiscal burdens, the explicit or implicit logic and policy prescription being that workers in the low-wage sectors with migrant background should receive less or no access to the welfare state or, in cases when they do enjoy such access, be deprived of such welfare access. Such "findings" then travel or are commissioned to serve as politicians' favourite soundbites, reverberating in claims that refugees and low-skilled migrants are costs and fiscal burdens, encroaching on the welfare of other vulnerable groups.

In adopting an MMT approach, however, we soon understand that the accurate way of perceiving refugee spending is not as a net drag on financial resources but, rather, as a net addition of real resources. Spending on refugee reception and integration, therefore, should not be approached as a challenge to fiscal constraints, hence jeopardizing fiscal sustainability. On the contrary, it should be approached as helping to alleviate real resource constraints; to quote the Swedish government (2018b: 16) again: "Without the foreign-born women and men, the elderly care would face significant problems in fulfilling its task."

# 4

# Demography, security and the shifting conjunctures of the European Union's external labour migration policy

The focus of this chapter and the following one is on the European Union's external labour migration policy. Whereas Chapter 5 takes a detailed look at this policy's directives and their strong correlation with sound finance logic, the present chapter delineates the general historical context of labour migration in the EU, surveying the developments from the early postwar decades to today. Below, I will devote most of my attention to the contemporary consequences of the major shift that took place around the turn of the millennium, when Brussels decided to scrap its three-decade-long "zero" external labour migration policy in favour of a policy able to attract tens of millions of labour migrants over the subsequent decades. Whereas to some this signalled a new openness and a less preventive approach to migration, I will show why it was actually premised on the opposite. More migration was thus perceived as requiring a larger security apparatus in order to ensure that those who come are of the right type and that the length of their stays, access to welfare benefits and other rights can be closely adjusted, monitored and controlled. As I will also elaborate on in the chapters ahead, many of the security measures have been aimed at preventing the entry of asylum seekers, as well as any other type of migrants seen as inflicting fiscal burdens on the welfare systems in the member states.

Before accounting for the broad historical and contemporary developments, a conceptual discussion of labour migration is necessary. This is to underline the importance of knowing what labour migration, as a policy term, really denotes in a European Union dominated by sound finance. How, for instance, should we understand the stratified character of current labour migration policy; and why does current labour migration policy have such an awkward relationship with social rights?

It is important to keep in mind that the European Union's supranational competence over external labour migration (ELM) is weak, to say the least. This is in stark contrast to "free movement", or EU-internal labour migration, which forms part of the EU's core competence – one of the "four freedoms". At the same time, the EU – the European Commission in particular – has invested an enormous amount of time and effort in the issue of ELM. This work, which consists of a huge output of studies and projections concerning demographics and labour and skills shortages, has been instrumental in unleashing the big and often alarmist debate over the EU's "demographic deficit", which got under way in the early noughties. For two decades Brussels has worked to convince the member states that, on account of the Union's dismal demographic outlook, they need to increase labour migration from outside the EU significantly. As part of this, and with limited success, the Commission has also worked hard to expand the supranational policy scope, making the most of the modest competence that is vested at the EU level. We will take a closer look at this effort in the next chapter.

## What is labour migration?

When we speak of labour migration and labour migrants today we are dealing with austere categories, denoting a paucity of the social embeddedness that citizenship offers, or what a path to citizenship through permanent residence offers. As such, labour migration and sound finance go very well together. Modelling the economy and the "budget constraint" on the private household, labour migrants who are "let in to our household" will, accordingly, be judged by the alleged sustainability of their tax contributions. Whether it is made explicit or not, this is one of the main ingredients in the policy debates around the pros and cons regarding foreign labour. We can spot this in policy-makers' preoccupation with calibration and fine-tuning: who can come; how many; with what type of skills; for how long they can stay; on what type of visa; whether they will be eligible for permanent residence; whether they can bring their families; whether they will have access to all healthcare, some healthcare or just emergency care; and what about unemployment benefits, family benefits and access to social allowances?

As we shall see in this and the next chapter, although decisions to allow for labour migration may highlight its benefits to the receiving society, the actual policies are often more preoccupied with hedging against its potential fiscal risks and costs. Under a sound finance regime this is bound to happen. Given that asylum seekers and refugees are not even seen as immediate labour, and thus as taxpayers from day one, we can also understand why, as discussed in the previous chapter, their fiscal position is considered to be particularly risky and unfavourable to the host state. This partly explains why policies targeting high-skilled labour migration offer more favourable conditions for the migrants than those targeting low-skilled labour migration. One of the most crucial dividing lines here concerns the prospects for permanent residence, and, with it, the prospects for social incorporation that are held out, or not held out, to the various categories of labour migrants (Castles & Davidson 2000: 94–5).

Most labour migration policies, then, are structured according to a set of explicit or implicit assumptions concerning the bargaining power of the prospective migrants. This is also the place where the true or concrete definition of labour migration and labour migrants can be spotted. If the bargaining position of the migrant is deemed poor we see a poor welcome, a welcome with the elbow or no welcome at all from the party – be it a state or a supra-state – that claims it needs more migrant labour to improve its growth, demographic structure and competitiveness. Indeed, there is often a sense that those migrating with their needed labour to the European Union should feel grateful for the opportunity to come, when, in fact, it should be the other way around: that is, those receiving *real* resources are the ones who should be grateful.

When the bargaining position improves, however, the downward spiral goes into reverse and better conditions are afforded to the migrants, sometimes even including paths to permanent residence. In this process, the category of "labour migration" will also start to be used interchangeably with nicer-sounding policy rubrics, such as "mobility", "free movement" or "talent attraction". Thus, when the term "labour migration" starts to blend with such nicer-sounding terms, and is used less frequently, or not at all, the true definition of labour migration comes into view as that which is mostly reserved for the less privileged, those with weak to non-existing bargaining power and those, often racialized, migrants, who move from poorer to richer corners of the world. In a report supported by the European Commission and prepared by the European Migration Network (2015: 2, emphasis added), for instance, we find the following telling formulation concerning bargaining power, under the heading "Attracting and retaining talent in Europe":

> Europe is currently less attractive than other developed regions when it comes to highly skilled migrants. One underlying question for attracting and retaining talented migrants, is do migration policies to attract and retain talents really matter? Many factors shape a decision to migrate to another country, based on more than just the promise

of a job – opportunities for a spouse and children, the quality of life in the destination country, *the possibility of being welcomed into a new community*. To have an impact, skilled labour migration policies depend on much more than just the setting of admission rules.

Similarly, the European Commission (2018a: 1) emphasizes that "for the EU to remain competitive in the global economy it also needs to attract qualified and talented people from around the world", adding:

> We therefore need to step up our work on legal pathways. We need to take forward essential measures such as the reform of the EU Blue Card proposed by the Commission, which would improve the EU's ability to attract and retain highly skilled third-country nationals, turning this targeted migration into an opportunity and benefit for the economy and society. We need to make legal pathways a compelling part of our partnership approach with third countries.

Although these statements indicate that highly skilled migrants are assigned better bargaining positions relative to labour migrants with less skills, it also makes clear that the EU feels outbidded by other players in the global skills and talent market. Apparently, these players have provided prospective migrants with more favourable conditions than they have vis-à-vis the EU, or, as put by the Commission (2018a: 3):

> So far, the EU has been less competitive than other OECD countries – the EU's most obvious competitors in terms of economic profile – in attracting workers, punching well below its weight, in particular in terms of attracting highly skilled migrants. Of all migrants residing in OECD countries in 2015–16, only 25% of those with a high level of education chose an EU destination, while 75% chose a non-EU destination (mainly US, Canada, Australia).

On the other end of the spectrum, however, where migrants' bargaining power is taken to be weak or non-existent, the European Union's approach shifts; as for unskilled migrants, the EU worries that it is too attractive. Consequently, a row of precautionary measures has to be installed to prevent this category of migrants from becoming socially incorporated and thus fiscally burdensome for the host states. Most of such measures revolve around preventing temporary stays from morphing into permanent residences, which would saddle the host state with a social incorporation obligation. In the context of unskilled and seasonal labour migration, then, and instead of fretting over skilled migrants ditching the EU for Canada, the Commission installs "incentives and safeguards to prevent a temporary stay from becoming permanent" (EC 2010b: 2). Member states, moreover, are told to "require that the seasonal worker will have sufficient resources during his/her stay to maintain him/herself without having recourse to the social assistance system of the Member State concerned" (EC 2010b: 19).

Finally, it is important to emphasize that, when labour migration is on the policy table, this is also tantamount to having an unequal relationship between sending and receiving countries, or regions, on the table. This should be obvious to all, but it is rarely acknowledged in the EU labour migration context. So, many places in the world suffer from labour and skills shortages, yet only a few of them can meaningfully adopt policies to remedy such shortages. To be sure, the Union is short of healthcare workers; yet this shortage is insignificant when compared to the shortages suffered by those very countries in the Global South from which many EU countries are recruiting doctors and nurses. Those countries most depleted of health workers are thus to be further depleted by having their labour shipped to the world's most affluent countries and, coincidentally, those least affected by healthcare worker scarcity (see, e.g., Siyam & Dal Poz 2014).

As noted in Chapter 1, this devastating dynamic has also become prevalent between EU member states, with peripheral members – such as Bulgaria and Romania – supplying core members with large numbers of doctors, nurses and care workers. Meanwhile, Romania is also hosting an increasing number of foreign medical students who exploit low tuition fees and living costs and who are treated to a rapidly expanding English and French teaching programme. According to the OECD (2019: 105), the English and French curricula now take up about "30 per cent of the total teaching capacity". The programme is particularly popular with French, German and Swedish students, the overwhelming majority of whom return to their home countries upon having finished their degrees (OECD 2019: 105–10). Between 2005 and 2015 the number of Romanian-trained doctors working in Germany grew by seven times (Lietzmann & Böök 2019: 30). As noted by a recent study, moreover, "The rate of personal care workers working in another country is extremely high among Romanians, with the number of those working in another EU country being higher (140%) than those (Romanian) personal care workers working in Romania. It is also quite high among Polish (around 65%) and Lithuanian workers (around 55%)" (Adamis-Császár et al. 2019: 54).

Although this is having a dire impact on healthcare systems and patient care in the sending EU members, receiving countries, such as France, Germany and

Sweden, are getting a huge break; they are being blessed with a net addition of valuable *real* resources. This notwithstanding, the lucky receivers retain the privilege to slander "EU migrants" as welfare burdens and benefit tourists. Conceptually as well as in policy terms, then, "labour migration" always harbours asymmetries of power between categories of labour migrants – with some categories (i.e. highly skilled) not even primarily referred to as "migrants" – and between sending and receiving countries. Those countries that need labour migrants the most cannot attract, whereas those with the least shortages can, often draining the former in the process.

## Migration policy, demographics and the welfare state

*A historical snapshot*

Ahead we shall reconnect with today's more concrete policy picture concerning the EU's approach to external labour migration. Before turning to this task, however, our current development and predicament needs to be situated historically.

Since the postwar era western Europe's perceived external labour migration needs have fluctuated, to say the least. In the immediate postwar period, and contrary to what most migration scholarship would have us believe, western Europe was largely seen as overpopulated and, as a consequence, much effort went in to having western Europeans emigrate overseas (to North America, Latin America, Australia, New Zealand or various settler colonies). The brunt of the alleged "overpopulation" related directly to the catastrophic refugee crisis that ravaged Europe in the wake of the Second World War (see Figures 4.1 and 4.2). The largest of the refugee cohorts consisted of the 12 to 14 million German minorities who were forcibly expelled to Germany from eastern, central and southern Europe (see Douglas 2012). To this we should add the millions of prisoners of war, concentration camp survivors, slave labourers and refugees who fled out of and into various European countries (see Cohen 2012; Zahra 2016). As opposed to the situation inside the EU in 2015/16, this was a *real* refugee crisis, taking place in a devastated, starving and bombed-out Europe. Today politicians, journalists, pundits and scholars routinely refer to 2015 as "Europe's worst refugee crisis since World War Two". If they were remotely acquainted with the situation around the end of the Second World War, they would not make such a ludicrous comparison. But, since neither they nor hardly anyone else seems to have a clue, they can say it, and continue to say it.

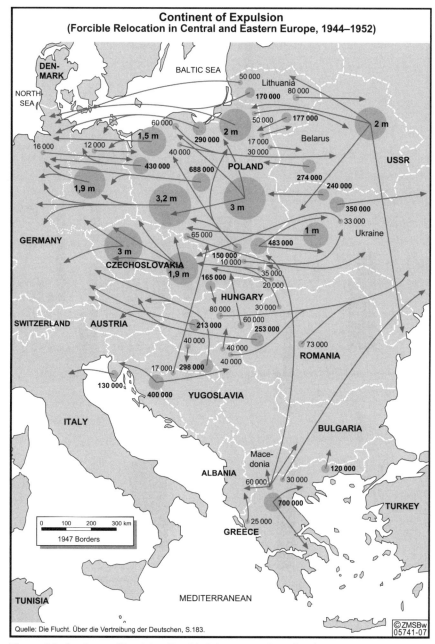

**Figure 4.1** Continent of Expulsion (Forcible Relocation in Central and Eastern Europe, 1944–1952) "Kontinent der Vertreibungen (Umsiedlungen in Mittel- und Osteuropa 1944 bis 1952)"
*Source*: Zentrum für Militärgeschichte und Sozialwissenschaften der Bundeswehr.

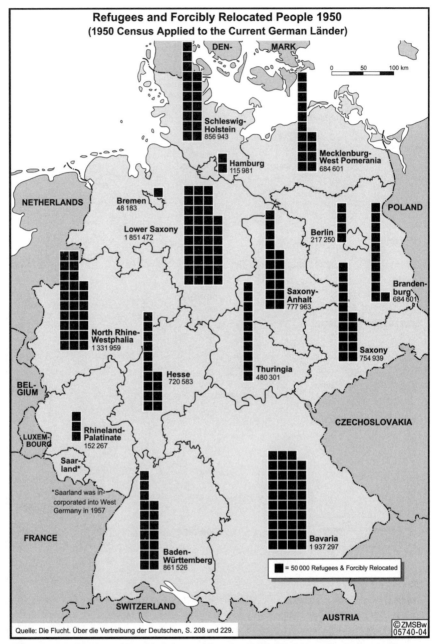

**Figure 4.2** Refugees and Forcibly Relocated People 1950 (1950 Census Applied to the Current German Länder) "Flüchtlinge und Vertriebene 1950 (Volkzählungsdaten von 1950 übertragen auf heutige Ländergrenzen)"
*Source*: Zentrum für Militärgeschichte und Sozialwissenschaften der Bundeswehr.

Reflecting this amnesia, today's students of migration have little or no knowledge about the great postwar refugee crisis and its consequences. As already noted, one such crucial consequence was the perception that western Europe was overpopulated and that this necessitated a large-scale emigration of Europeans. In its report *Migration from Europe* from 1951, the UN's International Refugee Organization (IRO) (succeeded by the UNHCR in 1952) stated that it had been set up "to solve that part of the world refugee problem represented by the 'displaced persons' who were uprooted by the second World War". In the early 1950s, however, the IRO stood ready to deal with what it claimed to be "the even larger problem of European over-population". "We know," the report went on,

> that the millions of "surplus" men, women and children who now burden the relief rolls and lengthen the queues of unemployed across the face of Europe, could and would contribute enormously to the wealth, the strength and progress of the free world if means could be found to transplant them to those broad areas where their talents and skills are in great demand. [...] Thus, for the second time within the memory of adults living today, the "West" is faced with the same dilemma: an excess of people in Europe whose very presence constitutes a threat to political and economic stability; a vast and growing demand in other parts of the world for the labor, the skill and the political and cultural assets possessed by these fretfully idle men and women.     (International Refugee Organization 1951: v–vi)

The IRO was not the only organization that worried about western Europe's alleged overpopulation crisis. The Council of Europe (established in 1949) also took pains to resolve it, by, among other things, examining "the extent to which a co-ordinated policy is likely to encourage emigration, particularly from Western Europe to overseas countries, to the benefit of all concerned" (Council of Europe 1952: 58). In its *Strasbourg Plan* from 1952, which drew up a blueprint for western Europe's collective exploitation of the resources in African colonies (see Hansen & Jonsson 2014), the Council cited estimates "that Western Europe now has a surplus population of 5 million people, including 3 million Italians, more than a million Germans and over half a million Austrians, Greeks, Turks and Netherlands nationals" (Council of Europe 1952: 58). "The settling of such persons overseas," the Council argued, "would help to solve one of Europe's most critical human and social problems" (Council of Europe 1952: 58). On account of the seriousness of the matter, the Council found it "encouraging that a number of European countries are prepared and indeed eager to foster overseas emigration of their nationals" (Council of Europe 1952: 58).

In the same year, 1952, *The Economist* reported on the "unsolved problem" concerning the refugee situation in western Europe, insisting that "emigration" constituted the "obvious solution" and the "principal hope" for "the able-bodied refugees remaining in Western Europe". West Germany was "overcrowded with 9 million German refugees", and the situation in Austria, Greece, Italy and elsewhere was described as unsustainable unless the obstacles to further emigration were removed. "Until emigration is made easier," *The Economist* (1952) wrote, the refugees' "only hope seems to lie in finding work in their present countries of asylum". In 1952, however – and similar to the mood in 2015/16 – it was pessimism that prevailed, and so the employment prospects were deemed to be very poor. As explained by *The Economist*, the refugees resided "in countries where unemployment, the presence of other refugees, or acute domestic economic difficulties provide serious obstacles to their assimilation".

The European Union's free movement, or intra-labour migration, provisions originated in the Treaty of Paris (1951) and its institution of the European Coal and Steel Community (ECSC). Through persistent pressure from the Italian government, the ECSC opened up for the free movement of qualified coal and steelworkers. Italy saw itself as suffering from an acute problem of overpopulation and was, therefore, very anxious to secure means for emigration in order to, as the expression often went, export its "surplus population", and, with it, its unemployment problem. This also constituted one of the main reasons behind the Italian support for and participation in postwar European integration (Willis 1971).

Italian "overpopulation" problems also influenced the Treaty of Rome's (1957) institution of free movement for labour. This time, however, it was easy to persuade the other five signatories of the benefits of more open intra-EEC labour migration. But for them, and in contrast to Italy, it was labour shortage, rather than unemployment, that prompted their approval. It took only a few years, then, for western Europe to move from a perceived overpopulation crisis to a looming labour shortage crisis. At this point in time the five other members, West Germany in particular, had difficulties in meeting what had emerged as the 1950s' great labour demand, and thus they saw free movement of labour as a means to amend the problem (Collins 1975: 13). The motives are clearly mirrored in the migration statistics for the years immediately following the ratification of the Treaty of Rome, when Italian workers made up over a half of all labour migrants admitted in the six EEC countries, while fewer than two-fifths came from countries outside the

EEC. At the beginning of the 1960s almost a half of West Germany's labour migrants came from Italy (Ascoli 1985: 186–7). This soon changed, however, with labour migrants from outside the EEC and western Europe taking over the majority share.

Interestingly enough, the great postwar labour migration to western Europe's rapidly growing economies coincided with the building of western Europe's welfare states. The large-scale immigration of often low and unskilled labour from southern Europe, Yugoslavia, Turkey, Ireland, Finland and a number of colonies and former colonies (where many of those arriving were not immigrants but citizens: Bhambra 2017) thus walked in tandem with the birth and expansion of the welfare state in the receiving countries. According to the trade-off theory, as described in Chapter 2, this should not have been possible, unless restrictions had been imposed on labour migrants' access to the welfare state's social rights, benefits and insurance systems. To be sure, welfare restrictions did exist in some western European welfare states, but they were less common or even non-existent in others.

Sweden belongs to the latter category. Sweden's postwar governments built one of Europe's most comprehensive and, as they like to say, "generous" welfare states – whatever the latter means, because generosity in Sweden was never economically unsound, as the "generosity" label is supposed to make us feel (think of "handouts"). At the same time, Sweden ranked among the largest recruiters of foreign labour and, subsequently, receivers of refugees (proportionally speaking); and by providing permanent residence for the often poor and low skilled migrants it also let them reap the benefits of the welfare state (see Schierup, Hansen & Castles 2006). This, moreover, would continue after the recessions in the 1970s set in, when unemployment and employment gaps were to open up between natives and the foreign-born. In the 1970s migrants' access to the welfare state was also expanded more generally in western Europe (e.g. Guiraudon 2000). From the standpoint of the sizeable trade-off literature, both the pre- and post-1970s developments in Sweden and elsewhere should have been impossible, because of their supposed unsustainability; yet they happened, and proved sustainable.

In relation to these historical circumstances it should also strike us as peculiar that the trade-off literature posits a trade-off between the welfare state and migration when, in fact, the birth and development of the western European welfare states are empirically inseparable from large-scale migration. They grew up together, and there are few empirical examples of a western European welfare state that expanded without also expanding the recruitment of labour migrants. Indeed, some welfare states also started their careers as hosts of massive numbers of refugees. In 1950 the West German population of 50 million included no fewer than 8 million refugees, or 16 per cent of the total population (Münz & Ulrich 1997: 68–9).

In 1973, however, most western European governments decided to formally end the recruitment of external labour migrants from non-OECD countries. The recession in the early 1970s and the higher rates of unemployment that followed in its wake were major factors influencing the rather uniform decisions, across western Europe, to halt the recruitment. Similar to the 1950s, then, an abrupt shift in policy orientation took place. In the early 1970s, however, it was not a surplus population problem but a labour shortage emergency that was dropped from the policy agenda. Yet this did not mean that immigration into western Europe would end; instead, it changed character, with family, refugee and, soon, irregular migration increasing. True, there was return migration taking place, but the majority of labour migrants decided to stay. Even in countries with so-called guest worker programmes, it was becoming obvious already in the 1960s that their temporary status no longer applied in reality. As pointed out above, permanent residence and hence incorporation into welfare state arrangements became the norm in many countries (for an overview of the post-1973 development, see Castles, de Haas & Miller 2014).

## The contemporary development

The roughly three decades running from the early 1970s to the late 1990s have subsequently been named the era of "zero labour immigration" by the European Commission. During this period, and in sharp contrast to today, the Commission championed an official line of policy that advised against labour migration to the EU from non-OECD countries. In its "comprehensive approach" to migration, presented in 1994 (and originally drafted in 1991), the Commission advocated a three-pronged migration strategy, calling for (1) "Taking action on migration pressure"; (2) "Controlling migration flows"; and (3) "Strengthening integration policies for the benefit of legal immigrants" (EC 1994: 11).

That said, it is of course crucial to make clear that, in practice, the 1980s and 1990s were by no means characterized by "zero" labour immigration to the European Union (see Figure 4.3). On the contrary, several million new labour migrants from around the world arrived during these decades. Most of these new arrivals were not legal or regular labour migrants, however. They were irregular, undocumented or "illegal". An important enabling factor for this development is to be found in the liberalization of the EU economy that got under way in the 1980s. Weakened labour unions and labour laws and pressure for low-skilled production and low-wage and temporary employment, in

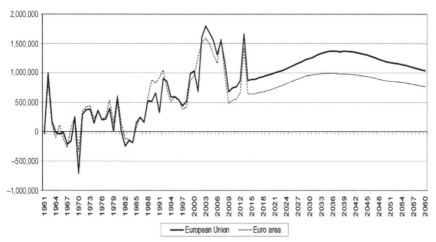

**Figure 4.3** Net migration flows, European Union and euro area, 1961–2060
*Source*: EC (2015a: 17).

conjunction with a fast-growing service sector and informal labour market of outsourced and sweated labour, were factors fuelling the EU's growing demand for irregular labour migrants – that is, the type of labour often most suited for such economic and labour market conditions (see, e.g., Anderson 2010; Castles 2004; Menz 2009; Samers 2010; Schierup, Hansen & Castles 2006; Schierup *et al.* 2015). In the official rhetoric, Brussels and EU governments have refrained from acknowledging that they, in fact, have been advancing policies that are conducive to "illegal immigration". As Stephen Castles (2004: 223) puts it, "Policies that claim to exclude undocumented workers [or 'illegal immigrants'] may often really be about allowing them in through side doors and back doors so that they can be more readily exploited."

Described as the only "realistic" option at the time, this "zero migration" policy also served as an important public relations tool from the mid-1980s and onwards, promising EU citizens that the transformations brought about by the Single Market would not lead to an increase in external migration (Hansen & Hager 2012). In an information booklet from 1996, for instance, addressing the "European citizens", Brussels took care to note that many "are concerned about immigration [...], thinking that this could increase once internal border controls have been fully swept away". The question that many EU citizens were asking, according to the Commission, could thus be phrased as follows: "Will the eventual dismantling of all internal borders lead to an increase in levels of immigration to my country, both from inside and outside the Community?" To this the Commission could give a reassuring answer: "No, it should not. The fundamental point about dismantling the Community's internal borders is that this process must be accompanied by the synchronized tightening of all external borders" (EC 1996: 13–15).

By the turn of the millennium this (by now) habitual policy picture was to be significantly revised. This was already well under way in certain member states, most notably in Germany, which had begun to institute temporary labour migration schemes with eastern neighbours. To be sure, the revision did not affect the build-up of measures to prevent the arrival of asylum seekers that had become an EU policy pursuit as part of the Single Market conversions in the mid-1980s; this pursuit would continue unabated (Hansen & Hager 2012). But it did involve a remarkable reversal of the EU's stance on external labour migration. All of a sudden Brussels would start issuing statements such as the following: "The Commission considers that the zero immigration mentioned in past Community discussion of immigration was never realistic and never really justified" (EC 1999: 2); and "it is clear from an analysis of the economic and demographic context of the Union and of the countries of origin, that there is a growing recognition that the 'zero' immigration policies of the past 30 years are no longer appropriate" (2000: 3).

Yet again, a new great European demographic crisis was brewing, and Brussels was soon to clarify that the Union's need for third-country labour migrants was not just any type of need. According to estimates put forward by the European Union (and also by the OECD, the UN and others) the figures ranged in the tens of millions for the coming five decades. In its 2005 "Policy plan on legal migration", the European Commission (2005: 4) warned that, unless the Union managed to increase external labour immigration, its working-age population was said to be expected to contract by some 52 million by 2050. In the Commission's *2012 Ageing Report*, looking only to 2020, it was held that the EU needed a net migration of 25 million individuals in order to keep the working-age population stable at the then current level (EC 2012b: 51–6). Three years later, in the *2015 Ageing Report*, the Commission painted an even bleaker picture, stating that "the age structure of the EU population is projected to change dramatically" in the coming decades (EC 2015a: 20). The old age dependency ratio was thus projected to take a huge turn for the worse over the period from 2013 to 2060, moving "from having four working-age people for every person aged over 65 years to only two working-age persons" (EC 2015a: 22). In the most recent *Ageing Report*, from 2018, the Commission points to a Union that is "turning increasingly grey in the coming decades", where "the working-age population (15–64) will decrease significantly from 333 million in 2016 to 292 million in 2070 due to fertility, life expectancy and migration flow dynamics" (EC 2018b: 3). For those aged between 20 and 64 the projected fall is even steeper, or close to 10 per cent, which should be seen in relation to a parallel drop in net migration, which is projected to decline (annually) from 1.5 million in 2016 to about 800,000 in 2070 (EC 2018b: 4, 19).

This provided, economic growth and external labour migration growth have become two sides of the same coin in the EU's economic and political ambitions. This was made clear as early as in the Lisbon Strategy (2000–2010) and it went on to become one of the cornerstones of "Europe 2020", the EU's subsequent ten-year plan for growth (EC 2010a: 18; 2011a: 4). From the perspective of the Commission, a large-scale increase in labour migration was becoming so urgent that the then home affairs commissioner, Cecilia Malmström, proclaimed: "We need migrants to ensure our economic survival" (quoted in Euractiv 2010). In 2017 the commissioner for employment, social affairs, skills and labour mobility, Marianne Thyssen, issued a similar warning:

> There are already more people aged over 65 than children under 14 living in the EU. By 2050, almost a third of Europeans will be aged 65 or more, compared to less than a fifth today. In comparison to the rest of the world, Europe will be the "oldest" region, with a median age of 45 by 2030. Europe has an interest in becoming an attractive destination for the talent our economies need. By improving opportunities for migrants, we can ease the pressure our labour market is facing because of demographic change. (Thyssen 2017)

The 180-degree policy shift on ELM in 2000 formed part of the larger conversion of EU migration policy brought about by the Amsterdam Treaty in 1997 (ratified in 1999)[1] and the Tampere European Council in 1999, the latter

---

1. The Amsterdam Treaty marked a historical shift towards a significantly augmented role for the EU and the supranational level in migration policy. Amsterdam laid down the broad outlines for a future EU policy on asylum and migration. Some of these changes were spelled out under Amsterdam's new Title IV (articles 61–9). Article 62 specified that measures should be adopted granting certain limited intra-EU mobility rights to "nationals of third countries". Article 63 outlined a series of measures on asylum and immigration, calling for the adoption (within a period of five years) of a set "minimum standards" in the area of asylum as well as "measures on immigration policy within the following areas: (a) conditions of entry and residence, and standards on procedures for the issue by Member States of long term visas and residence permits, including those for the purpose of family reunion, (b) illegal immigration and illegal residence, including repatriation of illegal residents'; and "measures defining the rights and conditions under which nationals of third countries who are legally resident in a Member State may reside in other Member States". As part of this reshuffling, Amsterdam also incorporated the Schengen *acquis* into the treaty framework. Owing to British, Irish and Danish opposition, and in order not to derail the negotiations, it became necessary to allow these countries to opt out of the new provisions.

marking the first European Council ever devoted to justice and home affairs (and thus to migration issues).[2] Looking at the policy development since Amsterdam and Tampere, however, the achievements with regard to ELM have been both meagre and fragmented. As put by Malmström in 2011: "When I meet ministers responsible for labour policies, they almost all speak of the need for immigrant workers – and it's true, we need hundreds of thousands, millions in the long term. But when the ministers go and speak in front of their national publics, this message is not to be heard at all" (quoted in Barber 2011). As such, ELM has clearly taken a back seat to the far more prioritized and interrelated areas of asylum, "illegal migration", border security, visa, return and readmission. The caption of chapter 2 under Lisbon's Title V, which reads "Policies on border checks, asylum and immigration", thus serves as an accurate description of the ranking of policy preference within the Council.

## Brussels' rationale and objectives for increasing external labour migration

In this context, "meagre results" of course relate to the Commission's object-ives. But what are these more precisely, and how should we construe them in more analytical terms?

As already seen, medium- and long-term demographic projections con-stitute the foundation for the Commission's outlook. They have been used con-sistently throughout as justification of Brussels' stance and to drive home the point that ELM is above all structurally determined, and, as such, should not be allowed to be compromised by immediate business cycle and unemployment concerns (EC 2012c: 4; see also Malmström 2012).

Besides expanding ELM as such, the Commission is also aiming to increase the admission of students, researchers and other categories of third-country nationals (TCNs) more indirectly related to the labour market; this in order to cope with a severe shortage of researchers, in particular, and to facilitate these groups' future labour market participation and contributions to innovation and entrepreneurship, in general.

Integral to the goal of increasing ELM is also the goal of increasing the internal labour mobility of TCNs in the European Union. This requires that

2. At the Tampere European Council in 1999, the Council decided that "a common European asylum system" gradually should be put into operation. Tampere also established that the EU should focus on establishing a "more efficient management of migration flows at all their stages", on more effective external border controls and on combating illegal immigra-tion (European Council 1999).

both long-term residents and newly arrived TCNs are provided with free movement rights that are more in line with those of EU citizens. For the Commission, this is crucial in order to optimize the allocation of labour and to ensure greater flexibility in the Union's labour market.

The rationale and goals relating to ELM are embedded in the "overarching framework of the EU External Migration Policy" (EC 2011b: 5), entitled the Global Approach to Migration and Mobility (GAMM), which was first adopted in 2005 and renewed in 2011, now with a more marked ELM profile (EC n.d.–b). Here, "all relevant aspects of migration" vis-à-vis third countries are accounted for and brought together into a "comprehensive", "coherent" and "balanced" framework for the purpose of managing migration and mobility to the benefit of both the EU and the sending countries (EC 2011b, 2014d).³ GAMM thus explains how to construe the links between ELM and all the other prioritized areas of EU migration policy (i.e. asylum, "illegal" migration, border security and visa policy); but it also underlines ELM's close alignment with EU foreign and development policy. As such, GAMM contains and seeks to develop in concert everything from supranational legislation and instruments with a firm treaty basis, on the one hand, to more loosely defined policy proposals, unbinding declarations and future plans, on the other.

In the wake of the upheavals in north Africa (the Arab Spring) and the war in Libya, EU migration policy activity targeting north Africa has grown exponentially. According to the Commission, the crises and transformations taking place in north Africa have accentuated the need for improved migration management in the Mediterranean area, so as to facilitate, within the GAMM framework, legal migration for north Africans in need of work and to help the EU meet key labour demands and amend its demographic problems. In order to set in train such a mutually beneficial dynamic, the Commission proposed, in March 2011, to develop "a partnership on migration, mobility and security with the Southern Mediterranean countries" (EC 2011c). The focus here is to promote circular labour migration to the EU, built on "real" and "clearly identified labour demands", which will "help to meet the need for highly skilled workers in the expanding sectors of the EU's economy but also help fill many jobs requiring a mix of lower skills" (EC 2011c: 7; 9). The Commission stepped up these efforts further following the refugee catastrophe at Lampedusa in 2013, which gave rise to the Task Force Mediterranean, calling for safe legal

---

3. GAMM consists of four pillars: "[R]egular immigration and mobility, irregular immigration and trafficking in human beings, international protection and asylum policy, and maximising the impact of migration and mobility on development" (European Parliament 2019a).

migration channels to the EU (EC 2013c), and even more markedly, of course, following the 2015/16 refugee crisis.

Within various bilateral frameworks under GAMM, such as the European Neighbourhood Policy and the EU–Africa Strategic Partnership on Migration, Mobility and Employment,[4] policies have been developed to facilitate ELM, mostly focusing on so-called circular migration. According to the Commission, circular migration refers to "migrants coming to the EU for short periods and going back to a third country after the end of the contract" (EC 2014b; see also EC 2007c, 2011b).[5] Besides the directive on seasonal migration, which we will look at in more detail in Chapter 5, the most important concrete policy instruments in this context are the bilateral and unbinding Mobility Partnerships that the European Union has signed (to date) with nine third countries,[6] as well as the Common Agendas on Migration and Mobility, which have been signed with two countries[7] (EC n.d.–b, 2011c).

In the wake of the developments since 2015, the Commission has sought to promote the partnership approach with third countries even further, and with a more marked focus on "maximising the synergies and applying the necessary incentives and leverages". "Acting jointly", the Commission (EC 2018a: 6) argues, the EU can have a stronger position vis-à-vis third countries in cooperation on migration management. Included here is an effort to tie trade and migration more closely together, particularly with regard to the service sector and cross-border service provision and investment (EC 2018a: 6–7).

As part of this, Brussels has also continued to invest heavily in its attempt to create stronger migration cooperation with African countries. In its communication "Enhancing legal pathways to Europe", presented in September 2018, the Commission thus called on "Member States to *fully engage and cooperate* on developing *pilot projects on legal migration with* specific *African countries*" (EC 2018b: 7, emphasis in original). To further boost this agenda, Brussels simultaneously launched a new Africa–Europe Alliance for Sustainable Investment and Jobs (EC 2018c).

---

4. Other similar cooperation frameworks are, for example, the Rabat process for western Africa; the Prague and Budapest processes; and the negotiations with Turkey and western Balkans countries.
5. For in-depth accounts on circular migration as it relates to EU policy, see the contributions in Triandafyllidou (2013); Cassarino (2008); Venturini (2008); Feldman (2012); Carrera and Hernández i Sagrera (2009).
6. These are Armenia, Azerbaijan, Belarus, Cape Verde, Georgia, Jordan, Moldova, Morocco and Tunisia.
7. These are Ethiopia and Nigeria.

## Security first

As noted initially in this chapter, and as we will be able observe in more detail ahead, the Commission's effort to persuade the member states to open "legal pathways to Europe" was soon eclipsed by an effort to ensure that all the possible measures to close migration paths were in place. Hence, the Africa–Europe Alliance makes up a central component of a "strategy combining in a coherent and balanced way the different elements of our joint approach to migration". These elements are outlined as follows:

> [A] shared responsibility for addressing the root causes of irregular migration and forced displacement, effectively managing borders, preventing and fighting migrant smuggling and trafficking of human beings, rescuing and protecting lives, offering paths for legal migration, and ensuring improved cooperation on return, readmission and reintegration of irregular migrants in line with the established principles and international law obligations, as well as agreed arrangements. As part of this comprehensive approach, legal pathways to the EU should be enhanced in order to offer safe and viable alternatives to dangerous routes and irregular migration.
>
> (EC 2018c: 2)

Caught in this barrage of measures inimical to migration and asylum, it is hard to see how the Commission's strategy is going to widen the "legal pathways" to the European Union. Although the EU has cooperated very successfully with Libya – currently as well as during Muammar Gaddafi's rule, and in flagrant violation of human rights[8] – in an effort to prevent migrants and asylum seekers from reaching the EU, even narrow legal pathways have yet to see the light of the day.

When Brussels speaks of a "balance" between policies on irregular migration, border security and readmission, on the one side, and ELM, on the other, this should not be understood as a symmetric relationship. Rather, it is a highly asymmetrical one whereby the latter is to be made compatible with the former. This could also be expressed as the golden rule of "security comes first" in EU migration policy – a rule that has been criticized from within the European Parliament and by numerous NGOs and scholars since the supranational level first tried to gain a say over external migration policy in the mid-1980s (see Hansen & Hager 2012; European Parliament 1990).

---

8. See, e.g., United Nations (2018); Human Rights Watch (2019); Campbell (2019).

It should also be mentioned that many analysts assumed that the Commission's new affirmative position on ELM at the turn of the new millennium would (logically) induce a toning down of the strong emphasis on migration security. Why roll out more barbwire carpet for those you say you desperately need? These hopes where soon frustrated, however, by Brussels' decision to make sure that its repeal of "zero immigration" was combined with a renewed pledge to EU citizens of strengthening migration security even further. This was visible early on, such as in 2002, when the European Commission (2002: 8) pointed to the merits of "forced return of illegal residents", arguing that this could "help to ensure public acceptance for more openness towards new legal immigrants against the background of more open admission policies particularly for labour migrants".

Security (as in border security) policy, then – to prevent temporary stays from becoming permanent and to combat "illegal" migration – serves as the primary rationale and objective that both practically and principally overdetermines ELM in all its forms, although it is less emphasized in migration policy involving the highly skilled. As stated in the Union's "Key messages" to the UN High-level Dialogue on International Migration and Development in 2013: "All states should review existing barriers to human mobility, with a view to remove barriers which are not justified from a security point of view and are unnecessarily hindering economic competitiveness and regional integration" (EC 2013a: 11). "Citizens need to feel reassured that external border controls are working properly", moreover, and authorities thus need to demonstrate that "[p]reventing irregular migration and maintaining public security are compatible with the objective of increased mobility" (EC 2011a: 7; 11; see also EC 2014a: 2; Council EU 2012). If not carefully governed, Brussels warns, "the costs of migration may be significant, and can include social tensions with host populations – often exploited by populist forces – and pressure on scarce resources" (EC 2013a: 4). More often than not, then, the Commission conveys the impression that the primary purpose of legal labour migration is not to serve labour needs but, rather, to serve as leverage against unwanted migration:

> Enhanced and tailored cooperation on legal migration with third countries of origin and transit of migrants will help reduce irregular migration by offering safe and legal alternatives for persons wishing to migrate; it will contribute to bridging gaps in certain sectors of Member States' labour markets; and will be an incentive to facilitate cooperation on issues such as prevention of irregular migration, readmission and return of irregular migrants.     (EC 2018b: 6–7)

To the extent that the Commission is determined to create a productive dynamic between the security-oriented prevention of "illegal immigration" and asylum seekers, on the one side, and the growth- and competitiveness-oriented aspiration for a large-scale increase in ELM, on the other, this dynamic needs to be construed as being founded on an asymmetrical relation in which security is squarely in control.

## Conclusion

Taken together, all this is indicative of how extremely high the stakes are when it comes to designing and adopting policy that will actually allow people from the Global South and non-OECD area to enter the European Union. The stakes remain awesome even when ELM has been elevated to a matter of "economic survival". As seen here, this also helps explain why security and control become even more emphasized when migration is set to increase. Before Brussels decided to discard its "zero" external labour migration policy some 20 years ago, policy was less complicated, in the sense that it could be consistently reluctant, at least officially, towards all types of external migration. These days the policy picture is variegated; many types of migration should now instead be encouraged, but they should be encouraged in extremely different ways – something we shall become painfully aware of in the next chapter. Since these differences pivot on a highly stratified set of rights of residence and access to welfare benefits and family migration, the control and monitoring of migrant numbers and categories become all the more crucial. The only thing that has remained constant over time is the Commission's and the member states' unfavourable disposition towards refugees and asylum seekers. A failure to control numbers here would risk upsetting the stratifying logic inherent to labour migration policy. In other words, it would mean that those with the least to offer, at least initially, in terms of tax contributions and valuable skills and talents, would be offered the most in terms of residence and welfare benefit access. This offers important clues as to why the situation in 2015 was deemed to be so utterly out of control and so wholly at odds with the EU's approach to migration. Tens of millions of migrants, Brussels claims, are indispensable in order to stave off an otherwise imminent demographic disaster. Yet, when a fraction of that number arrives in the form of young and working-age refugees, Brussels deems this a disaster that calls for hermetic border controls.

As with Brussels and member state governments, the trade-off literature also has a penchant for playing the "migration out of control" card. "Unlimited migration," Guiraudon (1998: 273) maintains, "would undermine the high level of benefits in advanced industrialized countries; thus, the replacement of porous geographical borders by a guarded entry to the welfare state would seem logical." Similarly, Joppke (1998: 7) posits that "rights are costly, and they can never be for the whole world. Spreading rights more evenly requires slashing existing privileges. […] This is precisely why immigration is even more jealously rejected by developed welfare states, which would go bankrupt overnight if literally everyone could reap its benefits."

When Guiraudon writes that "a guarded entry to the welfare state would seem logical" in the context of large numbers of migrants and asylum seekers wanting to get in, this captures very well how the logic runs when the EU and its member states conceive of labour migration. The problem arises when Guiraudon, Joppke and others within the literature impregnated with trade-off and sound finance thinking promote this logic and lend it an aura of sound science. In their quest to appear realistic, however – as opposed to "democratically minded social scientists", who, according to Joppke (1998: 7) find this realism "irritating" – they set out from a totally unrealistic scenario of "unlimited migration". It is a scenario in which the whole non-OECD world would show up in, let us say, Sweden to "reap its benefits", which, in turn, would make Sweden "go bankrupt overnight". Why not instead account for the fact that welfare states in western Europe have incorporated millions upon millions of poor migrants and refugees since the very inception of these same welfare states, without anyone being able to show that this has ever threatened the fiscal sustainability of the welfare state, let alone been responsible for its current dilapidation and subjection to austerity. Yet, as we shall see in the next chapter, the fear of having to socially incorporate labour from poorer parts of the world continuous to be profound, even when the labour is held forth as a primary means of survival for the rapidly "greying" Union.

# 5

# Labour migration in a sound finance policy logic

In the previous chapter I sketched the broad contours of the European Union's approach to external labour migration. In this chapter I will provide a more detailed description and analysis of the EU's legislation and actually existing policy in the area. As already clarified, the EU's supranational influence on external labour migration policy is very limited. Nevertheless, over the past couple of decades the European Commission has managed to get concrete policy on the ground, backed by a set of binding EU directives. These directives are the fruits of drawn-out negotiations and compromises between member states and EU institutions. As such, they help us ascertain the common denominators and conceptions underwriting the Union's external labour migration policy. Indirectly, they also help us get a sense of the stakes involved in national policy-making on labour migration.

Rather than following the common approach of mainly attending to the many and deep disagreements within the European Union on external labour migration, what I will do here is to look for the common ground. In other words, I try and answer the question: what are the consensual views that have made the actually existing common policy possible in the first place? Instead of getting stuck on the *obstacles* to common policies, then, I will focus on the *enablers*. I will do that not only to understand the dynamic and logic of the EU's ELM policy but also because I am convinced that these enablers offer us important clues as to what it is that disables the EU from working out an asylum policy focused on reception rather than prevention.

Of great significance, too, is the fact that the EU policy package contains both extremes in labour migration policy, as described in Chapter 4. That is to say, the EU has adopted policies covering both highly skilled (Blue Card) and unskilled labour migration (as part of a directive on seasonal migration). Consequently, a study of the EU's ELM directives also offers us the opportunity to analyse the differences with regard to the rights of welfare and residence that exist between the various categories of labour migrants.

Before turning to the actual legislation that has been achieved up to this point, something should be said too about how the Commission has gone about its task of initiating legislation and getting directives adopted on ELM. Put simply, the Commission has been pursuing two approaches or strategies. The one launched initially, referred to as the horizontal approach, sought to create a broad general common framework for the admission, residence conditions and rights granted to any third-country nationals engaging in paid work and self-employed economic activities. The first major directive proposal on ELM, presented by the Commission in 2001, aimed for a high level of harmonization and transparency and as little differentiation as possible among third-country workers – hence the horizontal approach. To be sure, member states were to retain "the right to limit admission" as well as being provided with other forms of discretion; and the principle of the preference of the domestic labour market's workers over TCNs was also to apply (EC 2001b).

Although the Commission's first directive proposal was given a favourable response by the European Parliament and the European Economic and Social Committee, the Council would have none of it. The proposal was, as Peers (2009: 410) puts it, "dead on arrival in the Council".[1] In order to break the deadlock with the Council over ELM, the Commission went on to present a sectoral approach as its second main option (EC 2005), and it did so on the merit of having already presented two separate sectoral directives, in 2002 and 2004 respectively, for the entry and residence of third-country students and researchers (as discussed below). In the public consultation process on Brussels' ELM plans, several of the stakeholders expressed scepticism towards the new sectoral approach, cautioning that it would create a differential and fragmented policy picture whereby rules and rights would apply differently and unequally to different categories of TCNs. The European Economic and Social Committee (2005: 4) went as far as stating that, "[i]f the European Council were to opt for a sectoral approach (geared towards highly skilled migrants), it would be discriminatory in nature" (see also European Parliament 2005: point 26).

Such objections notwithstanding, the "Policy Plan on Legal Migration" confirmed the sectoral approach as the Commission's new strategy. More specifically, the policy plan outlined a roadmap for the next four years, specifying that the Commission's priority would be to table a set of directives that were to address sector-specific categories of migrants: i.e. highly skilled, seasonal, intra-corporate transferees and remunerated trainees, as attended to below.[2]

---

1. The directive proposal was officially withdrawn in 2006.
2. In addition to this, a framework or single permit directive, defining basic rights for labour migrants, would also be adopted as part of this plan (Directive 2011/98/EU).

As already noted above, directives were also enacted to cover researchers and students from third countries; and one directive targeted the intra-EU mobility rights of already resident TCNs.

In what follows, I will discuss these directives, focusing on their objectives, their content and how they relate to migrants' rights and to sound finance logic. The chapter concludes by providing a more comprehensive picture of external labour migration in the EU, one that also draws together the threads from the previous chapter.

## The Long-Term Residence Directive

The directive concerning the status of third-country nationals who are long-term residents was adopted in November 2003. The LTR Directive (Directive 2003/109/EC)[3] establishes the conditions under which a member state confers (and revokes) long-term resident status and accompanying rights to legally resident TCNs.[4] The directive also lays down the rules concerning the rights of residence for TCNs in member states other than the one that has granted them long-term resident status. As stipulated in the directive, the status of long-term resident should be given to applying TCNs "who have resided legally and continuously" in a member state for five years. Other key requirements relate specifically to issues of welfare access and to measures relieving member states of welfare obligations. To qualify for the status, TCNs must, therefore, be able to demonstrate "stable and regular resources" that are adequate to support themselves and their family dependants, "without recourse to the social assistance system of the Member State concerned". TCNs must also confirm that they have sickness insurance, and that they abide by national integration obligations where such apply.

Although this directive does not speak directly to the Commission's objective of increasing ELM – it exclusively addresses the conditions for TCNs already residing in the EU – it aligns very well with Brussels' long-standing goal of closing the labour mobility gap between member state nationals, or EU citizens, and legally resident TCNs. In the LTR Directive proposal, the Commission (2001a: 8) contended that to continue barring legally resident

---

3. Council Directive 2003/109/EC of 25 November 2003 concerning the status of third-country nationals who are long-term residents. Denmark and Ireland (and the United Kingdom) do not take part in this directive.

4. As of January 2018, according to Eurostat (2019c), TCNs made up 4.4 per cent of the EU's population (or 22.3 million out of a total population of 512.4 million).

TCNs from the free movement provisions ran counter to "the demands of an employment market that is in a process of far-reaching change, where greater flexibility is needed". For the Commission, permanently settled TCNs suffered disproportionately from unemployment and thus constituted an untapped labour reserve that, once unhampered by the EU's internal borders, could help remedy recurrent labour shortages in growth industries and other labour market distortions across the Union (EC 2001a: 8).

It needs to be emphasized, however, that the mobility rights offered to TCNs by the LTR Directive are nowhere near those contained in EU citizenship provisions. As with all the directives covered here, moreover, the LTR Directive is fraught with exceptions and red tape, and, with regard to rights and equal treatment for the long-term resident TCNs, numerous disparities prevail, concerning both the situation in the granting member state and the conditions applying to a long-term resident who wishes to move to another member state. In the latter case, just to point to one of many derogations, non-granting member states are allowed to "limit the total number of persons entitled to be granted right of residency" (article 14: 4), a derogation highlighting member states' refusal to give a blank cheque to TCNs' intra-EU movement.

## The Researchers Directive

The Researchers Directive (Directive 2005/71/EC)[5] was adopted in October 2005. Aiming to attract third-country researchers to the EU, the directive was also launched for the more particular purpose of contributing to the target (set in 2003) of having an additional 700,000 researchers working in the Union by 2010 (via a goal of earmarking an amount equivalent to 3 per cent of GDP for investment in research).

Conditional on a hosting agreement with a research organization, the directive establishes the admission terms for researchers from third countries who are to carry out research in a member state for more than three months. The researchers are granted rights comparable to those of member-state nationals in a number of areas (much in line with the LTR Directive), but in contrast to students and doctoral students (under the Student Directive, which was adopted a year earlier)[6] they are afforded more favourable intra-EU mobility

---

5. Council Directive 2005/71/EC of 12 October 2005 on a specific procedure for admitting third-country nationals for the purposes of scientific research. Denmark and Ireland (and the United Kingdom) do not take part in this directive.
6. Council Directive 2004/114/EC, of 13 December 2004, on the conditions of admission of third-country nationals, for the purposes of studies, pupil exchange, unremunerated

rights and both family reunification and EU mobility for family members (neither of these applies to students). As Chou (2012: 1062) notes, moreover, and contrary to future ELM directives (e.g. the Blue Card Directive), the principle of Community preference, or labour market test, does not apply to the directive.

Although third-country researchers, by definition, will always comprise relatively few people, this directive nonetheless answers directly to the Commission's goal of increasing ELM, at least in the high-skilled category; it does this too, since it exclusively addresses third-country nationals (and their family members) who will migrate to the EU, as opposed to TCNs who are already EU residents.

In the subsequent reports on the application of the directive, the Commission voiced its dissatisfaction with its performance (EC 2011d, 2011e). Among other things, it drew attention to the dismally low number of third-country researchers who had been admitted under the directive.

In the spring of 2013, therefore, the Commission decided to table a proposal to amend both the Researchers and Student Directives and merge them into one directive, calling for improvements and additions regarding a number of key components, such as admission procedures, rights and intra-EU mobility. Most of all, the Commission (2013b) intended to make the directives more compatible with the Europe 2020 Strategy and the EU's Global Approach to Migration and Mobility.[7] The directive proposal also sounded the alarm over the EU's alleged "innovation emergency" vis-à-vis the United States and Japan, its shrinking working-age population and structural demographic and economic challenges that risked growing worse unless the EU managed to compete successfully for global talent: "Thousands of the best researchers and innovators have moved to countries where conditions are more favourable" (EC 2013b: 2).

The proposal is also much more explicit than the two original directives in its emphasis on the labour migration aspect: "One of the key elements of this proposal would be to better tap into the potential of students and researchers upon finalizing their studies/research. They constitute a future pool of highly skilled workers as they speak the language and are integrated in the host society" (EC 2013b: 8). The amended directive thus intended to provide students with more possibilities to work while studying as well as giving both students and

---

training or voluntary service. Denmark and Ireland (and the United Kingdom) do not take part in this directive.

7. As part of GAMM, the European Neighbourhood Policy (ENP) and the bilateral Mobility Partnerships signed with a growing number of non-EU countries are specifically mentioned as means by which the Union could increase its intake of researchers and students.

researchers the right, upon completion of their studies/research, to stay for an additional 12 months in order to seek work and to start a business. The new directive also added new categories of TCNs to the directive's admission conditions, but member states kept the right to choose whether or not they wanted to include these categories; these are labour migrants admitted to work as au pairs and remunerated trainees.

The new directive was adopted in 2016,[8] and the migration and home affairs commissioner, Dimitris Avranopoulos, greeted it as "modernising EU-wide rules for welcoming talents from abroad". Besides what has already been mentioned, the new directive added provisions for third-country researchers and their families with regard to family members' access to the labour market and to intra-EU mobility. This points to the highly stratified rights distribution between the directive's different target categories, ranging from highly quali-fied researchers to unqualified au pairs. This notwithstanding, no category escapes the requirement to "provide the evidence requested by the Member State concerned that during the planned stay the third-country national will have sufficient resources to cover subsistence costs without having recourse to the Member State's social assistance system, and return travel costs" (article 7: 1e).

As for equal treatment, the directive allows for many derogations and much discretion to the member states, and these apply also to the researcher cat-egory, the most vaunted category and the one that the EU has a particularly poor record in attracting.

## The Blue Card Directive

The Blue Card Directive (Directive 2009/50/EC),[9] which was adopted in May 2009 to attract highly qualified labour migrants to the European Union, is arguably the EU's most publicly well-known labour migration directive to date, immediately acquiring a flagship status because of the fact that the Commission finally could point to an instrument with a potential (at least ostensibly) to involve fairly large numbers of new labour migrants.

---

8. Directive (EU) 2016/801 of the European Parliament and of the Council of 11 May 2016 on the conditions of entry and residence of third-country nationals for the purposes of research, studies, training, voluntary service, pupil exchange schemes or educational projects and au pairing (recast).
9. Council Directive 2009/50/EC of 25 May 2009 on the conditions of entry and residence of third-country nationals for the purposes of highly qualified employment. Denmark and Ireland (and the United Kingdom) do not take part in this directive.

The general context for the Blue Card, according to the European Commission (EC 2007b: 3), could be described as a "need scenario" with regard to highly skilled labour. Reflecting the "very high international competition" for such migrant labour, this need scenario was said to pose a particular challenge for the EU (EC 2007b: 3; 2007a: 1). In order to face up to this challenge, the Commission thought it was high time to start phasing out one of the EU's major comparative disadvantages vis-à-vis its global competitors: the fact that high-skilled migrants had to wrestle with 27 different national systems for admission as well as facing several layers of red tape when trying to move jobs within the EU (EC 2007b: 3). "Europe," the Commission (2007a: 3) insisted, "can only succeed in attracting 'the best and brightest' if it speaks with one voice."

At the same time, the Commission also qualified that the Blue Card by no means was intended to be "a blank cheque" to all highly qualified workers (Goldirova 2007a). As such, the then home affairs commissioner, Franco Frattini, underlined that "the blue card is not a permanent card like the American green card" (Goldirova 2007b). That is to say, the card "does not create a right of admission" (EC 2007a: 2). Instead it was intended to be "demand-driven," invariably requiring that highly qualified third-country migrants show proof of a "job contract" or "binding job-offer" before a Blue Card is issued (EC 2007b: 9). By these means, member states "maintain control on which type – and how many – highly qualified workers will enter their labour markets" (EC 2007a: 2; see also EC 2007b: 7). The big irony here, then, is that Brussels wants the sensation of the Green Card but not its content. It is introducing something it has chosen to call the Blue Card – which it has copied from the Green Card – and then, in the same breath, goes ahead and tries to distance the card from the only thing people can associate it with after having heard the name "Blue Card", namely the Green Card. This is yet another illustration of the European migration policy taboos. Brussels has to make it absolutely clear that it is neither loosening admission rules, nor is it frivolously clearing paths to permanent residence and costly welfare commitments.

This is further underlined by the fact that the Commission's proposal steered clear of any mention of permanent residence, let alone the prospects thereof, for the would-be Blue Card holders. Instead, it emphasized that the work permit conferred by the card was to be limited to a maximum of two years' stay in a member state, whereupon the Blue Card migrant would be granted the opportunity to move to another member state provided that "certain conditions" were met, including the mandatory requirement of a valid work contract (EC 2007b: 6).

Tailored to amend projected labour and skills shortages, the directive lays down the terms of entry, residence and intra-EU mobility for highly qualified third-country workers and their families. As with the Long-Term Residence and Researchers Directives, it stipulates rights in a number of areas, including a set of labour rights. The directive also provides – although it hardly highlights it, as seen when the directive proposal was made public – a path to long-term resident status in the EU, in keeping with the rules of the LTR Directive.

Although the directive is promoted for its rights provisions and commitment to making the European Union the most attractive destination for highly qualified migrants, it also contains numerous complicated requirements and restrictions as well as many discretionary and derogative powers for the member states. As a result of this, as many scholars pointed out early on, the directive's facilitating impact on the harmonization of the different member states' admission systems, which made up one of the Commission's main rationales for the Blue Card (EC 2007b: 3), could only be meagre at best.[10]

Many limitations also apply to intra-EU mobility, another of Brussels' key motivations for launching the Blue Card.[11] As article 18 has it, before a Blue Card holder and his/her family "may move to" another member state, the card holder must have resided at least 18 months in the first member state. Yet, as the "may" clause indicates (and the directive contains many of these), even then their intra-EU mobility is not guaranteed, since the directive specifies that member states "may continue to apply volumes of admission as referred to in Article 6". As article 6 establishes, restating the Lisbon Treaty's article 79, this directive

> shall not affect the right of a Member State to determine the volume of admission of third-country nationals entering its territory for the purposes of highly qualified employment. This is of course the most crucial impediment to making due on the Commission's main objective of stimulating a large increase in ELM. Member States will therefore maintain control on which type – and on how many – highly qualified workers will enter their labour markets.      (EC 2007a: 2)

In effect, this means that member states retain the option of not issuing any Blue Cards at all, thus defeating the purpose of the directive.

---

10. For more on the limited scope and impact of the Blue Card, see, e.g., Cerna (2014); Eisele (2013); Gümüs (2010); Peers (2009); and the contributions in Grütters and Strik (2013).

11. As stated by the EC (2007b: 6) in the directive proposal: "Intra-EU mobility would be a strong incentive for third-country highly qualified workers to enter the EU labour market, and could play a primary role in relieving the labour shortages in certain areas/sectors."

This was also illustrated by the many restrictions that were imposed on equal treatment for card holders and their families. Member states were also entitled to introduce scores of other constraints, many of which were directed at the key nexus of welfare and permanent residence (Friðriksdóttir 2017: 160–1).

In its "5th annual report on immigration and asylum (2013)", published in May 2014, the Commission (2014b: 13) took note of the low number of Blue Cards that had been issued until then: 3,644 in total for 2012, of which Germany accounted for 2,584. According to the most recent data, 24,310 Blue Cards were issued in the EU-28 in 2017 (up from 20,979 in 2016), whereof 20,541 were issued in Germany (Eurostat n.d.–b). In its implementation report from May 2014, the Commission pointed to the already operating and competing national systems for high-skilled migration as one possible explanation (EC 2014c: 10).

In view of the dismal record, the Commission put forward a new proposal for a Blue Card directive in 2016, one that aimed for less red tape, a further harmonization of rules and more rights for card holders and their families. The proposal (EC 2016b), which soon was to stall in negotiations, formed part of the 2015 European Agenda on Migration and spoke with great urgency about the increasingly difficult demographic situation and "structural skills shortages" in the EU. Equally troublesome, the Commission highlighted, was the Union's lack of a system to attract enough highly skilled third-country immigrants. In 2014 the Blue Card and the various national programmes managed to produce only a dismal inflow of fewer than 40,000 such migrants, numbers that were "by far insufficient to address the existing and projected future labour and skills shortages in the EU in highly skilled occupations" (EC 2016b: 3; see also EC 2018a).

Given the urgency of the situation and the poor record, one would expect the new proposal to zoom in on making the Blue Card far more attractive with regard to rights. Yet, as Bjarney Friðriksdóttir (2017: 163) reveals in her meticulous study of the Blue Card and other labour migration direct-ives, the new directive proposal entails "no substantive changes" that would narrow the equal treatment gap between Blue Card holders and member state citizens. The directive proposal does, however, aim to give card holders and their families more access to EU free movement provisions; it seeks to simplify admission rules and it aspires to lift the restrictions on a card holders' right to change employer (see, further, Friðriksdóttir 2017). The proposal also adds new categories of TCNs that should be made eligible for the Blue Card. This "novelty", as the Commission terms it, is particularly interesting for our purposes here, and I thus wish to quote at length:

> The proposed Directive continues to not apply to persons seeking international protection and awaiting decision on their status or to

those who are beneficiaries of temporary protection or residing in a Member State on a strictly temporary basis. As a novelty it does cover, however, beneficiaries of international protection under Directive 2011/95/EU ("Qualification Directive"). They will be able to apply for an EU Blue Card like any other third-country national, while retaining all the rights they enjoy as beneficiaries of protection. Also third-country nationals to be resettled in Member States under future EU schemes, who will be granted similar rights as those laid down in Qualification Directive, are to be given access to the EU Blue Card. Highly skilled beneficiaries of international protection will thus become more accessible to employers and be able to take up employment in a more targeted way in accordance with their skills and education, filling shortages in sectors and occupations in any Member State. This allows them to actively participate in the labour market, which favours their integration, and to more easily secure their own livelihood. Furthermore, it avoids wasting their skills if there are no vacancies in their specific field in the Member State that granted them protection, leading to a more efficient labour market allocation.

(EC 2016b: 14)

Like the proposal in general, the tone in this passage bears the mark of the post-2015 atmosphere. Since a strong EU consensus prevents the uttering of anything that could be interpreted as mildly beneficial to refugees, the passage ensures that it is the EU, and only the EU, that will reap the benefits from the addition of two categories of refugees to the directive. As for the refugees, who will amount to a small number under the Qualification Directive and unspecified future resettlement: they get to "secure their own livelihood" (a recurring formulation), and so will not burden the host state.

Although this is in full compliance with both the political sloganeering of anti-immigration and sound finance principles, one may ask how it squares with Brussels' quest to boost the European Union's attractiveness for "global talent". The new Blue Card proposal's emphasis on attractiveness is thus soon overshadowed by provisos aimed at preventing the highly skilled migrants from becoming unattractive and costly. "Unemployment in itself," the proposal states, "shall not constitute a reason for withdrawing an EU Blue Card, unless the period of unemployment exceeds three consecutive months, or where the unemployment occurs more than once during the period of validity of an EU Blue Card." Brussels wants to recruit the world's very best and brightest, but somehow feels obliged to hedge against the risk of having hosting states foot the unemployment bill, as if that constitutes a real risk and as if the card holder would come to the EU for the unemployment benefits. For all the rhetoric of making the EU "more effective in attracting talent to Europe" and giving the "clear message to highly skilled workers that the EU welcomes them" (EC 2016b: 2, 6), what the proposal for a new Blue Card directive reveals, rather, is this: even those at the very top of the global labour migration or mobility pyramid cannot escape being designated as potential welfare liabilities and fiscal burdens.

## The Seasonal Workers Directive

After nearly four years of negotiations the Seasonal Workers Directive (Directive 2014/36/EU)[12] was adopted in February 2014. It specifies the terms of entry and stay and the rights of TCNs who apply to be employed as seasonal labour in the European Union for a maximum stay of between five and nine months within a 12-month period. Although the directive leaves decisions about volumes of seasonal labour to be admitted exclusively in the hands of member states, this, together with the Blue Card, is the only directive to date that at least nominally aligns with the European Commission's goal of significantly increasing the admission of third-country labour migrants to the EU. Industries employing seasonal migrant labour (tourism, agriculture and horticulture are mentioned in the directive but member states are entitled to define additional ones) are by nature labour-intensive, since costs can be kept to a minimum, and they have obvious growth potential given the pull of the high unemployment of unskilled labour in countries close to the EU. Most of all, as the Commission (EC 2010b: 2–3) makes clear, the directive has its basis in a structural predicament regarding the labour supply in the EU:

> EU economies face a structural need for seasonal work for which labour from within the EU is expected to become less and less available. [...] [T]he structural need for low-skilled and low-qualified workers is likely to continue expanding. It should also be pointed out that there is a more permanent need for unskilled labour within the EU. It is expected to be increasingly difficult to fill these gaps with EU national workers, primarily owing to the fact that these workers consider seasonal work unattractive.

---

12. Directive 2014/36/EU of the European Parliament and of the Council of 26 February 2014 on the conditions of entry and stay of third-country nationals for the purpose of employment as seasonal workers. Ireland and Denmark (and the United Kingdom) do not take part in this directive.

As a partial solution to the problem of high unemployment in north African countries and elsewhere, the Commission has, within its framework of the Global Approach to Migration and Mobility (as discussed above), made repeated calls for better migration management in the Mediterranean and for more legal migration channels to the EU. The directive fits with this objective by being the first one to be promoted in terms of *circular migration* and by being specifically designed to support development and prevent "illegal immigration" and employers' exploitation of TCNs through a set of "fair and transparent rules for admission and stay". In turn, these are intended to work by legalizing work in industries heavily staffed by undocumented migrants. As part of this, the directive puts much emphasis on "providing for incentives and safeguards to prevent overstaying or temporary stay from becoming permanent" and for "such temporary stay turning into unauthorised stay" (preamble: 7; see also the Commission's directive proposal: EC 2010b). As such, it is also adapted to the previously adopted Employers Sanctions Directive.[13] As the European Parliament's (2014) press release highlighted on the passing of the directive, the rules established "aim both to end exploitation and to prevent temporary stays becoming permanent".

Although they take note of "fair treatment" of TCNs and grant a set of minimum basic rights to seasonal workers, the directive's rights provisions also differ significantly from most of the other EU directives relating to ELM. For instance, the directive does not provide for intra-EU mobility, something that facilitated the adoption process (Lazarowicz 2014: 1); and it allows member states to restrict the right to unemployment and family benefits (Friðriksdóttir 2017; Fudge & Herzfeld Olsson 2014). It is noteworthy too that the directive allows member states to impose limits on migrants' further education and vocational training (Zoeteweij-Turhan 2017). As expected, it does not grant family reunification rights and it limits equal treatment in a number of areas (see, further, Friðriksdóttir 2017), restraints that NGOs lobbied against during the negotiation period (see, e.g., La Strada International *et al.* 2011). As the directive's preamble puts it:

> Due to the temporary nature of the stay of seasonal workers [...], Member States should be able to exclude family benefits and unemployment benefits from equal treatment between seasonal workers and

---

13. Directive 2009/52/EC of the European Parliament and of the Council of 18 June 2009, providing for minimum standards on sanctions and measures against employers of illegally staying third-country nationals.

their own nationals and should be able to limit the application of equal treatment in relation to education and vocational training, as well as tax benefits.                                                                 (preamble: 46)

By the same token, the welfare systems are basically off-limits to seasonal migrants. As the directive stipulates, "Member States shall require that the seasonal worker will have no recourse to their social assistance systems" (chapter II, article 5: 3). Furthermore, "Member States shall require that the seasonal worker will have sufficient resources during his or her stay to maintain him/herself without having recourse to their social assistance systems" (chapter II, article 6: 3). This includes an admission requirement on the migrant to have acquired sickness insurance and accommodation (chapter II, article 5: 1).

In contrast to other ELM directives, there is no mention of migrant integration in this directive. Even though neither the Commission nor the directive explains this, the temporary nature of seasonal work and the fact that the migrants formally remain residents of the sending countries while in the EU may provide sufficient clarification. Hence, as occupiers of the lowest rung in the EU's labour migration hierarchy, these migrants are to remain perpetually unincorporated, with no opportunity to receive permanent residence, let alone earn it. Formally speaking, these migrants do not even qualify as temporary residents.

The absence of any integration endorsement can also be construed, however, as contingent on the fact that the migrant labour addressed in this directive will enter highly segregated labour markets that, as noted above and as the Commission has underlined time and again, face a permanent and growing "structural need for low-skilled and low-qualified workers" that cannot be satisfied by "EU national workers, primarily owing to the fact that these workers consider seasonal work unattractive" (EC 2010b: 2–3). If this explains the non-appearance of migrant integration in the directive, its absence as well as the Commission's sanction of segregated labour markets nonetheless contradict sharply with the Commission's overall emphasis on the crucial importance of migrants' successful integration into EU host societies. The Commission's position, stated on numerous occasions, is that "[a]dmission of economic immigrants is inseparable from measures on integration" (EC 2005: 4) and "better migration management can only be achieved if the EU and its Member States also enhance efforts on the integration of third-country nationals staying legally in the EU" (EC 2018a: 7). Indeed, migrants' "successful integration into society in the host country is the key to maximising the opportunities of legal migration and making the most of the contributions that immigration can make to EU development" (EC n.d.–c).

As with the other directives discussed here, finally, mainly as a result of Council resistance, this directive also fails to meet the harmonization goals set up initially. Many of the administrative components related to admission, for instance, are to be kept within the purview of the member states, and the directive allows for a number of different admission terms (Delaney 2013; Jonjić & Mavrodi 2012; Monar 2013).

### The Intra-Corporate Transferees Directive

Finally, let us also take a brief look at the Intra-Corporate Transferees Directive (Directive 2014/66/EU), which, after some four years of very difficult negotiations, was adopted in 2014. The directive lays down the terms of entry, residence and rights of third-country managers, specialists and trainee employees who apply to be admitted as intra-corporate transferees (ICTs).[14] As the then home affairs commissioner Cecilia Malmström (EC 2014f) put it upon the adoption of the directive in 2014:

> Despite the crisis and the high unemployment, many highly qualified jobs currently remain unfilled in the EU due to the lack of adequate competences and skills. Europe needs to attract more highly skilled workers from outside the EU to match the needs of EU businesses and who can bring jobs and investments to our continent.

By facilitating the entry and stay of ICTs (defined as temporary workers),[15] the EU is to benefit from the added competence, skills, knowledge and innovation capacity that these migrants bring. At the time, the Commission expected the directive to apply to some 15,000 to 20,000 new ICTs annually. Symptomatically, the implementation of the directive was delayed in most member states – in Sweden, for instance, the directive did not go into effect until March 2018 – and as a consequence the EU-wide numbers as to how many people are making use of the directive are not in yet (see Eurostat 2019a).

Predictably, the most contentious aspects of the proposal revolved around rights for the ICTs, in general, and intra-EU mobility rights, in particular. The

---

14. Directive 2014/66/EU of the European Parliament and of the Council of 15 May 2014, on the conditions of entry and residence of third-country nationals in the framework of an intra-corporate transfer. Denmark and Ireland (and the United Kingdom) do not take part in this directive.

15. The maximum duration of stay is limited to three years for managers and experts and one year for trainee employees.

Council insisted that ICTs should be placed on a par with posted workers, whereas the Parliament argued for equal treatment along similar lines to that given to member state nationals (Monar 2013; Kostakopoulou, Acosta Arcarazo & Munk 2014: 144; Peers *et al.* 2012b). As Steve Peers and colleagues (2012b: 105) have it, however, the Council and Parliament positions were "not radically far apart", and in the end a compromise was struck. Here, and in accordance with the Council's position, it was agreed: "Intra-corporate transferees should benefit from at least the same terms and conditions of employment as posted workers whose employer is established on the territory of the Union" (article 15). At the same time, the Parliament managed to incorporate the right to equal treatment into some areas (Brieskova 2014).

Provided that it was the Council that carried most of the day in the negotiations, the directive's list of rights turned out to be quite short, including no more than three items. On the other hand, and in contrast to seasonal workers, ICTs were granted family reunification rights, although not to the same extent as applies to third-country workers in some other directives. Also in contrast to seasonal workers, ICTs and their families were given intra-EU mobility rights. These came with many strings attached, however, as the Council prevailed over the Parliament's request for less member state discretion in this area. Together with numerous other derogations, highly complex rules and much leeway for the member states, this diminished the directive's harmonization effect.

## Conclusion

Judged by the European Commission's yardstick of what needs to be done in order to stimulate a large-scale increase of external labour migration, the EU policies and legislation enacted over the past two decades are nothing short of disappointing. An increase in labour migration through concerted EU action, then, seems as "politically impossible" today as it was when Malmström complained about it back in 2013 (quoted in Larsson 2013). Or perhaps even more impossible. In the post-2015 political climate, the conflicts over migration between member states and between member states and the Commission are hardening and effectively halting the little progress there had been on EU policy on ELM. Other than the Commission's proposal for a new Blue Card directive, there has been very little activity in the area of ELM since the adoption of the ICT Directive in 2014. And at the time of writing the negotiations on the new Blue Card have been mired in deadlock since 2016. In fact, things were stalling even prior to 2015. At the European Council meeting in June 2014, for instance, the member states were making it clear that they would not reconsider and allow for more EU influence over ELM (European Council 2014). At the same time, the Commission clarified that the focus from then on should not be on new legislative initiatives but, rather, on ensuring the implementation and consolidation of existing legislation and frameworks (EC 2014e).

But, if there is no impetus for a supranational ELM regime at the moment, this, as I touched upon in Chapter 1, is not the same as saying that ELM is not happening in the European Union. As acknowledged by the Commission in its assessment of the Blue Card Directive, several member states have invested quite some effort in getting their own ELM policies up and running. Consequently, they have little inclination to scrap these for EU policies that may be less sensitive to national interests (see European Economic and Social Committee 2016: 3). After all, we are talking about 27 members, all with highly diverse labour needs, unemployment levels, industrial structures, welfare regimes, positions in the business cycle and political leanings.

To illustrate a little further, the most recent Eurostat (2019b) and pre-Covid-19 figures may be instructive. They show that EU member states issued 3.1 million first residence permits in 2017, which is the highest since 2008 and up by 3.7 per cent compared with 2016 (in 2013 the number was 2.36 million, which was a 12 per cent increase as compared to 2012). Of these residence permits, 32 per cent were specifically issued for employment purposes; in 2013 the figure for employment purposes was only 23 per cent. In 2017 family-related residence permits came in second, with 26.5 per cent; "other reasons", mainly asylum, claimed 24.5 per cent; and education-related issuance accounted for almost 17 per cent. Compared to 2016, work-related permits were up by more than 18 per cent in 2017; in sharp contrast, permits agreed for "other reasons" were down by almost 14 per cent (Eurostat 2019b). The latter reflect the steep decline in the number of asylum seekers entering the EU. Declining asylum entries and, with them, declining numbers of people receiving international protection has also meant that the EU has seen a steep decline in permanent migration, starting in 2017 (OECD 2018a: 19–20).

Somewhat contrary to the impression the "demographic deficit" debate often gives, then, these figures show that external labour migration to the EU is anything but insignificant, although it is far from meeting Brussels' projected needs. Moreover, with labour migration increasing, both in terms of real numbers and proportionally, and with asylum migration decreasing significantly, this corresponds perfectly with Brussels' preferred policy. Yet, when this data is disaggregated to the member state level, it is also possible to discern a highly varied picture, both number-wise and proportionally speaking, with seven member states accounting for more than 80 per cent of the total issuing of new residence permits in 2017. Countries such as Bulgaria and Romania barely register here. As for the number of external labour migrants in 2017, the ostensibly "anti-immigration" Poland is the unchallenged leader, with almost 600,000 temporary work permits issued. Germany and Spain trail far behind, with 53,000 and 43,000 respectively. The bulk of the permits were issued to Ukrainian and Syrian citizens, the former increasing and the latter decreasing (Eurostat 2019b).

In all, the development of ELM and its lack of a strong supranational component reflect country-specific preferences that – together with the range of economic and political factors mentioned above – speak to the fact that, as long as enough member states feel they have more to gain from staying in control of ELM, they will allow only for so much common EU policy and legislation (see, further, Paul 2015).

As noted in the introduction, however, the development accounted for here is not only reflective of negativity or the absence of consensus. Most of all, rather, the ELM directives are the results of a negotiated consensus that, in turn, reveals, in a rather distilled form, what all EU parties actually *can* agree on, what the particular requirements are that need to be satisfied for directives to be given a green light. So, what are these requirements? First, and needless to say, member states have to remain in control of how many external labour migrants are granted admission. Since the outset two decades ago, Brussels has never challenged this prerogative. As should also be clear by now, EU policy needs to make sure to avoid obligations to grant permanent residence, which, if redeemed, would generate automatic access to welfare provisions for the migrants. What raises the stakes around permanent residence is that it also entails a right to family reunification. Consequently, family members would also be entitled to social rights – family members who may not work and who may be children entitled to "costly" child care and schooling.

In every directive analysed here, permanent residence and, to a lesser extent, family migration have proved to be *the* most consensual issues among the member states. (As I will discuss further below, Brussels has challenged member states on family migration; this has happened only when highly skilled migration has been on the table, however.) On the face of it, the Blue Card includes both family migration and the prospect for permanent residence. In reality, however, member states have ensured that too many strings remain attached for permanent residence to be more than just that: a possibility. And this, of course, also impacts negatively on family migration. Member states, then, want to hedge against the risk of having Blue Card holders become fiscal burdens on the hosting state's welfare system. Even here, with the highly skilled and the highly sought-after who sit atop the labour migration pyramid and who often are spared the "migrant" epithet – yes, even here – sound finance has more than one finger in the pie.

This shows just how high the stakes are; and it also helps us understand to the full why, at the other end of the spectrum, the directive on seasonal labour migration rules out migrants' access to social assistance and why it pledges to "prevent overstaying or temporary stay from becoming permanent". As Friðriksdóttir (2017: 260) notes, the Commission's directive proposal on seasonal migration "was silent on the right to family reunification for seasonal workers and there were no references made to it in the accompanying impact assessment". In the first exchange of positions on the proposal, Sweden actually did propose that seasonal migrants should be given the right to bring their families. But, as Friðriksdóttir (2017: 260) is able to show, this proposal was "not discussed at all during the negotiations", which is ample proof of just how solid the consensus is on this issue.

As seen, member states are also sceptical towards intra-EU mobility rights for external labour migrants. This relates to member states wanting to avoid a situation in which they have to foot the welfare, healthcare or unemployment bill for migrants admitted by other member states. Although Blue Card holders and their families have better access to mobility within the EU, many obstacles remain and, in fact, there are no guarantees. Given the premier status of the Blue Card, applying only to the highly skilled, this again goes to show the extreme fiscal cautiousness with which member states approach also those migrants whose fiscal riskiness (viewed from a sound finance perspective) is negligible.

Interestingly, the ICT Directive also imposed restrictions on both intra-EU mobility and family benefits. Initially, both Austria and Germany had pushed for the "full exclusion of family benefits" for transferees; as it turned out, benefits were made conditional on length of stay (Friðriksdóttir 2017: 306). As with the Blue Card holders, the ICT Directive applies to, should we say, the migrant business class of managers, experts and specialists working for multinational corporations. During the difficult negotiations over the ICT Directive, the then commissioner in charge, Cecilia Malmström, vented her frustration: "What the Council and Parliament are arguing over concerns the extent to which intra-EU mobility will apply. If a computer engineer from New Delhi is going to work in Stockholm then we want it to be possible for that person to bring the family and that they should be able to take a weekend trip to Copenhagen" (quoted in Larsson 2013). The scandal was thus that the Council would spoil weekend trips for IBM's computer engineers and their families, as if the Council had failed to understand that these were not your regular migrants; in fact, they were not even called migrants – they were managers, experts and specialists. All the same, the member states wanted to hedge.

I am well aware that this chapter may come across as unnecessarily wonkish at times, with all the detailed references to directive preambles and paragraphs. But, as they say, the devil is in the detail, and this applies to policy guided by sound finance too. What is interesting, and perhaps surprising at first sight, is the fact that those directives drawn up for the upper echelons in the labour migrant hierarchy are those that contain the most devilish details. Upon closer consideration, however, this is simply logical. It is logical because it is only the researchers, the managers, the specialists and the other highly skilled migrants who are being provided with any meaningful access to the welfare state. In stern contrast to the near-total exclusion that applies to seasonal migrants, the former migrants' incorporation, however gradated, qualified and conditional it might be, does raise the spectre of full incorporation, with all the automatic fiscal obligations that this places on the hosting state. Once member states concede – rather than simply refuse – some type of partial or substantial access to their welfare systems and benefit schemes, this raises the stakes and hence the concerns of being stuck with fiscal obligations should things not go according to plan. And, as the stakes rise, so does the propensity to hedge against potential fiscal risks.

Some may conclude that the problems addressed here mainly result from penny-pinching member states. As noted, Brussels' original ELM scheme advocated a horizontal approach that contained a stronger commitment to rights and equal treatment for TCNs. This was rejected by the member states in favour of a discriminatory and stratifying sectoral approach that compromised many of the Commission's original objectives. Hence, the narrative about parsimonious member states is not without merit. It applies almost exclusively to the directives and policies targeting the highly skilled segments, however, for which most member states' fiscal risk analysis differs from the Commission's. Certainly, Commissioner Malmström was greatly annoyed over the fact that the Council did not find it as natural as she did that IBM's ICT engineers and their families should receive full intra-EU mobility rights and be able to enjoy a weekend in their EU city of choice. Brussels vented no frustration over the meagre rights rationed to the seasonal migrants, however. In fact, when dealing with the Seasonal Labour Directive, the Commission could be seen to be even more austere in its approach to migrants' rights than many member states. As already shown above, Brussels did not propose any family migration rights to seasonal workers. Neither, and much more remarkably, did its proposal include equal treatment for the migrants in working conditions and terms of employment. This was opposed by both Finland and Sweden. Subsequently, after several other member states (but not Germany) and the Parliament followed Finland and Sweden's lead, equal treatment in working conditions was adopted into the directive (Friðriksdóttir 2017: 253–4, 262; Fudge & Herzfeld Olsson 2014).

Whereas Brussels and member states may have issues over highly skilled labour migration, they are, on the whole, in agreement when it comes to low-skilled migrants. Here, sound finance's austere rights regime rules supreme and no risks are taken. This was clear already in the build-up to what became the seasonal migration directive. At a G6 migration ministers meeting held in the United Kingdom in 2006, France and Germany jointly presented a document, entitled "New European migration policy". In this subsequently leaked document, which Carrera and Hernández i Sagrera could pass on a few years later, the following position on circular migration was presented:

> We do not want uncontrolled immigration into our labour markets and our social security systems. In order to promote circular migration, quotas should be set for the migration of labour into certain occupations ... in order for the concept of circular migration to succeed, it is important that migrants return to their countries of origin after their stay in an EU member state. [...] Finally, we also have to make sure that the countries of origin unconditionally comply with their obligation to readmit those migrants who do not want to return voluntarily.
>
> (quoted in Carrera & Hernández i Sagrera 2009: 11)

In the Commission's (2007c: 8) communication on circular migration a year later part of this message was reaffirmed:

> Circular migration is increasingly being recognized as a key form of migration that, if well managed, can help match the international supply of and demand for labour, thereby contributing to a more efficient allocation of available resources and to economic growth. However, circular migration also poses certain challenges: if not properly designed and managed, migration intended to be circular can easily become permanent and, thus, defeat its objective.

Provided that this consensual position has hardened further in recent years, it is now high time to ponder how it can help us understand the EU's hardening approach towards refugee reception and its ultimate stance on the watershed 2015 refugee crisis, in particular.

**6**

# Why EU asylum policy cannot afford to pay demographic dividends

"*Flüchtlingshilfe: Unser Land überrascht sich selbst*" – "Help for refugees: our country surprises itself." So ran the headline on *Die Zeit*'s web edition in the evening of 18 September 2015 (Liebsch 2015). Underneath the headline, a photo showed volunteers distributing water and other necessities to newly arrived refugees at Munich's train station. The volunteers' expressions suggest that they know they are doing something meaningful.

I have lost count of the number of times that I have opened a presentation or a lecture with this front page. Usually, I have to help the audience to get what I am after. Once they do, people sigh in disbelief, laugh in a subdued manner or shake their heads. We are surprised when we do good deeds. How did it come to this: that we find it surprising when people do the right thing and help foreigners in need?

*Die Zeit*'s headline captures succinctly the hardwiring of sound finance in societal cognition: that foreign refugees in need should be received warmly and enthusiastically is a surprise precisely because it contravenes everything we have been taught about sound national bookkeeping. According to the fiscal impact literature, with more people to house, feed, school, train and provide social assistance to, there will be less tax money to spend on everyone else. Whereas the admission of a small number of refugees may be regarded as a legitimate human rights tax by some, the mass enthusiasm for the arrival of hundreds of thousands (in Germany and Sweden) should strike us as unusual. Society has been taught that refugee admission is an expense, which, consequently, translates into a socio-economic sacrifice by the host population. If conceived of as a *sacrifice*, we also know that popular sacrifices on such a scale are rare, even non-existent, today. People generally do not smilingly volunteer in large numbers to become materially worse off. In this sense, the 2015 refugee response was Janus-faced; for some it was a nice surprise, while for others it was the opposite: the manifestation of mere delusion and foolhardiness.

But, as I will show, there is also a historical pattern that explains why a country in the European Union surprises itself when it helps refugees. The EU's persistent work, starting in the 1980s, to prevent the entry of refugees makes the "Refugees welcome" actions of the summer and autumn of 2015 even more surprising. At that point, there were even a few political leaders – in Germany and Sweden, to be precise – who took the unprecedented step of supporting the reception of large numbers of refugees. "*Wir schaffen das,*" said Angela Merkel, famously, of the refugee admission on 31 August 2015. Her counterpart in Sweden, Stefan Löfven, a week later addressed a large crowd in central Stockholm: "Once more we have to decide the type of Europe we want to be. My Europe receives refugees who flee from war, in solidarity and jointly. My Europe does not build walls, we cooperate when distress is severe" (Regeringskansliet 2015).

For the first time since EU cooperation on asylum matters began in the mid-1980s, it might have seemed as if two countries were about to call for a change of course, shifting from a focus on refugee prevention to one such that admissions into the EU would be a real option. The situation was extraordinary. In the autumn of 2015 Germany had received hundreds of thousands, and soon maybe over a million, of refugees and yet, surprisingly, many high-rank politicians kept their cool and did not succumb to the usual panic mode of branding refugees as threats, burdens, terrorists and "illegals".

But, if the situation was extraordinary, it was also short-lived. Below I start out by accounting for 2015's aftermath and the unambiguous demise of whatever prospects there were of the EU contributing to a resolution of the global refugee crisis by, as a first requirement, agreeing to serve as a real sanctuary for refugees. To make sense of the current development, however, and also to grasp EU policy conceptually, a brief look at the historical trajectory and logic of EU asylum policy is necessary. We need this historical context, too, in order to dispel the long-standing notion that "Europe", as opposed to "selfish" nation states, somehow harbours a cosmopolitan and humanitarian teleology, according to which "More Europe", or an increase in supranational influence over asylum policy, somehow should result in a more humanitarian policy.

From here the chapter moves on to resolve the puzzle that I pointed to in Chapter 1 concerning the simultaneous goals of blocking asylum seekers while at the same time seeking to attract millions of labour migrants to mitigate the EU's demographic crisis. Among other things, I discuss the fact that both Germany and Sweden momentarily (in 2015) referred to the Syrian refugees as a demographic boon and dividend that added an economic rationality to the humanitarian justification for the refuge reception. Almost immediately, however, both countries would revert to the familiar depiction of refugees as a fiscal burden and use it to justify the efforts to put an end to the EU's refugee intake. In beginning to make sense of this volte-face I set the scene for the following chapter's detailed study of both the fiscal and real impact of Sweden's large refugee reception in 2015.

## EU asylum policy: built to prevent

The EU's moment of welcoming refugees was brief and, from the outset, it was engulfed in a barrage of intergovernmental vitriol. It triggered the reintroduction of border controls between EU members as the Dublin and Schengen systems collapsed. In the late autumn of 2015 the German and Swedish governments decided to normalize and thus Europeanize their positions. They called it quits, and things went back to business as usual – or, rather, a *new* normal – with the swift implementation of a battery of anti-asylum measures at both national and EU levels. Many of these measures formed part of the multi-annual European Agenda on Migration, which was launched in May 2015. The crisis mood also propelled many new measures into necessity status. In Sweden, for instance, the long-standing policy and principle of granting permanent residence and family reunification to refugees were suddenly scrapped and the meagre social allowances were further reduced or cut altogether.

Similar "reforms" were passed in Germany. In January 2016 finance minister Wolfgang Schäuble thought the time ripe for some measured vindication of Viktor Orbán: "To be honest, we have to admit that not everything Hungary has done has been wrong" (quoted in *Süddeutsche Zeitung* 2016). Instead of being proud of behaving humanely, moreover, *Die Zeit*'s feature article on 28 January 2016 was headlined "Are the Germans insane? Or is it the rest of the world that does not admit any refugees?".[1] In fact, 85 per cent of the world's forcibly displaced population of roughly 70 million are sheltered in the Global South and not in Germany and the EU (UNHCR 2018). The signal sent by *Die Zeit*, therefore, implied that Germany was foolhardily taking on the whole refugee "burden" alone and that, because of its altruism, it had lost touch with its own best economic and societal interests.

---

1. My translation; "Sind die Deutschen verrückt? Oder ist es der Rest der Welt, der keine Flüchtlinge aufnimmt", *Die Zeit*, 28 January 2016.

In 2017 the head of the centre-left Democratic Party and former Italian prime minister, Matteo Renzi, decided to have his moment of exculpation, stating: "We need to free ourselves from a sense of guilt. We do not have the moral duty to welcome into Italy people who are worse off than ourselves." People in Africa should not migrate to Italy and the EU, he went on, but remain where they are and the EU should assist and encourage them to stay. Said Renzi: "We need to escape from our 'do gooder' mentality" (Reuters 2017).

At the EU level, meanwhile, matters were unequivocal. In contrast to Germany and Sweden, the Commission and European Council were never in a welcoming mood. In September 2015 Donald Tusk, head of the European Council, made the Council's position crystal clear: "It is clear the greatest tide of refugees and migrants is yet to come. So we need to correct our policy of open doors and windows. Now the focus should be on proper protection of our external borders" (quoted in *The Daily Telegraph* 2015a).

Although Tusk was candid about the real objectives of EU asylum policy, he was, like so many other officials and politicians, amateurishly deceptive about the past. Since cooperation on asylum policy began in the late 1980s, EU policy has always been to prevent asylum seekers from entering the Union.[2] This has been the bottom line among the member states, and thus the lodestar for the common policy that has been enacted since the 1980s. First developed via intergovernmental agreements, but, as explained in Chapter 4, modified with the Amsterdam Treaty and the Tampere Programme, asylum policy was gradually subjected to supranational competence and policy-making via the Community method. We need to remember that, although there were refugees coming to the EU in the early 1990s, very few perished in the Mediterranean (Guild *et al.* 2015: 4). But since then there has been a steady increase in casualties, and this has proceeded in tandem with an EU approach bent primarily on devising policies, systems, legal instruments and third-country cooperation for the purpose of denying asylum seekers entry into the EU.[3] The common visa policy and carrier sanctions legislation have been particularly culpable in precluding legal and thereby safe access to the EU for asylum seekers (Guild *et al.* 2015).

Contrary to what Renzi, Tusk and others have claimed, therefore, EU asylum policy has never suffered from a do-gooder mentality but has always striven to close doors and windows to asylum seekers. It is true that borders between Turkey and Greece, and then onwards through Balkan non-EU members, were

---

2. For a detailed account of this policy development, see Hansen and Hager (2012).
3. The literature corroborating this point is extensive, and I have therefore chosen not to cite any one in particular.

temporarily forced open thanks to the exceptional refugee situations in Syria and Turkey. But this was not EU policy as such; rather, it is seen by Brussels as a mammoth policy failure, and hence the enormous efforts on the part of the EU, starting in the late summer of 2015, to negotiate a refugee-blocking settlement with Ankara. "We face two possibilities, and these are the options," European Commission president Jean-Claude Juncker told the European Parliament in October 2015:

> We can say that EU and the European institutions have outstanding issues with Turkey on human rights, press freedoms and so on. We can harp on about that but where is that going to take us in our discussions with Turkey? [...]. We know that there are shortcomings but we need to involve Turkey in our initiatives. We want to ensure that no more refugees come from Turkey into the European Union.
>
> (quoted in *The Daily Telegraph* 2015b)

Faced with having to choose between human rights and the barring of refugees, Juncker made sure to leave no one in doubt where Brussels stood. "Europe's most ardent courtship of a Turkish leader in the post-Ottoman era" was how the *Financial Times*' Alex Barker (2015) described the spectacle.

But the "EU–Turkey statement",[4] as it came to be named, had a precedent in the EU's courtship of Gaddafi, which officially began in 2004 and lasted until 2011, when the EU supported the NATO operation that helped overthrow Gaddafi. In fact, as late as October 2010 home affairs commissioner Cecilia Malmström and enlargement commissioner Stefan Fuele were in Tripoli to conclude the negotiations of a new "border management" deal with Libya, supplying Gaddafi with aid in return for his promise to block migrants and asylum seekers from travelling on to Europe (BBC 2010). Less than a year later Malmström (2011) wrote on her blog that she was "following the developments in Libya with great interest" and went on: "At the moment, it is not yet clear if Gaddafi, one of the cruellest dictators in the world, has been overthrown, but it does look like his days in power are numbered. Gaddafi and his government

---

4. In short, the EU–Turkey Statement, which was agreed in March 2016, authorized the return of "[a]ll new irregular migrants crossing from Turkey into Greek islands as from 20 March 2016". It also stipulated that "Turkey will take any necessary measures to prevent new sea or land routes for illegal migration opening from Turkey to the EU"; and it laid down that, "[f]or every Syrian being returned to Turkey from Greek islands, another Syrian will be resettled from Turkey to the EU". The EU also pledged €6 billion to be spent on improving the situation for refugees in Turkey (European Council 2016). The Statement was immediately subjected to fierce criticism from numerous NGOs, scholars and legal experts (e.g. Amnesty International 2017; Peers 2016).

must now be held accountable for what he has done to his own people during the 42 years his terror regime has held on to the power." In less than ten months Gaddafi had gone from being an EU "partner" to being "one of the cruellest dictators in the world". Yet for years EU leaders had taken Gaddafi's "terror regime" to be the perfect holding pen for the EU's unwanted asylum seekers and migrants.

The anarchy following in the wake of the EU-supported and NATO-led demolition of the Libyan state soon led the Union to search for new migrant-blocking instruments to be applied in the Mediterranean. In June 2015 Operation Sophia, formally the European Union Naval Force Mediterranean (EUNAVFOR MED), was launched in the southern central Mediterranean (Council EU 2015). According to the European Union External Action Service, "The aim of this military operation is to undertake systematic efforts to identify, capture and dispose of vessels as well as enabling assets used or suspected of being used by migrant smugglers or traffickers" (European Union External Action 2015). Subsequently, Sophia was expanded to also include cooperation with the UN-backed Libyan regime in Tripoli, primarily to train and boost the capacity of the regime's coast guard so as to prevent migration to the EU. If the EU's migration cooperation with Gaddafi was incessantly criticized for its blatant violations of human rights (e.g. Human Rights Watch 2008), the subsequent cooperation with the UN-backed Tripoli regime has fared no better, with frequent reports confirming the EU's complicity in the deaths, torture and generally grisly conditions that migrants face in Libya (e.g. Carrera 2018; Human Rights Watch 2019; Pillai 2019; Refugees International 2017; UN 2018).

## The historical logic of EU asylum policy

Before delving further into the contemporary developments, I owe the reader a few glimpses of EU asylum policy history and some of its key dynamics and logics, which, taken together, help explain and put into perspective the surprise of 2015. Again, Sweden and Germany will serve as illuminating cases.

Let us turn back the clock a little more than decade and check in with the developments in Sweden between 2006 and 2008 and what the government and many others at the time described as an untenable refugee problem. Around 2006 an increasing number of Iraqis had started to flee their country as a result of escalating fighting and civilian suffering. For those who managed to flee to the EU, Sweden soon became the main destination country. Under the headline "Sweden offers safe haven to Iraqi refugees", CBC/Radio Canada

(2007) extolled "generous Sweden", emphasizing: "No country outside the Middle East has been as welcoming to the refugees of this war." Similarly, Spiegel Online (2007) depicted Sweden as a land of milk and honey for Iraqi refugees: "Life is so good in Sweden that families are encouraging their relatives and friends to follow their example and move there." Scores of other reports from, among others, ABC News (2007), *The New York Times* (2007) and *The Washington Post* (2007) all commended Sweden for its generosity towards fleeing Iraqis.

Needless to say, the global media's rosy depiction of Sweden belied a long list of wrongs committed by the Swedish state against individual asylum seekers. Nevertheless, when speaking of asylum policy in the EU – then as now – it must be kept in mind that adjectives such as "welcoming" and "generous" long ago lost their applicability as descriptors. When taking this into consideration, the media's depiction of Sweden's handling of the Iraqi refugee crisis in 2006 and 2007 had some validity. During this period some 30,000 Iraqi refugees came to Sweden; Sweden took 60 per cent of all Iraqi asylum seekers who arrived in the EU during this period. In 2006 over 80 per cent of those Iraqis whose asylum applications had been processed were granted permanent residence in Sweden, jumping to more than 90 per cent the following year. This can be compared to the situation in Germany, where just over 1 per cent of roughly 2,000 Iraqi asylum seekers had their applications granted in 2006. As the European Council on Refugees and Exiles (ECRE) reported, since 2004 Germany had repealed the refugee status of approximately 18,000 Iraqis, "leaving them no means of supporting themselves". At the time, similar conditions and treatment of Iraqi refugees constituted the norm across the EU (ECRE 2007).

Although the Swedish government steered clear of many of the hostile speech acts directed against asylum seekers by most other EU countries, it still voiced alarm and irritation concerning the alleged "flood" of Iraqi asylum seekers. The minister for migration and asylum policy, Tobias Billström, blamed the large increase in Iraqi asylum seekers on the former Social Democratic government and its enactment of a temporary asylum law, in force from November 2005 to March 2006. The law's introduction was pushed forward by a grand coalition of grass-roots movements, religious communities, labour unions and political parties, with the exception of Billström's own right-wing Moderate Party and, ironically enough, the Social Democrats. According to Billström, the law – which, thanks to the Moderates and Social Democrats joining forces, was a watered-down version of what the coalition had advocated – "gave thousands of Iraqi people, who had previously received negative responses to their asylum application, a second chance. Their applications were heard again and many of them received positive responses" (Middle East Online 2007).

In the government's view, it was precisely such positive responses that Sweden payed dearly for in 2006 and 2007. In other words, they helped spread the word that Sweden was a sanctuary – or, to use Billström's expression, they "created a signal effect" (Middle East Online 2007). This also meant that many more refugees were given permanent residence in Sweden, a development that the government wanted to halt. As put by the migration minister in a speech at a Paris ministerial conference on migration and development in 2008: "We must recognize that the old paradigm of migration for permanent settlement is increasingly giving way to temporary and circular migration" (Billström 2008).

When asked in an interview for Middle East Online in 2007 whether the "signal effect" was causing problems, the minister answered that the government was worried, foreseeing problems in the labour market, in schools and with welfare costs and integration. Given the sombre mood of the minister, the interviewer then asked if this should be taken to mean "that Sweden is slowly turning away from its much-lauded, liberal Swedish immigration policy". The migration minister's answer is very interesting also for our current predicament, and so worth quoting at length:

> We do not have immigration laws that are more liberal than any other European country. However, the effect of our laws was, unfortunately, that people who left Iraq and came to Sweden were given a resident's permit sooner or later. This was an unfortunate signal because it meant that the shared responsibility [...] also means that we have to have the same set of rules and the same kind of practice in applying these rules. And this is something that Sweden works hard for in the EU. I never go to a council of ministers' meeting in Brussels without speaking about the importance of creating this common asylum policy for Europe. (Middle East Online 2007)

Then, as today, it was the EU that was taken to be the solution to Sweden's "refugee problem". "More Europe", in other words, was the recipe for fewer refugees.

To illustrate the EU factor in this a bit further, we should turn to the German refugee situation in the early 1990s, one that shared some important similarities with the Swedish one in 2006/7. Germany then took in the great majority of the refugees coming to western Europe. As put by the interior minister at the time, Wolfgang Schäuble, Germany had become the "reserve asylum country of Europe" (quoted in Joppke 1999: 93). This was largely attributable to its then uniquely liberal asylum policy, laid down in article 16 of the Basic Law (constitution) and instituted as a response to the lessons of Nazism. As put by Neuman (1993: 509–10), article 16 "was adopted in reaction to the fate of those who were unable to find refuge from the Nazi regime". As in Sweden in 2006, German politicians in the early 1990s were not thrilled with the country's "reserve" status, and hence they were annoyed with their fellow EU members for failing to share the "refugee burden". Although EU governments were panicking over the Yugoslavian refugee crisis, Germany felt it had to shoulder a highly disproportionate part of the "refugee burden". Some may recall the dire headlines from 1992: "Yugoslav refugee crisis: Europe's worst since 40's" (*New York Times* 1992); "European divisions persist over Yugoslavia's refugees: Germans criticize other Europeans for not taking in more displaced by war" (*Christian Science Monitor* 1992).

In 1992, and much like Sweden 15 years later, Germany received two-thirds of all the asylum seekers who came to (what would subsequently be) the EU-15, or a total of 440,000 (Eurostat 2007). This was a predicament that came to work in favour of those advocating the abrogation of article 16. After a long and agonizing domestic debate over refugees from the Yugoslavian wars and an upsurge in neo-Nazi violence against asylum seekers, Helmut Kohl's government finally managed to strike a deal with the Social Democrats that resulted in an amendment of article 16 that enabled Germany's asylum policy to be tightened up. Germany then gained full access to the restrictive instruments provided by the Schengen Agreement and the Dublin Convention (Joppke 1999: 93), something that it had been "constitutionally disabled" from doing prior to the amendment of article 16 (Neuman 1993: 509).

In consequence, this also meant that Germany fell into line with regular EU asylum policy and was no longer "burdened" with limitations imposed by its Nazi past. Even though the debate triggered by German reunification in the early 1990s pointed to the importance of establishing a normalized "European Germany" rather than a portentous "German Europe", few heeded the fact that Germany's compliance with the European norm on asylum policy was tantamount to a violation of the memory of the stateless in Europe's refugee catastrophe of the 1930s and 1940s. If governments in the EU had wanted to honour this memory, one option would have been to call for the opposite: the "Germanization", paradoxically, of EU asylum policy rather than the Europeanization of German asylum policy.

But Germany was not alone in deciding to leave behind the lessons of the past. Indeed, it was actually one of the last to do so; other EU governments had already produced asylum policies and rhetoric that did not betray the slightest remorse over their own behaviour during the refugee crisis of the 1930s. Germany thus decided to turn its back on history in order to emerge as a fully fledged member of the new Europe. Interior minister Schäuble's explanation of this decision to join Europe reads like a lesson in the art of realpolitik: "If we change our constitution," he stated, "*we*, and not the others, would profit from our geographical location. Then our European neighbours, and not only we, would quickly want to find a joint solution" (quoted in Joppke 1999: 93, emphasis in original). As legal scholar Kay Hailbronner (1994: 179) wrote at the time, in his defence of the amendment of article 16: "The change has been highly successful, stemming the burgeoning immigration into Germany." Making sure to avoid any mention of asylum seekers or refugees, he added crucially that, in order "[t]o guarantee a continuing control of immigration, the nations of Europe should provide for a harmonized asylum system"; hence his call for "a more effective border control" and "rules on European burden sharing" (1994: 177).

## Then as now: borders, burdens and external solutions

Indeed, what topped the EU agenda 25 years ago continues to do so today: the need to seal borders, avoid refugee burdens and establish refugee preventive cooperation with third countries. And, if there has always been consensus and action on border reinforcements and third-country cooperation – one of the prime results being their effectiveness in increasing the death toll in the Mediterranean – the sharing of the "refugee burden" remains stuck in political deadlock. As should be clear by now, this is fundamentally related to the fact that refugees are perceived as a "burden" in the first place: a fiscal burden, or an ethno-cultural burden, or both. If refugees and other categories of migrants seen as too fiscally burdensome or too ethno-culturally different are defined as burdens, it seems obvious that no EU member state should feel the urge to assume this burden.

Above Hailbronner spoke about the early 1990s change in German asylum policy as having "been highly successful" precisely because it was "stemming the burgeoning immigration into Germany". Such a definition of what makes up a successful asylum policy tallies exactly with the one currently subscribed to by policy-makers at both EU and national levels. This is why the arrival of substantial numbers of refugees in the EU immediately gets articulated in crisis terms.

But there have also been moments of lull, even moments when politicians have pointed at asylum policy success. The years following the wars in the former Yugoslavia and the Bosnian refugee emergency saw a sharp drop in asylum seekers in the EU-15. From then on Brussels and member states stepped up their efforts at preventing asylum seekers from entering the European Union. Around the turn of the millennium, however, the number of asylum seekers increased again. This is the time period during which refugee boats and deaths in the Mediterranean emerged as regular features in the news reporting. More importantly, the refugee plight in the Mediterranean now also emerged as a EU policy problem and, at times, emergency, climbing to the top of the EU agenda. Then, as now, there was only one set of measures and solutions on the table; that is, border security to "fight illegal immigration", the targeting of smugglers and the implementation of external solutions, such as the striking of trade- and aid-leveraged migration deals with the regimes in sender countries. To these we should also add policy to facilitate and increase the return of declined asylum seekers and "illegal migrants".

From 2002 onwards, however, the arrival of asylum seekers dropped again and stayed at historical lows until about 2013, when the war in Syria escalated and Syrian refugees started to arrive in the EU. This decline occurred in parallel with the EU's enlargement from 15 to 27 member states; more members did not impact positively on the EU's refugee reception. As already noted, there were exceptions to this picture, such as Sweden, where the refugee population grew. Yet, in 2006 – at the height of the Iraqi refugee crisis – the EU recorded the lowest number of asylum applications in 20 years (Eurostat 2007). The years from 2002 to 2006 saw a 50 per cent drop (Eurostat 2007: 1). In 2007, moreover, Germany, the former "reserve asylum country of Europe", processed the lowest number of asylum requests in 30 years. Likewise, the United Kingdom had a record-breaking fall in asylum seekers in 2004, prompting the Labour home secretary, David Blunkett, to issue the following, apparently exuberant, statement: "These figures show the very significant progress that has been made in dramatically reducing the number of asylum seekers entering the UK last year as a result of the tough reforms we have put in place." Blunkett was also very pleased to announce that asylum "costs" were coming down: "The progress we are making will soon begin to bring down the costs of asylum support" (*The Independent* 2004).

The logic and trend of refugee prevention that has characterized the past decades help us understand why the European Union always comes across as so utterly unprepared whenever refugee crises hit – or, better, why it is that refugee arrivals, even in low numbers, are framed in crisis terms. The wrangling between EU governments over Iraqi refugees in the mid-noughties could be intense, yet the numbers were minuscule. And just recall the virtual panic that broke out in the EU during the winter of 1998 – triggering a succession of crisis meetings in Brussels and elsewhere – following the disembarkation of just over 1,200 Kurdish refugees onto Italian shores. The German interior minister at the time, Manfred Kanther, declared: "In view of this threatening situation, western Europe must view itself as a security community." Kanther also referred to the Kurdish refugees as representing a "criminal wave of migration" (quoted in *International Herald Tribune* 1998a, 1998b).

Even in 2015/16 the crisis was *not* driven by numbers alone, as most politicians and media outlets made it appear. First and foremost, it was politically driven, unless we think it outlandish to suggest that 28 member states with a combined population of some 500 million should have been capable of handling the roughly 2 million refugees that arrived in the course of 2015 and 2016. Politically speaking, of course, it was an outlandish thought. This does not detract from the fact, however, that several EU countries lacked the financial, material and administrative capacity to admit and shelter large numbers of refugees. But, again, this problem is directly linked to the long-standing *political* consensus around refugee prevention as the primary objective and driver of EU asylum policy. The Common European Asylum System (CEAS), which was launched as part of the Amsterdam Treaty and Tampere Programme in the late 1990s, was never geared towards creating a robust asylum system inside the EU and within each and every member state. To be sure, directives on so-called minimum standards in a number of areas have been adopted,[5] but these never addressed the core issue of how capacity for reception could be built in every member state so as to have the EU help alleviate the global refugee predicament. By building such a capacity within the EU, the toxic political crises of refugee arrivals could have been avoided. But the creation and deployment of such an internal capacity would also have required a significant increase in government spending and hence a reform of the EU's sound financial policy framework.

Although Brussels and the member states have always pointed to the "external solution" as the only road worth pursuing, let me just give one poignant example of how this has been expressed along the way. In 2003, and as part of the work in developing the Common European Asylum System, the Commission (2003) launched a "new approach" to asylum policy. At the same time as pledging to continue the work on harmonizing the "in-country [asylum] process in the EU" – i.e. the work on minimum standards, which did not involve raising the internal reception capacity – the new approach was to "move beyond the realm of such processes" and focus even more forcefully on "the phenomenon of mixed flows and the external dimension of these flows". The Commission also stated that this new focus was not going to render in-country harmonization

---

5. For example, minimum standards on "temporary protection" (Council EU 2001); the "reception of asylum seekers" (Council EU 2003); "the qualification and status of third country nationals or stateless persons as refugees" (Council EU 2004); and "minimum standards on procedures for granting or withdrawing refugee status" (Council EU 2005).

"obsolete", since "spontaneous arrivals" of asylum seekers in the EU would continue to occur. Nevertheless, "the new approach would reinforce the credibility, integrity and efficiency of the standards underpinning the systems for spontaneous arrivals, by offering a number of well-defined alternatives" (EC 2003: 3). Such "well-defined" alternatives were all pointing in the direction of externalization – the project of having third countries, such as in the current cases of Turkey or Libya, strike cooperation agreements with the EU on control, prevention and return.

In understanding this, it becomes clear why it is mistaken to claim that the CEAS was not prepared for the refugee arrivals in 2015/16. It was never intended to be prepared for an influx of refugees in the first place. The failure, as Brussels and member states have never stopped repeating, consisted, rather, in not having prepared the barriers against refugees in the eastern Mediterranean well enough. It was a failure of prevention, not of reception capacity. The CEAS was thus never really designed to provide for its eponymous policy, namely asylum in the EU.

## "DROP OF 98%"

Let me illustrate this a bit further by turning to post-2015 developments. The following quote is a good place to start.

> Many people in need of international protection are coming to the EU to seek asylum. Protection is given to people fleeing their home countries who cannot return due to a well-founded fear of persecution or risk of suffering serious harm. The EU has a *legal and moral obligation* to protect those in need. EU Member States are responsible for examining asylum applications and for deciding who will receive protection.                              (EC 2017c: 2, emphasis added)

This quote is from a European Commission factsheet, entitled "The EU and the migration crisis", published in July 2017. It forms part of the wider information series entitled "The EU and", and it aims to explain the so-called migration crisis to the general public as well as to outline the EU's various responses to it.

The Commission's factsheet is very indicative for at least two reasons. First, it captures in a nutshell the contradiction that has been plaguing EU asylum policy cooperation, harmonization and supranationalization over the past 35 years: the contradiction between a rhetoric saluting human rights and refugee protection, on the one side, and a practice working towards entirely opposite ends, on the other. Reading past the initial nod to human rights and the EU's "legal and moral obligations to protect", we thus discover that the factsheet soon turns to a diametrically different set of objectives, policies and achievements. Under the headings "Reducing flows" and "Protecting our borders", the Commission changes track and turns its attention from protection to prevention. Much space is devoted to the EU–Turkey Statement and what is presented as its accomplishments, most importantly the fact that "[t]he numbers of refugees and migrants coming from Turkey have been significantly reduced as a result" (EC 2017c: 3). The reduction of refugee arrivals into the EU is presented as a major achievement: "From a high of 10,000 in a single day in October 2015," the Commission boasts, "arrivals to Greece have averaged less than 74 a day since March 2016." In what seems to be an attempt to make absolutely sure that no EU citizen fails to take note of the achievement, the bar chart illustrating this steep decline has been adorned with an enlarged, capitalized caption, which (as in triumph) reads: "DROP OF 98%."

Just as EU governments celebrated significant drops in asylum seekers some 15 years ago, so Brussels takes this opportunity to do the same. In the factsheet, Brussels can also take credit for having "increased the return of irregular migrants" and for having adopted measures "to ensure that Europe can protect its common external borders and face the new migration and security challenges together" (EC 2017c: 3). We should note too that this factsheet is an updated version; the first edition was published in July 2016, but under the slightly yet significantly and, most of all, tellingly different title: "The EU and the *Refugee* Crisis" (EC 2016c, emphasis added).

At the same time as Brussels affirms the "legal and moral obligation to protect those in need" it pats itself on the back for having drastically reduced refugee reception from Turkey, or the "flows" of "irregular migration", which is the altered designation of Syrian refugees. This highly contradictory picture owes very little to changes taking place outside the EU; rather, it has everything to do with an intra-EU dynamic. As everybody knows, while the EU is working around the clock to scale back its commitment to host and protect refugees, the global refugee crisis shows no signs of abatement. Yet many poor and resource-depleted countries continue to open their borders to refugees. In less than six months in 2017, for instance, Bangladesh received some 655,000 Rohingya refugees from Myanmar. In the same year Sweden admitted an exceptionally low number of asylum seekers, counting only 25,000 and mainly coming from Syria, Iraq, Eritrea and Afghanistan. Fredrik Bengtsson, communications director at the Swedish Migration Agency, commented on the decline: "This is of course resulting from the political decisions that have been made, both at national and EU levels. The situation for refugees in the world has not improved. Millions of people are still fleeing.

What has changed are the possibilities to come to Sweden and Europe" (Swedish Radio 2018).

To the satisfaction of Brussels and governments, then, the number of asylum seekers coming to the European Union has declined sharply since 2015/16. Compared to 2016, 2017 saw a decrease in asylum seekers of 560,000. In its "Progress report on the implementation of the European Agenda on Migration" from October 2019, the Commission (2019b) hails the sharp drop in asylum seekers reaching the EU. Reporting "the lowest figure in five years", refugee numbers top the list in terms of "Key progress" indicators (2019b: 1). The report refrains from any explicit mention of asylum seekers and refugees in this context, however; rather than asylum seeking, it instead refers to "irregular border crossings". As "Key" to this progress, the Commission (2019b: 1) cites "innovative approaches to partnership with third countries, such as the EU–Turkey Statement of March 2016".

In the report, the Commission also hails "EU action" for saving lives in the Mediterranean, but fails to mention that such action was suspended earlier in the year, after already having been scaled back since the termination, in 2014, of Italy's EU-supported rescue programme, Operation Mare Nostrum. This has been repeatedly slammed by numerous human rights organizations, including a European Parliament (2019a) "resolution on search and rescue in the Mediterranean", which was released in late October 2019. The resolution highlights the fact that migration from Libya to the EU still constitutes "the migration route with the highest death toll in the world (646 deaths in the first nine months of 2019) and was five times deadlier in 2018 than in 2015. This was due to a reduction in search and rescue activities off the Libyan coast." Amnesty International's migration researcher, Matteo de Bellis, goes further: "Having already used every excuse in the book to banish NGO rescue boats from the Mediterranean, and having already stopped carrying out rescues several months ago, EU governments are now removing their own ships, leaving no one to save the lives of women, men and children in peril" (quoted in Hall 2019).

The International Organization for Migration (IOM) has announced that a reported 3,116 refugees and migrants died in 2017 in their attempts to reach the EU by sea. This was down from a reported 5,143 deaths in 2016. But, since the total arrivals by sea was lower in 2017, dropping from 363,504 in 2016 to 171,635, the ratio of deaths actually turned out to be higher in 2017 (IOM 2018). According to the IOM, 2018 saw 2,299 deaths in the Mediterranean, with 1,041 deaths reported for the first nine months of 2019. Starting in 2014, this brings the total known death toll to some 19,000 people (IOM 2019).

## Less migration, more migration

If "Fortress Europe", or the objective of minimizing "inflows", has its merits when it comes to asylum policy, we know from the preceding chapters that this metaphor fits poorly with EU labour migration objectives. This brings us to the puzzle that I spelled out on the first pages of this book: the seemingly contradictory goals of *less migration* as a resolution to the refugee crisis versus *more migration* as a resolution to the demographic crisis. If the Commission mourns the political impossibility of launching large-scale labour migration to the European Union, we must ask: why did it not celebrate the large-scale refugee migration of 2015/16 as a compensatory gift from heaven? In other words, what is preventing the Commission from making up on the swings what it loses on the roundabouts? If the objective is to increase the working-age population, then refugees should come in very handy given that the overwhelming majority are young and of working age. Certainly, the number of refugees is nowhere near what is needed to satisfy the Commission's labour migration demand projections. Even so, should the refugees not be greeted as a promising first step in the right direction?

Given what we know from the previous chapters, it is not difficult to formulate a solution to the puzzle, at least on a *principal level*. That is to say, the labour migration model, or regime, that Brussels and many member states have adopted (or want to adopt) is simply incompatible with the institution of asylum. As detailed in Chapters 4 and 5, the EU's labour migration policy is extremely austere and does its utmost to hedge against labour migrants becoming fiscal burdens on the host state. This means that welfare entitlements and permanent residence are persistently avoided. As was also demonstrated earlier, the precautionary approach towards welfare provisions and permanent residence comes close to an obsession, and, as such, it does not stop short of the obvious category of low-skilled labour migrants but also makes its mark, albeit to a lesser extent, on policy for the highly skilled. Within this sound-finance-impregnated framework, asylum seekers and refugees obviously make for an extremely poor fit. Besides all the initial reception and integration costs, potential expenditures for children and the hosting and return costs for failed asylum seekers, it can take a long time before refugees enter the labour market and start paying taxes. Until then they are dependent on (allegedly) burdensome welfare "handouts". Refugee protection and the asylum system also have a penchant for long-term stay. Although temporary protection has become the norm in most places, once people are incorporated into the asylum system they tend to become less deportable as compared to temporary labour migrants. In addition, the asylum process is seen as slow and administratively costly as a result of a burdensome legal apparatus.

In its 2016 "Proposal for a regulation on standards for the qualification of third-country nationals or stateless persons as beneficiaries of international protection",[6] the Commission does not mention permanent residence as an option under "Rights and obligations related to residence and stay". Instead, it stipulates:

> (a) For beneficiaries of refugee status, the residence permit shall have a period of validity of three years and be renewable thereafter for periods of three years. (b) For beneficiaries of subsidiary protection status, the residence permit shall have a period of validity of one year and be renewable thereafter for periods of two years.
>
> (EC 2016d: 45–6)

In the proposal, which forms part of the push to reform CEAS, the Commission (EC 2016d: 4, emphasis added) also cautions that "[t]he absence of checks on the continued need for protection *gives the protection a de facto permanent nature*, thereby creating an additional incentive for those in need of international protection to come to the EU rather than to seek refuge in other places, including in countries closer to their countries-of-origin".

The prospect of permanent residence and, with it, access to welfare provisions are thus deemed pull factors and incentives that need to be short-circuited. For the past couple of decades practically all EU member states have been pursuing this objective; and since 2015 they have stepped up their efforts further. These efforts do not aim simply to make it more difficult for asylum seekers to enter; by reducing asylum seekers' access to welfare and sustainable living conditions, they also aim to make the internal situation act as a deterrent to asylum seeking (see, e.g., Mayblin 2020). In January 2018 the Danish liberal-conservative government issued a statement congratulating itself for succeeding in reducing the number of asylum seekers to its lowest level in nine years. The integration minister, Inger Støjberg, who gained international notoriety for introducing what became Denmark's so-called jewellery law in 2016, was elated: "I have no doubt that our restrictive migration policy has become known far beyond our borders, and that's exactly the effect I sought." She went on to add: "I have never second-guessed my certainty that refugees make their choices based on the types of welfare benefits they receive in the

---

6. Amending Council Directive 2003/109/EC.

different European countries, and now the Danish government has terminated its handout policy" (*Berlingske* 2018).

In all, this should provide enough clarity as to why Brussels and the member states, *as a matter of principle*, do not greet refugees as a much-needed demographic labour boost. Refugees depend on access to social welfare, their labour market participation is delayed and their stay often ends up being permanent. This set of circumstances is in conflict with the criteria set for how low-skilled labour migration should be managed. The migrants falling into this austere category are admitted for immediate work, they have little access to social welfare and their prospects for permanent stay, and hence substantial rights and paths to citizenship, are insignificant. Although much work is now being devoted to weaken the asylum institution, as seen above, asylum law and policy are still largely incompatible with Brussels' favoured labour migration regime. The same applies to the relationship between the model circular labour migrant and the asylum seeker.

## Demographic deficit, demographic dividend

This covers both the principal and most of the practical approaches at the EU level. But I have already indicated that there were things happening in 2015 that markedly diverged from this. Previously, home affairs commissioner Malmström had been very pessimistic towards the prospects of getting the member states to understand the necessity of a massive increase of labour migration to the EU. She went as far as saying that such an undertaking was "politically impossible to attain in today's Europe". Yet, in 2015, just such a window of opportunity seemed to have opened, with the two main receivers of asylum seekers, Germany and Sweden, invoking what we may term a "refugee dividend" to defend and explain why their large intake was not only justifiable from a humanitarian standpoint but also demographically and economically rational. The dismal demographic outlook, they claimed, simply spoke for itself. It was done, as one leader in *The Economist* (2015) put it at the time, "not just for moral reasons but for selfish ones, too", adding: "Europe's labour force is ageing and will soon begin to shrink. [...] Immigrants, including asylum-seekers, are typically young and eager to work. So they can help ease this problem: caring for the elderly ... Africans and Arabs are young. Europe can borrow some of their vitality."

Hence, my question above about Brussels' unresponsive approach towards a refugee dividend is not a contrived one but a claim that figured prominently in Germany, Sweden and elsewhere during the early stages of the crisis. As Germany's interior minister, Thomas de Maizière, stated when defending the refugee admission in early September 2015: "We are a country of immigration. We need people. We need young people. We need immigrants." He added: "All of you know that, because we have too few children" (quoted in *The Independent* 2015). "A country with a decreasing population is a stagnating country," said Sweden's minister of justice and migration, Morgan Johansson, when endorsing Sweden's large reception of asylum seeking unaccompanied minors in August 2015: "In about 20 to 30 years the share of the elderly will grow more and more while the share of the working age will decline. Those young people arriving now will soon be of working age. That's why we should not look at this only as a cost but instead see it as an investment for our country." The minister, who today claims Sweden cannot afford refugees because of its fiscally corrosive impact, also underlined this by going on to say that, "when we discuss increasing costs, we need to remember that we need labour and will need more in the long term. It is important to be clear about that." For Johansson, the large spending increase on the unaccompanied minors was thus a smart investment: "If we play our cards right, this will be something that strengthens Sweden" (Swedish Radio 2015a).

Commenting on Sweden's high number of asylum admissions, the Swedish prime minister, Stefan Löfven, put it similarly at an EU meeting in Brussels in June 2015. Despite the fact that the undertaking was not frictionless, the prime minister urged his colleagues to perceive of the refugees as "an asset": "We must recognise that if we do not do this now, we are going to have a gigantic problem in a few years" (*The Guardian* 2015b). Finally, even the finance minister, Magdalena Andersson, admitted in the parliamentary budget debate in September 2015 that, although the refugee reception would "put a strain on our society", "we should remember one thing: even though no country in Europe is doing this [admitting refugees] for their own private gain, the arrival of working age families is not to the disadvantage for an ageing Europe" (Andersson 2015a: 4).

In the business press and parts of the corporate world, meanwhile, something of a buzz was created around the refugee dividend and the seeming ease with which it could be realized. Daimler CEO Dieter Zetsche spoke of young and skilled refugees as "just the sort of people we're looking for" (*Financial Times* 2015); or, as one columnist in the *Los Angeles Times* (2015) phrased it: "[H]elping to alleviate Europe's refugee crisis could help defuse Germany's demographic one." A triple win was in clear sight: labour for business, demographic relief for states and protection for refugees. Researchers chimed in too, some claiming that the business community was leading the way in showing governments the upside posed by refugee migration, hailing humanitarian efforts extended by corporate giants such as Google, Norwegian, Federal Express, Facebook, American Express and JP Morgan Chase. Such charitable contributions walked hand in hand with "a business opportunity, as new arrivals offer their talents and knowledge to forward-thinking firms". In this way, Khalid Koser (2015) and others argued, corporations were doing what "politicians in fear of (or in thrall to) xenophobic currents have struggled to accomplish", namely to "make the case for the bright side of the refugee influx: it can help close Europe's demographic deficit, plug gaps in the labour market, and supply a cohort of young workers and taxpayers for the future".

## From demographic assets to fiscal burdens

What is overlooked here, however, is that this was precisely the message that the *governments* of Germany and Sweden kept repeating ... until they stopped repeating it. In September 2015 the sentiment was that "Germany's generosity towards the refugees shows no sign of abating" (Godin 2015). By December this had changed, with Angela Merkel imparting the view that "we took on board the concerns of the people, who are worried about the future, and this means we want to reduce, we want to drastically decrease the number of people coming to us" (Reuters 2015b). A couple of months later Germany's deputy finance minister, Jens Spahn (2016), had this to say: "If we do not manage to reduce the numbers coming in significantly, and soon, the refugee crisis has the potential to tear German society apart, politically and culturally." Similar statements were made by the Swedish government. This U-turn emphasizes just how radical the initial governmental responses in Germany and Sweden were. They stood in glaring contrast to the rhetoric of fear and rejection – or the plain indifference – exhibited by most other EU members.

As already noted, Brussels was not swayed by Germany and Sweden's invocation of a refugee dividend. But how do we account for these two countries' abrupt volte-face? Why did they stop invoking the refugee dividend; why did that which seemed possible in September metamorphose into an impossibility in December? To begin with, the sudden policy shift in Germany and Sweden is not satisfactorily explained with reference to a simple caving in to racial austerity *à la* Denmark, Poland or Hungary. Neither Germany nor Sweden went this far. This does not preclude a *political* explanation for the sudden shift, however – because Berlin and Stockholm's rapid change of approach could very well be interpreted as a reaction out of "fear of [...] xenophobic currents", as Koser put it (2015). In other words, in seeking to fend off the challenge from the extreme right, they were adapting to its policies, and, to some extent, to its rhetoric, as seen for instance in Jens Spahn's statement above.

Even so, this goes only so far in terms of understanding the abrupt shift from a policy of welcome to one of rejection. If we accept the major explanation to lie in the political fear of the extreme right, Berlin and Stockholm were using the extreme right's overtly racist or anti-Muslim card very sparingly. Instead, their preferred vocabulary centred on economic, fiscal and welfare matters. So, even if we were to accept the political explanation, we are still left with the crucial fact that this political causality for the most part was framed as an economic causality. The admission of refugees had to be curbed not because they were deemed racial or cultural threats but primarily because they jeopardized fiscal stability and welfare sustainability. We could take this one step further, and say that *economic* causality may be the wrong word and that *objective* causality may be the most accurate term. The claim that the admission of large numbers of refugees is fiscally costly is, after all, accepted by all, whether a Harvard economist, mainstream media or politicians from the left to the extreme right. The argument is, rather, whether, or the extent to which, it can be afforded or not.

In adopting this perspective, we do not have to decide whether the shift from welcome to rejection was instigated primarily by political *or* economic concerns. What has already been decided for us, however, is the fact that the Swedish and German governments made very frequent use of sound finance reasoning when arguing and explaining why refugee admission had become unsustainable and thus a bad idea. Indeed, affordability, fiscal costs and welfare trade-offs became their preferred arguments. There have been counterclaims, to be sure, but none of these has fundamentally questioned the seeming neutrality and factuality of the cost perception per se. The next chapter probes further into this matter, focusing on sound finance reasoning as well as the fiscal and real impact of Sweden's large refugee reception in 2015.

## Conclusion

In Chapter 1 I drew attention to European Commission president Ursula von der Leyen's open praising, in February 2020, of the Greek border guards for their service as "our European shield". As the international press reported, what the Greek guards were shielding Europe from was refugees, mostly Syrian, who wanted to seek asylum in Greece and the European Union. The Commission president was openly praising a violent crackdown against unarmed women, men and children in dire need of protection. This should have been the final nail in the coffin for the conviction that "More Europe" in asylum policy somehow proffers a progressive and humanitarian counter to the excluding, parsimonious and often xenophobic member nation states.

But, as I have shown here, this conviction should have been tested much earlier. As noted above, the Amsterdam Treaty (ratified in 1999) and the EU's Tampere Programme (agreed in 1999) paved the way for more supranational EU influence over asylum policy. As a consequence, these landmark agreements were received fairly positively by many of those who had earlier been worried by the detrimental consequences of the EU's intergovernmental asylum policy cooperation. Many suggested that the introduction of supranationalism would beget a less restrictive and more human-rights-based approach to asylum in the Union. Trimming the national influence on what was always a delicate issue for the nation state, it was argued, held out the possibility of subduing the inherent nationalist and xenophobic impulse. On this view, which was put forward by many prominent scholars and NGOs working in the field of asylum and migrants' rights, supranationalization could produce a counterweight to the kind of national and intergovernmental decision-making that was built around the lowest common denominators of each member state. For example, the European Council on Refugees and Exiles, one of the principal migra-tion NGOs, saw the supranationalization of migration and asylum policy "as a favourable development, as more progressive, and as a positive restraining force on member state actions that have tenuous regard for international legal standards" (Geddes 2000: 640). In contrast to many scholars, however, ECRE's optimism soon gave way to resentful pessimism. In its 2004 evaluation of the development of migration policy after the Amsterdam Treaty and the Tampere Programme, it did not mince its words:

> The promise of protection delivered by the EU Heads of State at the Tampere Summit in 1999 left many of us full of hope that harmoniza-tion would bring better protection for persons fleeing persecution … ECRE's assessment finds that the EU has adopted a package of laws that will not ensure that asylum seekers and refugees will get effective protection across the whole of the newly enlarged European Union.
>
> (ECRE 2004: 3)

As I have stressed in this chapter, and contrary to what many had predicted or hoped, supranationalization, or "More Europe", has so far not reversed the national "race to the bottom" set in train in the 1980s. Nor has the increased mandate of the supranational European Commission shown any sign of pro-ducing a more human-rights-oriented asylum policy.

As a final illustration, let me also give a brief, yet very telling, glimpse of Brussels' push for an increase in returns of failed asylum seekers and irregular migrants. A controversial EU directive on "returning illegally staying third-country nationals" had already been enacted in 2008 but because of Brussels' dissatisfaction with what it considered to be too low return numbers it decided to launch an "EU action plan on return" in the autumn of 2015 (EC 2015b).[7] To increase returns, the plan proposes a whole battery of new measures and ways to strengthen old ones. It speaks in terms of the "returnable", of the EU's surroundings in terms of an "Eastern flank" and a "Southern side", of the enterprise to "muster adequate leverage" vis-à-vis countries in north and sub-Saharan Africa, of "brisk action", "swift legal procedures" and "forced return", and says that "removal should not be undermined by a premature ending of detention" (EC 2015b). The Commission does not hide its frustration with tardy member states, and thus anticipates "*infringement procedures* against Member States that do not fully comply with all its provisions including the obligation to issue and enforce return decisions" (EC 2015b: 4–5, emphasis in original). This also goes for third countries that drag their feet in signing readmission agreements with the EU, these agreements being held up as one of *the* chief instruments in significantly increasing the number of returns.[8] In this context, and "[w]hile the EU's Eastern flank is now well covered through readmission agreements", it is the task of getting north and sub-Saharan African countries to sign that appears in the limelight. Among the priority countries to be added to the list of signatories are Morocco, Egypt, Ethiopia and Afghanistan (EC 2015b: 12), all in line, we must assume, with today's EU standards of human rights, the rule of law, democracy, refugee rights and overall state stability.

As if this was not enough, the action plan also takes us down the whole Freudian slippery slope when it states that the reason for having an asylum system in the first place is to ensure an efficient return policy: "An effective return policy requires the existence of a *functioning asylum system*, to ensure that unfounded asylum claims lead to swift removal of the person from the European territory" (EC 2015b: 5, emphasis in original). Asylum policy has thus been turned on its head, now to primarily serve as a handmaiden to return policy. The plan does not waste any time in promoting this precise transformation, instructing, for instance, that "[a]sylum seekers need to be informed of the possibility of assisted voluntary return early on and at all stages of the asylum procedure, to provide a sound alternative to rejected asylum-seekers and to those who wish to discontinue their claim to return to their countries in

---

7. For a discussion of the "Return Directive" (Council Directive 2008/115/EC of 16 December 2008 on common standards and procedures in member states for returning illegally staying third-country nationals), see, for example, Hansen and Hager (2012: ch. 6). In 2018 the Commission issued a proposal for a recast Return Directive, with the stated purpose "to significantly step up the effective return of irregular migrants" (EC 2018d: 1).

8. As of today, 17 countries have signed readmission agreements with the European Union, including human rights abusers such as Pakistan, Turkey and Sri Lanka.

dignity". Described in this fashion, it should be obvious that we are no longer dealing with an asylum system; what we have, rather, is a return system. The Common European Asylum System is built to prevent and return – but not to admit and protect.

This chapter also tasked itself with resolving the puzzle or seeming contradiction between the EU's simultaneous fixation with the alleged menace of refugee migration and the EU's rapid demographic ageing. After all, refugees are predominantly young and will contribute to alleviating the negative effects of ageing. As shown in Chapters 4 and 5, however, the labour migration regime propagated by Brussels and member states is premised on an austere rights regime, one that harmonizes with the overall sound finance regime that governs fiscal policy in the Union. In this picture, the catalogue of welfare and residence rights inherent to the asylum institute appears as both too fiscally burdensome and as utterly anachronistic. True, the EU wants millions of low-skilled migrants as replacement labour, but it wants this labour in an austere or – to borrow from Karl Polanyi (2001 [1944]) – fictitious commodity form of temporary and circular labour, *not* in the socially embedded form that would apply to refugees on a path to citizenship. The mismatch between the rights conferred to highly skilled labour migrants and refugees is of course less stark, but here also EU policy, as seen, for instance, in the Blue Card case, is extremely reluctant towards automatic residence and welfare provisions. In addition, refugees, even if highly skilled, do not start work immediately and so have little choice but to rely on welfare assistance at first.

The answer to the puzzle thus rests with an austere calculus, ultimately dictated by the EU's sound finance framework, which effectively thwarts the type of expansive public investment and citizenship regime that would be required to allow the EU's demographic deficit to be perceived as congruent with the global refugee surplus. Instead of seizing the moment to try and persuade the member states to perceive of refugee arrivals not as a crisis but, rather, as a demographic gain, the Commission has spent all its energies on devising new measures to make it harder for refugees to enter the EU.

Nonetheless, we must not forget that refugees have come and continue to come to the European Union. It is thus high time to attend to the consequences thereof, to the demographic, fiscal, welfare and real resource impact of refugee migration. In the next chapter, we examine these effects by looking at Sweden – the country that, proportionally speaking, has admitted the most refugees in the EU over the years.

**7**

# "We need these people": refugee spending, fiscal impact and refugees' *real* bearing on Sweden's society and economy

For a few short months in 2015 Germany and Sweden approached their large refugee reception as if this was the right thing to do. In doing so, the two countries broke one of the European Union's core taboos, namely that of saying "Yes" – or, at least, not emphatically "No" – to the admission of refugees. But, in initially agreeing to receive a significant number of refugees, this also meant that Germany and Sweden had to violate another of the Union's principal taboos (at least prior to Covid-19), namely that of agreeing to fiscal expansion. Germany and Sweden's massive spending (starting in 2015) created an MMT, or Keynesian, laboratory environment. The two EU governments that were arguably the most wedded to the doctrine of sound finance thus felt compelled to practise, de facto, *functional finance*: they spent to resolve a real problem instead of creating a problem by trying to guarantee fiscal balance – or, as in the Swedish case, surplus – at the end of the year. Both governments were soon to agonize over this issue vociferously, bracing their citizens for potentially perilous deficits, spending cuts and borrowing. Although both governments would subsequently revert to sound finance, this did not change their functional approach during the period in question.

In discussing these issues further this chapter will mainly focus on the Swedish case, just briefly commenting on Germany. The first part takes a close look at the fiscal impact of Sweden's increased spending on refugee reception and integration in the period from 2015 to 2017. What really happened? Did the spending lead to the allegedly dangerous deficits and borrowing that the government and the economic expertise had predicted? How did the government and economists reason when they made their predictions and forecasts;

and why did they routinely present these as foregone conclusions and not as the predictions and forecasts they were?

The second part of the chapter then goes on to examine further the real resource impact of Sweden's refugee migration, an exploration that I began in Chapter 3. This means that we will look at refugees' demographic and labour market impact. As part of this, the chapter also highlights the significance of refugee migration and refugee spending for the depopulating and revenue-constrained Swedish municipalities that received many of the refugees. In tracing the municipal impact, I will also reveal a growing conflict over public finance between the central government and the municipalities, one that we could conceptualize as a conflict between sound finance (the central government perspective) and functional finance (the municipal perspective).

### Refugee crisis, fiscal crisis?

From the perspectives of Stockholm and Berlin, the large-scale admission of asylum seekers in 2015 would pose a real challenge to their respective fiscal frameworks. Welcoming refugees thus required saying goodbye to austerity, at least for the time being. Accordingly, by the early autumn of 2015 the finance ministries in Germany and Sweden were starting to grumble, and, with news media serving as their amplifiers, the refugee crisis soon became synonymous with a looming fiscal crisis. "Ballooning refugee costs threaten Germany's cherished budget goals," one headline noted. The article went on to inform readers that "[t]he unexpected cost of looking after a record influx of refugees in Germany could scupper Finance Minister Wolfgang Schäuble's cherished goal of achieving a balanced budget for the next five years, coalition sources said on Thursday" (Reuters 2015c). Thus, finance ministries' and their forecasting agencies' warnings went in tandem with images of refugees illustrating ill-boding headlines about "Asylum costs: Germany's budgetary burden". Underneath the latter headline in *Handelsblatt* (2016) the introduction read: "A surging population of refugees in Germany could burst its balanced budget with billions of euros in added outlays." The sense that Germany's fiscal health was hinged on a drastic reduction in refugee numbers was growing, with Schäuble's deputy, Jens Spahn, saying that "[m]oney for other things that we might want is simply not there" (*Irish Times* 2016).

This message of spending being reserved for unwanted refugees whose numbers had to be cut to salvage the German budget antagonized the Social Democratic Party (SPD), the junior coalition partner, at least for a little while. In February 2016 the SPD countered by proposing a "new solidarity project" that would allow for a general increase of social welfare spending. Sigmar Gabriel, the SPD leader and vice-chancellor at the time, warned that singling out refugees as the only spending item ran the risk of being divisive. By putting budgetary surplus before social cohesion, Gabriel claimed that Merkel's Christian Democratic Union (CDU), the major element in the coalition government, was becoming complicit in right-wing radicalization. Whereas Merkel's response reiterated the importance of sticking with a balanced budget, Schäuble was implacable, denouncing Gabriel's intervention as "pitiful" (*Die Zeit* 2016b).

The Swedish finance minister in the government led by the Social Democrats, Magdalena Andersson, adopted a similar outlook to Merkel and Schäuble. In the autumn of 2015 she reaffirmed the government's long-term commitment to a budget surplus and a budget ceiling while at the same time underlining that "the margins under the ceiling are way too thin" and that "[t]his [was] due to Sweden having admitted an exceptionally large number of asylum seekers" (Andersson 2015b). According to Andersson, the refugee reception was "financially unsustainable". "We will both have to reduce spending and borrow", she asserted in an interview in October 2015. "It's about cutting migration costs as well as looking into spending cuts in other areas. But we will also have to borrow money." The interview's introduction read as follows: "The big rise in costs for migration forces the government to make big spending cuts and a drastic increase in borrowing". The next sentence quotes the finance minister as saying: "This is not sustainable" (*Dagens industri* 2015). In November one headline in a major daily paper read: "The deficit is growing: government's expenditures sharply increase due to the growing number of refugees" (*Svenska Dagbladet* 2015a). Subsequently, Andersson explained Sweden's decision to curb refugee reception by saying that it had been necessary financially, and she also confirmed that a tight fiscal policy would be necessary to preserve the budget ceiling. As the government also announced, although the refugee spending would cause a deficit in 2015, the goal for the future was to have the budget return "to balance and surplus" (*Dagens industri* 2015).

## The fiscal impact of Sweden's refugee reception: the view from the government and the economic expertise

As asylum numbers in Sweden reached new highs in the autumn of 2015, it was not only the Finance Ministry that lost sleep; the government's research and forecasting agencies also issued recurrent salvos of warnings about the negative fiscal impact of the rising refugee spending. In its November

2015 report, the Swedish National Financial Management Authority (Ekonomistyrningsverket: ESV)[1] cautioned that the fiscal position would deteriorate significantly in the coming years, "primarily as an effect of the drastic increase in spending on refugee reception" (ESV 2015: 3). In the report the ESV prognosticated that the consolidated government sector would run fiscal deficits (as a percentage of GDP) for the next five years: 2015 (−1.0 per cent), 2016 (−1.3 per cent), 2017 (−1.3 per cent), 2018 (−1.1 per cent) and 2019 (−0.7 per cent) (ESV 2015). It made the same (what it deemed) gloomy forecast for the central government, with the exception for 2019, when a slight rebound into surplus territory was expected (ESV 2015: 36).

In its April 2016 report, the ESV continued to forecast deficits in the consolidated government sector for the period from 2016 to 2018 but thought 2019 could be a surplus year. It continued to cite increased spending on refugee reception as the major reason for the deficits. For the central government, however, the April report forecast surpluses for the entire period (2016 to 2020) (ESV 2016: 1, 2, 37). An increase in tax receipts was said to explain this, but in the same breath the report also maintained that the expenditures were growing rapidly, "mainly due to high migration costs" (ESV 2016: 38). It needs to be pointed out that the spending increases were known to the November 2015 report and that they, at the time, were said to be the main cause for the deficits in the consolidated as well as the central government sectors. The forecast costs for refugees in 2016 were about the same in the November 2015 report as they were five months later in the April 2016 report. Yet, strangely enough, the refugee-*caused* central government deficit for 2016 that the November 2015 report had predicted, or confirmed, was no longer anticipated to occur in the April report. On the contrary, and with everything else equal concerning the projected spending increases, 2016 was now said to be a surplus year for the central government. The April report also presented the final balance for the central government in 2015; the predicted deficit turned out to be much lower (0.3 per cent of GDP) than what had been anticipated in the November report (1.0) (ESV 2016: 39; 2015: 34). The actual result for the consolidated sector in 2015 followed the exact same pattern, the deficit landing at 0.3 per cent of GDP; six months earlier it had been forecast at 1.0 per cent of GDP (ESV 2016: 4; 2015: 4).

Jumping ahead to the ESV's November 2017 report, the ESV has made a 180 degree turn and forecast surpluses for the consolidated sector in all the years from 2017 to 2021. Likewise, it revised the final result for 2015 to record

---

1. ESV is a public agency under the Finance Ministry that is tasked with providing analyses and forecasts of the national finances.

a surplus of 0.2 per cent of GDP! The final result for 2016 was also revised upward, now showing a surplus of 1.2 per cent instead of the deficits of 0.3 and 1.1 per cent that had been projected in the April 2016 report and the November 2015 report respectively (ESV 2017: 3). As for the central government, 2016 was said to have posted the largest surplus in ten years, at 1.6 per cent of GDP (ESV 2017: 47). In the November 2015 report, the ESV (2015: 34) had projected a deficit of 0.6 per cent for the central government.

Forecasting is a tricky business, obviously, and forecasters are often the first ones to point this out. Yet, in the reports cited from 2015 and 2016, there is at least one thing that the forecasters appear to have been certain about, namely the undeniable fact that refugee spending would *cause* deficits for the foreseeable future. To be sure, there was uncertainty around the future number of asylum seekers, but no uncertainty about the damage – as deficits are always perceived to do damage – that had already been done by the large spending increases being made and by those that would have to be made in the near future.

But the ESV was certainly not alone in this conviction. The government and the Ministry of Finance, as already shown, were equally stubborn. In its budget proposal for 2017 (presented in September 2016), the government began by priding itself on having sharply reduced the budget deficit for 2015, a deficit it said it had "inherited" from the former government.[2] It had done so "despite the significant effect that the large number of asylum seekers had had on the public finances" (Swedish government 2016: 23). Nevertheless, the government expected the fiscal position to worsen again in 2016 and 2017. "The deterioration," the government (2016: 531) noted, "could mainly be explained by the expected cost increases for migration following in the wake of the great number of people who sought asylum in Sweden during the latter part of 2015." The government (2016: 175–6) thus stressed that, since "the large number of asylum seekers amounts to a burden on the public finances in the short term, it is reasonable that the return to the surplus target will not take place right away. As a consequence, the government intends to conduct a fiscal policy that can achieve the surplus target in 2020, at the latest."

As an EU member, Sweden abides by the EU's fiscal rules (see Chapter 3), but it also has its own fiscal framework, which was launched in the 1990s. With a current surplus target of 0.33 per cent of GDP for the consolidated government

2. In the budget proposal for 2017, presented in September 2016, the 2015 result had still to be corrected from the previously projected deficit to the surplus it turned out to be. Hence, this explains the budget proposal's conception that the *deficit* would increase in 2016, when, in fact, it was a *surplus* from 2015 that was to turn into a deficit in 2016. But this never happened.

sector over the business cycle, Sweden's "Fiscal Policy Framework" is actually more austere than the EU's. In fact, until 2019 the surplus target was set at 1 per cent, and had been so for two decades. The framework also includes an expenditure ceiling (seen as supporting the surplus target), a debt anchor and a balanced budget requirement for the municipal sector (Swedish government 2018c).

To be sure, government spending on refugee reception and integration grew significantly in 2016 and 2017, the two years for which the government predicted an increase in the deficit. Looking at the budget allocation for "Migration", spending grew from Swedish krona (SEK) 19 billion in 2015 to around 41 billion in 2016 and 40 billion in 2017 (ESV 2019: 75). The same applied to the budget area for migrant integration, which grew by 3 billion or 34 per cent in 2016 (Swedish government 2018a: 62). But there were significant, multi-billion-krona spending increases in addition to this. The large refugee reception prompted the government's amended extra budget in the late autumn of 2015 (as mentioned in Chapter 3), which was to pay out SEK 10 billion (per year) to the municipal sector. The government referred to this as "the largest ever single reinforcement of general government grants to the local government sector" (Ministry of Finance 2016).

In the budget proposal for 2016 (presented in September 2015), the government thus expected the deficit to grow in 2016, mostly as a consequence of increasing migration costs and despite, as it put it, "the upward economic trend" (Swedish government 2015: 425). But that calculation was made with the budget having allocated a mere SEK 19 billion to the migration area for 2016; as just mentioned, the actual allocation to this area *alone* ended up being 41 billion. Had this been known at the time, we must assume that the deficit estimate in the 2016 budget proposal would have been much larger.

Looking at the budget proposal for 2020 (presented in September 2019), it is evident that the government's predictions in the 2017 budget were wildly off the mark. 2016 and 2017 turned out to run up the largest surpluses for the consolidated government sector in many years: 1.0 and 1.4 per cent of GDP respectively. This meant that the surplus target was also met, four years ahead of the schedule set out by the government in its budget proposal for 2017.

The government's own fiscal watchdog was even more wildly off the mark. In its April 2016 report, the Swedish Fiscal Policy Council (SFPC)[3] pointed to "worrying developments in several expenditure areas", relating principally to "the cost of asylum immigration" (SFPC 2016: 12). The SFPC could be in no doubt that the government would run deficits in 2016 and 2017, and it thus acknowledged the government's view that "[t]he increased expenditure caused

---

3. The SFPC's job is to make independent assessments of the government's conduct of fiscal policy; for example, monitoring the surplus target and spending ceiling.

by asylum immigration will weaken the balance and delay the return to surplus" (SFPC 2016: 41). In relation to this, then, the SFPC (2016: 11, 99) criticized the government for missing the target, and even more so for making "no commitments as to when and how the surplus target is to be achieved". "Having a clear direction for the policy," the SFPC (2016: 99) argued, "is if anything more important right now because the high level of refugee immigration may be expected to create continued pressure for increased expenditure in some areas of the public sector." For that reason, the SFPC went on, "the government urgently needs to come back in BP17 [budget proposal for 2017] with a clear and credible plan containing a commitment as to how and when the variance in financial net lending is to be rectified". By the same token, the SFPC was displeased with the government's fiscally expansive policy, not least since the expansion was conducted in an economy that was already picking up speed. Fiscal policy should, instead, "be considerably more restrictive in the years 2016–2018 than the policy that the government is presenting in VP 16 [spring budget proposal for 2016]". The Council thus requested that the government immediately prepare for "active budgetary consolidation measures", or austerity (SFPC 2016: 99–100).

Although the SFPC's stern requests fell on deaf ears in the government, the fiscal results for 2016 and 2017 turned out to be just what the Council had ordered, namely sturdy surpluses and a swift return to its sacrosanct surplus target. But, again, the government did not follow the Council's advice. Hence, from the perspective of the Council, what happened should not have been possible. As I have shown, the government thought so too; it was just that the government found it more acceptable to miss the surplus target and run deficits in 2016 and 2017.

In its 2017 report, the Council no longer assumed that the consolidated government sector would run deficits in 2016 and 2017. With the definitive fiscal result for 2016 not being available when the report was written, however, it seemed as if the SFPC was not wholly convinced. The possible surpluses (if they were to materialize) were still projected to be very small and far below the surplus target. This seriously concerned the Council, and it reproved what it took to be the government's "fiscal policy stimuli", claiming that it "could cause the economy to overheat" (SFPC 2017: 23). The budget was said to include spending increases that were undermining rather than helping the return to the target, a conduct the Council took to be "remarkable". Hence, "the Government's active fiscal policy is not well-considered [sic]" (SFPC 2017: 112). The Council was thus adamant that the government tighten its belt and do everything it could to meet the surplus target. The Council did agree, however, with the government's position, in the 2017 budget proposal, that it was "unreasonable to expect the return to the surplus target to be *immediate*" (SFPC 2017: 121; emphasis in original).

The main obstacle to this was the extra spending allocated to manage the refugee situation. Nevertheless, the government could do so much more, and this was precisely why the Council had "argued in earlier reports for a tighter fiscal policy". "However," the reprimanding went on, "the Government has chosen not to follow our recommendation. It is now clear that the current surplus target will not be met in the current government's term in office, which is partly the consequence of its excessively expansive fiscal policy" (SFPC 2017: 121–2).

For the Council, then, this was not a prognosis but a certainty, and an unavoidable end result. We already know that the Council's confidence was unfounded. Yet again the government had failed to listen to the economists within the Council, and yet again that which the Council had said could not happen ... had happened: both 2016 and 2017 experienced surpluses and the restoration of the surplus target.

The National Institute of Economic Research (NIER) – another, much bigger state forecasting agency – basically took the same position as the other ones, claiming in its report from December 2015 that the rise in migration costs would worsen the government's fiscal position in the years to come, i.e. 2015 to 2018. "Despite a booming economy," the NIER also observed, "public finances will continue to show deficits in the coming years." It was therefore "clear" – and presented as a certainty rather than a prediction – that "the budget surplus target is no longer relevant" (NIER 2015: 9). In relation to this, the report stated that, in order to adhere to the current "public sector commitment", a significant rise in spending would be necessary in the next few years. In order to fund the increase without loans, the NIER (2015: 10) had calculated, "taxes will have to increase by around SEK 160 billion in 2016–2020". The spending increases on migration, the NIER assumed, would be debt-financed (2015: 26). In its subsequent report in 2016, the NIER assumed continuing fiscal deterioration because of migration spending, and, like the SFPC, it thus urged the government to consolidate: "Given the strength of the economy and the need to move back towards the surplus target, it would have been more expedient to tighten fiscal policy in 2017 and so reduce the need for more acute tightening in 2018 and beyond" (NIER 2016: 9).

Finally, the European Commission's forecasting predicted a deficit for Sweden in its June 2015 Country Report (consolidated government sector) of 1.6 per cent of GDP for 2015 and a deficit of 1 per cent for 2016. "Negative risks to the budget", it claimed, "could come from a potentially worse macroeconomic outlook and higher costs for integrating the large inflow of migrants" (EC 2015c: 6). In the report published in February 2016, the Commission continued to forecast deficits for 2016 and 2017, as well as citing "higher spending on refugees" as one of "the main negative risks for the budget" (EC 2016e: 7).

**Table 7.1** Consolidated government sector/general government balance in Sweden, forecasts and actual results (% of GDP), 2015–19

| Forecasting institution | 2015 | 2016 | 2017 | 2018 | 2019 |
|---|---|---|---|---|---|
| **Government** | | | | | |
| Budget proposal 2016; September 2015 | −0.9 | −0.9 | −0.5 | 0.0 | 0.3 |
| Budget proposal 2017; September 2016 | −0.1* | −0.2 | −0.3 | 0.0 | 0.8 |
| **ESV** (Swedish National Financial Management Authority) | | | | | |
| November 2015 | −1.0 | −1.1 | −1.3 | −1.1 | −0.7 |
| April 2016 | −0.3 | −0.3 | −0.7 | −0.3 | 0.2 |
| **NIER** (National Institute of Economic Research) | | | | | |
| December 2015 | −1.1 | −1.1 | −0.9 | −0.3 | 0.0 |
| August 2016 | −0.1 | −0.6 | −0.3 | 0.2 | 0.6 |
| **European Commission** | | | | | |
| June 2015 | −1.6 | −1.0 | | | |
| February 2016 | −1.0 | −1.1 | −1.2 | | |
| February 2017 | 0.2* | 0.5 | −0.2 | 0.2 | |
| **OECD** | | | | | |
| November 2015 | −1.1 | −0.6 | −0.35 | | |
| June 2016 | 0.0 | 0.2 | 0.06 | | |
| November 2016 | 0.2 | 0.2 | −0.06 | | |
| June 2017 | 0.3 | 0.9 | 0.95 | 1.0 | |
| **Riksbank** (central bank) | | | | | |
| September 2015 | −1.4 | −0.8 | −0.4 | | |
| April 2016 | −0.3 | −0.3 | −0.3 | −0.2 | |
| September 2016 | −0.1 | 0.1 | 0.0 | 0.2 | |
| **Actual result** | | | | | |
| ESV November 2019 | 0.0 | 1.0 | 1.4 | 0.8 | |
| Budget proposal 20, September 2019 | 0.0† | 1.0 | 1.4 | 0.9 | |
| European Commission, October 2019 | 0.0 | 1.0 | 1.4 | 0.8 | |

*Notes*: * Stated actual result. † In the budget proposal for 2020 (published in September 2019) the government stated that "[t]he general government sector had reported surpluses 2015–2018". Although this does not register as a percentage of GDP (and hence the "0.0" result for 2015 in the table), it does register as measured in krona, totalling SEK 2 billion (Swedish government 2019: 131, 11).

*Sources*: EC (2015c, 2016e, 2017a, 2019c); ESV (2015, 2016); NIER (2015, 2016); OECD (2015a, 2016a, 2016b, 2017b); Riksbank (2015, 2016a, 2016b); Swedish government (2015, 2016).

## Refugee spending and economic growth

All the forecasts failed to understand the fiscal impact of the refugee spending that got under way in 2015. They simply assumed that the spending would worsen the Swedish fiscal position. The more that was spent, the more severe the deterioration would end up being. Simple sound household logic: the higher the heating bill, the worse for the household budget. Conversely, if the spending were reined in, then the fiscal position would start to return to positive turf. It bears repeating, too, that many of these "predictions" were not expressed as such but, rather, were presented as established facts. That refugee spending would cause deficits and hence necessitate borrowing, tax hikes and budget cuts were thus regularly rendered as foregone conclusions, rather than as the projections they actually were.

It was also presented as a foregone conclusion by politicians, who deployed the forecasts to back up their claims about the unsustainability of the increased refugee spending and to justify turning their backs on asylum seekers. These conclusions were frequently headlines in the news media, further reinforcing the sound finance narrative about refugees' negative impact on the economy and welfare. We have also seen, as during the Swedish election campaign in 2018 (see Chapter 2), that politicians have continued to peddle this narrative, long after the conclusive refutation of their certainties about refugee-induced deficits. News media have followed suit. In Chapter 2, I quoted *The Economist*'s (2018: 26) November 2018 verdict on Sweden that "refugees tend to drain the public purse". But, when *The Economist* published its alarming verdict, Sweden was on course for a fourth consecutive year of fiscal surpluses and, with it, a rapid reduction of its accumulated public debt. Had *The Economist* stuck to its own sound finance principles, it would have noted that Sweden's finances were at their "soundest" in many years precisely at the height of the spending spree spawned by the refugee crisis. In fact, the two years 2016 and 2017, when Sweden spent the most, were also the years that recorded the highest surpluses in almost a decade.

So, what was going on here? We should begin by noting that not all headlines during this period harmonized with the narrative in which refugees spelled a negative fiscal and hence economic impact. "Refugee wave behind Sweden's GDP growth," ran the headline in Sweden's major business daily following the release of the exceptionally strong fourth quarter growth figures for 2015, showing a 4.5 per cent gain compared to 2014, whereas the growth figure for 2015 stood at 4.1 per cent (*Dagens industri* 2016). As reported by the *Financial Times* (2016a), "Economists credited the refugee crisis for helping boost growth as a record number of asylum seekers … led to an increase in consumption and government spending." Furthermore, in the OECD's early 2017 assessment of the Swedish economy, the positive impact of refugee immigration on overall economic growth took centre stage: "Population increases, to a large part related to immigration, have contributed significantly to growth. Even so, the country's GDP per capita has expanded faster than in most OECD countries" (OECD 2017a: 6). A similar dynamic between refugee spending and growth became equally apparent in Germany and, to some extent, in Austria (IMF 2016; *Financial Times* 2016b; Reuters 2016b). And, as was the case in Sweden, the dire predictions in the autumn of 2015 about the refugee reception's negative fiscal impact all came to nought, with Germany recording surpluses from 2015 and onwards (*Financial Times* 2017). Reports also corroborated the positive impact of refugee spending on economic growth in the EU *in general* (see, e.g., IMF 2016).

Noteworthy too is the fact that the Swedish government and its forecasting agencies were quite aware of this development and accounted for it in their reports cited above. Yet the knowledge about refugee spending's positive impact on growth, employment and investment did not make even a small dent in the perception that refugee spending would cause deficits that would have to be recouped through additional taxation, borrowing and austerity. In its March 2016 report, under the telling subheading "Booming economy in Sweden", the NIER noted as follows:

> Both fiscal and monetary policy will stimulate domestic demand in 2016 and 2017. Government consumption is forecast to grow by around 4 per cent this year, which is very high by historical standards. The increase is due largely to higher refugee-related costs. [...] The ever stronger economy means that firms' need to invest will continue to grow. Demographic developments will also exacerbate [*sic*] the existing major need for increased government investment and investment in housing. Investment will therefore continue to fuel growth in Sweden over the next couple of years. In addition, a strong labour market will lead to a relatively rapid rise in household income, with the result that household consumption increases in 2016 and 2017 at around the same rate as in 2015. (NIER 2016: 6–7)

Remarkably, however, this boom description did not at all complicate the NIER's conviction that refugee spending would generate deficits in 2016 and 2017. The SFPC was equally convinced, and this despite the fact that the picture it painted of the Swedish economy in its 2016 report smacked of a surge in tax receipts: "The stimulus to demand coming from the unexpectedly high level of asylum immigration is also expected to lead to higher employment, in both the public and private sectors, and hence also to lower unemployment in the short term" (2016: 24). As seen above, the European Commission also predicted a deficit for 2017, yet gave this upbeat assessment in its February 2017 report:

> The Swedish economy is continuing to perform well. Growth was 3.3% in 2016 – among the highest in the EU. [...] Solid investment growth and increasing household and government consumption are expected to support growth in the coming years. [...] After expanding at a rate of close to 7% per year in 2015-2016, investment is expected to keep increasing at a solid pace of around 3% in the coming years.
>
> (EC 2017a: 1)

Domestic demand was credited as the primary driver of growth, with the increased refugee spending playing a key role (EC 2017a: 1, 4).

Subsequently (and logically), practically all the reports acknowledged that they had underestimated the growth in tax revenue during the years when refugee spending was peaking. "During 2015–2017," the SFPC stated in 2018, "revenue from taxes and fees was significantly higher than estimated in the respective budget bill. By 2015, these revenues were about SEK 50 billion higher than estimated in BP15 [budget proposal 2015], and for 2016 and 2017 the outcome was approximately SEK 80 and 30 billion higher than estimated in the budget bills respectively" (SFPC 2018: 51). In the annual financial reports, similarly, the government reported an increase in tax revenues of SEK 97 billion for the consolidated sector in 2016 (compared to 2015) and SEK 81 billion in 2017 (Swedish government 2017a: 19; 2018a: 17).

And so it continues: report after report accounting for the "unexpected" growth in tax revenue. But should it have been so unexpected? Certainly not for the simple reason that the previous forecasts had reported on economic data and trends, all of which pointed in the direction of higher tax revenue – e.g. significant increases in public consumption, investment, employment and hence overall economic growth. Yet such trends and indications did not even make the government and forecasting agencies so much as toy with the idea that maybe, just maybe, refugee spending would not inflict the serious fiscal "damage" predicted initially.

I should mention, however, that, of the agencies and institutions surveyed here, the OECD stood out as never really worrying much over deficits and the fiscal impact of refugee spending. From the outset, the OECD instead had its focus on the economic growth opportunities created by the increase in government spending on refugee reception. Assessing the "additional fiscal measures" adopted to manage the large refugee reception in 2015, the OECD calculated that they "should provide a modest boost to aggregate demand, provided they are not offset by budgetary cuts elsewhere …. In the European economies as a whole in 2016 and 2017, the boost to aggregate demand could be worth between 0.1 and 0.2% of GDP" (OECD 2015a: 2; 2015b: 18). This was in line with the organization's "rethink", as it put it, of the one-sided priority that, for a long period of time, had been given to fiscal balance over economic growth (OECD 2016b: ch. 2).

As I noted in Chapter 3 – with reference to MMT – the fact that government spending often impacts positively on growth is downplayed within the sound fiscal frameworks that govern EU countries. Although it still adhered to sound finance principles, it was basically this problem that the OECD was addressing, believing that fiscal policy, rather than the exhausted monetary policy instruments, should be given some modest leeway to help aggregate demand. As we have seen here, in the context of the Swedish situation, the OECD's attempted "rethink" obviously fell on deaf ears.

## "We have not borrowed a single krona to finance the refugee crisis"

With the arrival of some 160,000 asylum seekers to Sweden in 2015, the Swedish government decided to temporarily depart from its fiscal framework. The finance minister, Magdalena Andersson, declared that the surplus target would not be met in the coming years because of the increased spending on refugee reception and integration. One interview with the minister summarized her outlook: "Magdalena Andersson's harsh reality message continues. It will take a long time until the budget reaches balance and much longer until the government's finances are in surplus" (*Svenska Dagbladet* 2015b). In the interview (conducted in November 2015), Andersson also noted that "it would be unwise to issue spending cuts to achieve the surplus target of one per cent in this situation" (*Svenska Dagbladet* 2015b). Important too was that the government suspended the "pay as you go" rule (or *krona för krona*), whereby all new spending increases in the budget have to be offset by tax increases or spending cuts. The Fiscal Policy Council referred appreciatively (and accurately) to the rule as "automatic austerity" (SFPC 2015: 49). The stated reason for the suspension was to allow for borrowing in the amended extra budget in November of 2015, which spent SEK 10 billion in the municipal sector, assisting local and regional governments with additional funds to ease the refugee situation.[4] At this point in time the government thus clarified that it was not going to increase taxes or implement any short-term spending cuts to offset the refugee-related spending increases (Andersson 2016: 14).

From the perspective of sound finance, all of this was bad news, of course, and the reports examined above as well as the news media made sure that they got this message across. The irony, however, is that the outcome turned out to be nothing but *good* news for those espousing sound finance. Just as the finance minister had buried any hope of surpluses in the near future and repeated the mantra of the need to borrow to "finance" the refugees, a veritable tidal wave of tax revenue had already started to engulf Sweden. "Borrowing will increase next year owing to the fact that we are getting higher costs for asylum seekers," said the finance minister to *Swedish Radio* (2015b) in December 2015. Borrowing to "finance" the refugees would thus *increase* in 2016, on top of the SEK 10 billion the government claimed it had already borrowed for this purpose in 2015. Yet, when presenting the new budget (for 2018) in September 2017, Andersson bragged about *not* having borrowed: "We have not borrowed a single krona to finance the refugee crisis, but instead we have been able to pay down the public debt during our whole term in office" (*Svenska Dagbladet* 2017a). As one of the main explanations, the finance minister cited the sharp drop in migration spending. In December 2015 Andersson was determined to inform the public that the government was borrowing some SEK 10 billion to finance the refugee spending. A little less than two years later Andersson was equally adamant that the government had borrowed nothing at all. Unfortunately, and symptomatically, there were no journalists available to call the bluff. What the finance minister still has not commented on, however, is the fact that the two years (2016 and 2017) when the refugee spending peaked also happened to be the fattest surplus years, from a sound finance perspective. After that, when refugee spending decreased significantly, the surpluses depreciated.

The finance minister thought it "unwise" to issue the steep cuts she claimed would have been necessary to honour the surplus target in the years following 2015. The Fiscal Policy Council commented on this in its 2016 report, saying that the government thought "a policy aimed at achieving 1 per cent net lending in its

---

4. As put by the Fiscal Policy Council (SFPC 2016: 91): "As a means of handling the urgent refugee situation, the Government decided to grant approx. SEK 10 billion to municipalities and county councils at the end of 2015. When new assessments of the economic situation were presented at the end of 2015, the Government announced that it could no longer insist that all reforms would be fully financed. This was a statement of fact in so far as the extra grant to municipalities and county councils was meant to be loan-financed."

term in office would be too austere and hence not feasible" (SFPC 2016: 90). The Council agreed, but, above, we also saw it express great frustration over what it took to be an "excessively expansive fiscal policy" (SFPC 2017: 121–2). Yet it was precisely this excess, the opposite of austerity, that facilitated what should have been an impossible, and impossibly swift, return to the surplus target.

The ironic lesson to be learned from the Swedish refugee crisis thus goes something like this: if you favour sound finance and high surpluses, please go ahead and welcome 163,000 refugees and then spend massively. The more serious lesson, however, should be the need to draw attention to the futility and erroneous nature of sound finance governance. As seen, all interested parties conceive of the nation's finances as analogous to a household. Hence, the government has to chase a surplus at the end of the year; it needs to approach much spending as wasteful, and also disregard the impact that government spending has on aggregate demand and economic growth.

From 2015 to 2017 Sweden partially put its sound fiscal framework on hold in order to deal with a serious situation that required a drastic increase in spending. The surplus target and the "pay as you go" rule were temporarily suspended. Although all stakeholders argued otherwise, the drastic government increases in spending and public consumption continued to do what they often do: they stimulated aggregate demand, investment and employment. In 2016 alone public consumption increased by 3.6 per cent (EC 2018e), a development not seen since the 1970s (Nilsson & Nyström 2016). The economy grew and tax revenue surged so much that successive surpluses were created, which is something that may happen, albeit not necessarily. But, as MMT explains, this is not important; what is important is *not* the fiscal balance at the end of the year but the overall balance and *real* health of the economy and society. Despite the fact that politicians and experts have squandered years – and still do – on trying to figure out ways to get out of the non-existent and, in any case, non-dangerous fiscal hole allegedly dug by refugee spending, very little thinking has been done with regard to the latter balance. Meanwhile, the wider political, academic and public debate has also continued to deem refugees a cost, even after their own trusted method for judging costs and benefits – i.e. the financial method – has proved them wrong. It is therefore high time to look at some of the *real* effects of Sweden's refugee reception and the spending that went with it.

## Financial and real resources, once more

Chapter 3 has already partially demonstrated and explained the real resource impact that refugee migration has had and will have on Sweden for the foreseeable future. Sweden suffers from record levels of labour shortages in several sectors and geographical regions (Swedish Public Employment Service [SPES] 2018: 30; EC 2019a), and in many of these refugees are instrumental in keeping production afloat both in the public and private sectors. Like all other EU countries, Sweden has a growing elderly population and its social care sector has become utterly dependent on people who have arrived as refugees. According to the Swedish Association of Local Authorities and Regions (Sveriges Kommuner och Regioner: SKR 2018: 6) – an employers' and advocacy organization for Sweden's local governments – the Swedish welfare sector will have to increase its personnel by about 200,000 people by 2026. It also needs to replace some 300,000 staff who will retire during this same period, however, which means that around half a million people need to be recruited in just a few years. Unsurprisingly, it is elderly care that faces the greatest recruitment needs. Since the home-grown labour supply is far from sufficient, SKR thus concludes that the foreign-born, or newly arrived refugees, "must rescue Swedish elderly care" (*Dagens Samhälle* 2019).

As described in Chapter 2, the government does acknowledge that Swedish elderly care is dependent on staff with a refugee background. But such an acknowledgement is reserved for internal reports; it is not something the government likes to emphasize in the public debate (see Chapter 2). Close to 30 per cent nationally, and about 55 per cent in the Stockholm region, of those working in the Swedish elderly care are foreign-born, of whom the overwhelming majority have a refugee background (Socialstyrelsen 2019: 47). A similar situation prevails within a number of other labour market sectors and industries. In 2018 60 per cent of all cleaners in Sweden were foreign-born. The same was the case for 51 per cent of bus and tram drivers; 49 per cent of taxi drivers; 68 per cent of maids, nannies and related personnel; 42 per cent of restaurant and kitchen assistants; 49 per cent of machine operators in laundering; 44 of machine operators in meat and fish processing; 42 per cent of newspaper deliverers; the list goes on (Statistics Sweden 2020, 2019a).[5] These statistics relate only to the lower end of the labour market, where the share of the foreign-born with a refugee background is high. This does not mean that people with a refugee background do not also perform middle- and high-income work. Of course they do. According to the OECD (2017c: 164), most of the foreign-born medical doctors in Sweden (over 30 per cent of the total) come from three countries: Germany, Poland and Iraq. Whereas the Germans and Poles are grouped as labour migrants, practically all Iraqis in Sweden came to Sweden as refugees.

---

5. For an in-depth study of refugee migration's impact on the Swedish labour market, see Scocco (2019).

Thanks to refugee migration, Sweden has experienced a unique demographic development over the past few decades. In 2000 the foreign-born population in Sweden stood at about 1 million people, or 11.3 per cent. At the end of 2018 it counted some 2 million people, or 19.1 per cent (see Figure 7.1). Only Austria can compete with this development in the European Union, but, if we consider the large proportion of refugees and people born outside the EU-28 among the foreign-born in Sweden, there is no counterpart to Sweden in the EU. And here we are talking only about the foreign-born. If we add the people who are born in Sweden to two foreign-born parents, those with a "foreign background" make up a quarter of the population (Statistics Sweden 2019b).

As a consequence, and as seen in the labour market statistics above, the real resource contribution from foreign-born nationals in Sweden has been nothing less than astounding. With fewer Swedish-born workers joining the labour force than leaving it, the entire addition of working-age people in Sweden has, since 2008, consisted of the foreign-born (SPES 2018: 54). Between 2010 and 2017 the number of working-age (16–64) Swedish-born people dropped by over 150,000 while the number of working-age foreign-born grew by some 360,000 people (SPES 2018: 71). In this period Sweden was thus able to increase its working-age population by more than 200,000. This growth will pick up even more until 2025, when the foreign-born share of the working age is set to hit 27 per cent, as compared to 18 per cent in 2010 (SPES 2018: 72). The figures for 2017 illustrate this well: the labour market added 94,000 jobs, of which 75,000, or 80 per cent, went to foreign-born workers

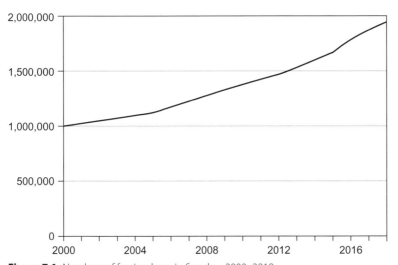

**Figure 7.1** Numbers of foreign-born in Sweden, 2000–2018
*Source*: Statistics Sweden (2019c).

(SPES 2018: 26). According to the Swedish Public Employment Service (SPES 2018), this pattern is likely to continue.

The rate of employment has thus improved for the foreign-born, yet the unemployment gap between the foreign- and Swedish-born is still staggering: around 15 per cent for the former and 4 per cent for the latter (prior to Covid-19). In order for Sweden to plug an already enormous recruitment gap that will continue to grow – not the least in the elderly care, healthcare and education sectors – increasing the employment rate for the foreign-born individuals will be crucial. This becomes all the more imperative given that Sweden has a high employment rate overall; at over 82 per cent for those aged 20 to 64 in 2019, Sweden has the highest employment rate in the European Union (Eurostat 2019d).

But Sweden's high net immigration is not just a benefit in terms of boosting the cohort of working-age people. Reflecting refugee migration's family character and family reunification component, Sweden has also added a large number of children and youth, who soon will further boost the working-age cohort. Because of this, Sweden is the only country in the EU (and beyond) that has not seen an increase in the median age over the last decade (see Figure 7.2).

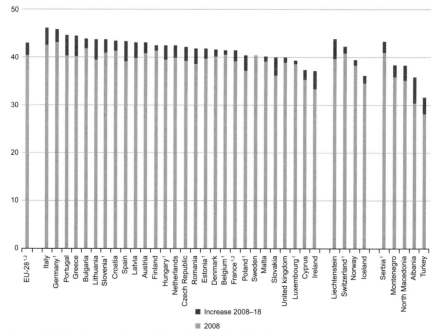

**Figure 7.2** Median age of population, EU-28 (+9), 2008–18
*Notes:* [1] Break in time series in various years between 2008 and 2018. [2] Provisional.
*Source*: Eurostat (https://ec.europa.eu/eurostat/statistics-explained/index.php?title=File:Median_age_of_population,_2008-18_(years)_.png).

Again, the Swedish government and all other interested parties are well aware of this. As noted in Chapter 3, the government acknowledges that the expected growth of 600,000 in the working age population between 2015 and 2035 will result solely from foreign born (Swedish government 2018b: 13–14). Yet such acknowledgments have failed to disrupt the policy focus on refugee migrations' alleged fiscal costs. In the public debate, refugee migration is framed only as something that subtracts *financial* resources when, in fact, what it really does is to add *real* resources. In short, refugee migration is rejuvenating Sweden's labour stock, and has therefore transformed Sweden into the only country in the EU that has halted the decline of the working-age population. But, rather than consider this as a real boon, the debate has framed it as a fiscal burden. The Swedish Fiscal Policy Council (SFPC 2017: 22) thus talks about "the increased demographic burden on the welfare system as the proportion of young and elderly people in the population rises". As the reader may recall from Chapter 2, this confirms the fiscal impact literature's notion that children indeed are the biggest fiscal burden of all. In the debate, politicians and experts label Sweden's extraordinary situation of being awash in children and youth as "the demographic challenge" – *den demografiska utmaningen* – and in nine cases out of ten the "challenge" has negative connotations. Rather than being viewed as the real blessing it is, it is thus treated as a fiscal hazard that conjures up bleak future fiscal scenarios. Children are considered to make for a bleak future.

In a representative piece of the current debate on Sweden's "demographic challenge", three economists point to the ten years between 2008 and 2018 as having involved a cost increase for all Swedish inhabitants of about SEK 90 billion. The cost increase is attributed to the rapid population growth, spurred mainly by refugee migration. The increase in migration, they go on, also means that the demographic group of those up to 19 years of age increased significantly and, with it, the costs. Within the 0–19 age cohort, they then separate out the foreign-born and those born in Sweden, and what they find is that between 2008 and 2018 the migrant group has incurred a cost increase of SEK 40 billion. In comparison, those aged 80 and older have contributed a cost increase of SEK 10 billion over the same time period (Gustafsson, Hultkrantz & Österholm 2020). This "cost problematic", the authors go on to argue, has to be dealt with, as, in the long term, "welfare has to be adjusted to the available revenue".

As I write (summer 2020), the debate has since long reached alarmist proportions, something that explains the finance minister's ominous warning in March 2019 that, on account of the "demographic challenge", "Sweden is heading for the most serious situation in a hundred years", and that this requires a "penny-pinching budget" and a set of "exacting prioritizations for many years to come" (*Dagens industri* 2019a). Similarly, in January 2020 the prime minister, Stefan Löfven, proclaimed migration to be one of the most important issues for the years ahead: "We should make sure to show that the number of asylum seekers gets fewer – significantly fewer so that we can handle integration. Then people will see that those who come here go to work in the morning and contribute – duty, right." When asked about the real meaning of the often mentioned "long-term sustainable migration policy and a [refugee] reception at a responsible level", Löfven said: "A responsible level is reached when those you admit can get a job, the children go to school and when we can cope with elderly care and all the rest. We should reduce the number of people who come, but those who do come should work" (*Dagens Nyheter* 2020).

Asylum seeking in Sweden has dropped to an historic low and has been at this low level for some years (Figure 7.3). Meanwhile, the number of people with a refugee background working in Swedish elderly care is at an all-time high – something the government is well aware of. Nevertheless, the prime minister's rhetoric suggests that a sharp reduction in asylum seekers is a prerequisite for sustainable elderly care.

In 2019 a parliamentary commission of inquiry was launched for the purpose of outlining a sustainable long-term migration policy with broad parliamentary support. As expressed by one of the Social Democratic representatives

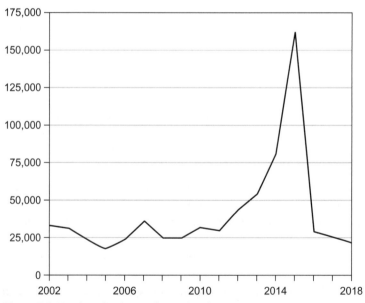

**Figure 7.3** Number of asylum seekers in Sweden, 2002–18
*Source*: Statistics Sweden (2019d).

at the inquiry, the party's main objective entering into this inquiry was to ensure a "continuation of a migration policy that is restrictive and which thus enables us to handle our welfare responsibilities in the municipalities" (Swedish Radio 2019c).

## Refugees' impact on municipalities

### The fiscal boon of refugee reception

Much of the current debate about the fiscal impact of migration and the so-called "demographic challenge" boils down to a question of the fiscal health of the Swedish municipalities. This has been the case since 2015, when refugee reception initially surged. With the dramatic drop in asylum seeking, however, the "refugee crisis" has subsided and given way to a "municipal crisis" and the "demographic challenge". But, as already seen, the two latter crises are still connected to 2015, in the sense that they are said to be partly caused by the large refugee intake. Social allowances for unemployed refugees and the increased welfare expenditures relating to the refugee-spurred demographic rejuvenation are all the financial responsibility of the municipalities. It is the surge of these refugee-related "costs" that municipalities are said to be unable to handle; hence the current fiscal crisis in the municipal sector.

In contrast to the central government, municipalities are revenue-constrained in a real sense, in that they spend from income, or tax revenue. In addition, municipalities abide by a balanced budget rule that forms part of Sweden's fiscal policy framework. In reality, however, few if any of Sweden's 290 mostly small municipalities have a tax base able to fund all the financial obligations that fall on them – and there are many. Instead, they rely on central government grants. Above, we saw this illustrated in the amended extra budget in November of 2015, which granted the municipal sector an additional SEK 10 billion per annum to finance refugee reception and integration. In fact, however, it was the municipal sector that received the brunt of all the other, and far higher, spending increases that followed in the wake of the refugee crisis. The European Commission's 2017 "Country report" for Sweden provides a neat summary of developments in 2015 and 2016:

> The high influx of asylum seekers in 2015 led to more spending on providing public services. […] Government consumption expenditure therefore surged in 2015 and 2016. Additional public consumption and investment is expected to support economic growth in the years to come. Local authorities will play a key role in the integration

> of refugees. They have been granted extra funding, some of which is earmarked for accommodating refugees, but have also received a general grant from the central government. This grant is intended to be spent on staff, welfare services and infrastructure, e.g. childcare facilities and hospitals.
>
> (EC 2017a: 4)

The spending increases impacted very positively on the municipal sector's financial situation. In the budget proposal for 2017 (presented in September 2016) the government acknowledged this, pointing to the fact the municipalities were in a position where they could both increase their consumption *and* improve their fiscal stance (Swedish government 2016: 182). In the subsequent budget proposal, the effects of the increasing central government grants and surging tax revenues became clearer, with virtually all the municipalities (97 per cent) reporting a surplus or balanced budget for 2016 (Swedish government 2017b: 218–19). The Swedish Association of Local Authorities and Regions (SKR 2017: 5, 35–6) spoke about a historical "record result", with only nine out of Sweden's 290 municipalities reporting a deficit for 2016. As noted by the SKR, the municipal costs grew considerably as a result of the refugee situation – but so did the state grants. The refugee-receiving municipalities collected some SEK 36.0 billion in 2016 and SEK 42.3 billion in 2017, which is to be compared to the little over SEK 15.2 billion that was paid out for refugee purposes in 2019 (Swedish Migration Agency 2020). For 2016, moreover, the municipalities received at least an additional SEK 10 billion for refugee reception and integration (SKR 2017: 39). The small municipality of Gnosjö in southern Sweden (with fewer than 10,000 inhabitants), for instance, went from a deficit of SEK 3.5 million in 2015 to a SEK 14.7 million surplus for 2016. The economic manager for the municipality explained the dramatic improvement as mainly an effect of the refugee-related support received from the state. Thanks to an increase in inhabitants, Gnosjö's tax revenue also increased by close to 5 per cent in 2016 (*Värnamo Nyheter* 2017).

Another important point to note is that smaller, rural and depopulating municipalities received the most refugees, proportionally speaking. This had a huge effect on the distribution of central government grants, with these municipalities receiving the most money in relative terms (Figure 7.4).

A key factor in this was that smaller and rural municipalities also received a disproportionately large share of the 35,000 unaccompanied minors seeking asylum in Sweden in 2015. Since the financial compensation for minors was much higher than for other asylum seekers, this helps explain why so much of the refugee money went to the smaller municipalities. As seen in Figure 7.4, there were municipalities in which the central government money came to

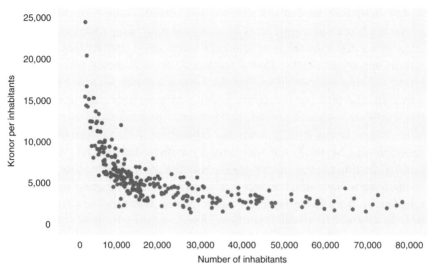

**Figure 7.4** Size of municipality and reimbursement in kronor per inhabitant, 2016
*Notes:* X axis: number of inhabitants (inhabitant size of municipality); Y axis: SEK 1,000 per inhabitant.
*Sources:* Swedish Migration Agency and SKR (2017: 40).

equate a net addition of more than SEK 20,000 per municipal inhabitant (SKR 2017: 40).

As emphasized in Chapter 3, central government spending cannot be conceptualized as a mere cost, following the flawed household analogy. The money spent ends up somewhere, and it ends up as income in the non-central government sector. As should be clear by now, the great increase in refugee-related spending in Sweden in the years 2015 to 2017 mostly ended up as income in refugee-receiving municipalities. Here, it was used to manage reception and integration, but it was also used for investment and spending on other municipal concerns. Last but certainly not least, municipalities used the money to save and to pay down debt; and many saw their liquidity improve. Hence, it soon became clear – as pointed to in the European Commission's report above – that the funds received by the municipalities by far exceeded that which was needed for strictly refugee-related matters.

## Small municipalities, huge examples

The fact that refugees disproportionately ended up in smaller and rural muni-cipalities also meant that poorer municipalities received a disproportion-ately large cash injection from the central government. These were the same ageing municipalities that had suffered from decades-long depopulation and whose tax bases had dwindled as a consequence. In many municipalities this coincidence fed a dynamic of goodwill and a sense that refugee reception was an opportunity rather than a burden. Apart from being rejuvenated by young working-age people and families, municipalities were also financially refreshed, and thus put in a better position to meet both current and future challenges with regard to welfare services and investment and savings needs. This – as we can call it – unintentional experiment in "functional finance" (as described in Chapter 3) was welcomed by many municipalities. "Functional finance" in this context simply means that the successful management of a challenging refugee situation was made an end in itself, whereas government spending to the refugee-receiving municipalities was a means to this end. It was the opposite of the normal sound finance approach, in which concrete needs related to the public good take a back seat to the superior goal of fiscal balance or surplus.

"Jämtland sidesteps law to receive more refugees": this headline from 2017 appeared in one of Sweden's largest dailies. The article concerned the numerous municipalities in the northern Swedish region of Jämtland that had grown increasingly dissatisfied with the sharp drop in the number of refugees that were allocated to them by the central government. Jenny Edlund, speaking for the County Administrative Board of Jämtland, explained the situation: "In Norrland's interior the population declines each year. But during the last few years we've finally recorded some positive signs due to migration." She continued, "We need these people," and stressed that "Jämtland has both work and housing for the newly arrived refugees" (*Svenska Dagbladet* 2017b). Another headline, this time in Sweden's largest daily, read "Municipalities worry about receiving too few refugees". The article, published in December 2017, took note of the Swedish Association of Local Authorities and Regions' observation that more and more municipalities were expressing concern over what they considered a too meagre allocation of refugees to them in 2018. The leaders of the municipality of Åre, with some 11,000 inhabitants, declared that they would have been very happy to receive around 100 refugees in 2018, instead of the 25 who had been allotted by the central government. Martin Söderström, head of the municipality's unit for economic growth, stated: "We are very pleased to receive new municipal citizens who contribute to our community and we have come up with an integration model that makes people feel welcome and at home here" (*Dagens Nyheter* 2017).

Although Åre received 50 refuges in 2017, it also attracted about 100 refugees who moved there voluntarily from other municipalities. Given Åre's small size and remote location, this unusual trend signalled that the municipality's integration model was bearing fruit, with many refugees finding work. The municipality, as Söderström emphasized, considers refugees who come to live there as absolutely crucial for the future: "We want to keep and expand our schools and daycare centres, we want grocery stores to stay open in the villages and we want our small businesses to find people to hire" (*Dagens Nyheter* 2017). Subsequently, Åre has persisted in trying to receive more refugees, and when it found out that it would receive only three refugees in 2020 it made its disappointment known. "We look at these people as resources who contribute to our population base," says Hanna Moback, who is establishment coordinator in Åre. The chief town in the region, Östersund, with some 50,000 inhabitants, agrees with this attitude, and in 2019 it decided to "share" some of the 60 refugees it received with smaller, depopulating municipalities in the vicinity. But the head of integration in Östersund, Jens Fladvad, says it would rather have kept all 60 of the refugees it received and that it wishes to receive as many as 250. "Östersund," Fladvad states, "wants to grow and therefore we are thinking the more inhabitants the better. We want to invest in the refugees and approach them as a resource for our local community" (*Dagens ETC* 2019).

Further north, in the 28,000-inhabitant-strong municipality of Boden, a similar development can be spotted. Like most rural municipalities in Sweden, Boden had been losing people for decades on end. In recent years, however, it has grown significantly, thanks solely to refugee migration, adding some 1,600 people, most of whom are working age and children (Bodens kommun 2019). In 2016 the Social Democratic chairman of the municipal council commented that, "[w]ithout these 1,600 people, we would be discussing which schools to close, which housing units that stand empty or which to tear down. Now, we are instead discussing which schools to expand, the building of new schools and housing" (Tidholm 2016).

Numerous Swedish municipalities, particularly in depopulating regions (which cover most of Sweden), have been happy to receive refugees. They are happy chiefly because refugees promise to mitigate three interrelated problems faced by most Swedish municipalities: (1) a severe and long-standing demographic ageing and depopulation; and, with it, (2) a continuous loss of municipal tax revenues, which forces an equally continuous reduction in welfare services; and (3) severe staff shortages and recruitment problems (e.g. in the care sector), a problem experienced by the public and private sector alike. With the increase in state transfers from 2015 to 2017 to assist municipalities' refugee reception and integration, many small to medium-sized municipalities saw a real chance to reverse this decades-long negative spiral. The central government is reluctant to acknowledge this positive dynamic, however. In all likelihood, this is probably because it challenges the logic of the fiscal framework and sound finance, as well as the narrative of refugees as fiscal burdens. Yet developments in many municipalities point to how a real refugee dividend can look.

In 2016 the tiny municipality of Laxå,[6] with some 5,700 inhabitants, hosted about 550 asylum seekers. Proportionally speaking, this was the fifth largest reception among Sweden's 290 municipalities; and Laxå had been receiving many refugees for some years – a total of over 900 between 2012 and 2016 (*Dagens Samhälle* 2016). Not long ago Laxå was rated the poorest of Sweden's 290 municipalities. With the positive economic dynamic that was put in motion by the refugee reception, this is no longer the case. In 2013 Laxå increased its population for the first time in over 40 years, a feat caused almost entirely by the municipality's increased refugee admission (Laxå kommun 2019a). In turn, this helped generate a surplus of SEK 7.8 million in 2013, equalling the municipality's largest since at least 2000. The positive trend continued in 2014 (SEK 9.6 million) and 2015 (SEK 10.3 million), and then it skyrocketed in 2016, when an unprecedented surplus of SEK 32.5 million was reported. 2017 and 2018 were also good years, with surpluses of SEK 15.2 and SEK 11.1 million respectively (Laxå kommun 2019b). Besides increasing tax revenues resulting from the population increase and the overall pick-up in economic activity, the surpluses mainly stemmed from the refugee money injected by the central government.

Before 2013 Laxå was heavily indebted; in 2012 the accumulated debt stood at over SEK 120 million. With the refugee money pouring in, however, Laxå has experienced a surge in liquidity, amounting to SEK 122 million at the beginning of 2018. Thanks to this, the municipality has managed to significantly reduce its debt, a development that began in 2013. In 2019 the debt had been reduced to just over SEK 20 million, and the plan is to have it eliminated entirely by the end of 2021 (Laxå kommun 2019a: 29–31). In fact, Laxå's liquidity position became so strong that it decided to invest some of the money in interest-bearing securities.

Most of all, however, the large increase in central government funds enabled Laxå to invest massively in both the refugees and the municipality's overall welfare and infrastructure. A large chunk of the government money was invested in a very ambitious integration programme, mapping the needs and skills of each individual refugee to ensure the best possible preparation for jobs, education and training. Clear and easily accessible information was also prioritized early on, and, therefore, Laxå immediately opened an information bureau for this purpose. As it turned out, the bureau catered to all inhabitants and proved

---

6. Located 200 kilometres west of Stockholm.

to be a very popular addition to the municipal services. As part of the integration programme and thanks to the generous amount of government funds, the mandatary hours of language training provided by the central government programme were practically doubled in Laxå. I learned this when interviewing the head of the labour and integration unit in Laxå.[7] As the head made clear, the approach was to give the refugees a head start, and minimizing the language barriers faced by the newcomers was a top priority.

Since the municipal leadership immediately approached the refugees as an opportunity and investment for the future demographic and economic sustainability of Laxå, there has also been an effort to make sure that refugees want to continue to live in Laxå after the state-financed integration period of two years is over. So far Laxå has been quite successful in this pursuit, and what is noteworthy too is that, as in the case of Åre above, quite a few refugees have chosen to move to Laxå from other municipalities (Laxå kommun 2019a, 2019c). The main reason for this probably has to do with the fact that Laxå has been exceptionally successful in ensuring that refugees become self-supporting once the two-year integration programme is completed. As of 2018, 42 per cent of refugees in Sweden are working or studying 90 days after the completion of the two-year integration programme. This should be compared to 2013 and 2017, when the figures stood at 27 and 31 per cent respectively (Nilsson 2018). The positive trend accompanies the general improvement in the employment rate for the foreign-born. In Laxå the rate is 50 per cent, which is extraordinary in its own right but even more so considering Laxå's small labour market (Laxå kommun 2019c: 4). Even more extraordinary is the figure for Åre, which is 70 per cent. The rate of self-support for those refugees who completed the two-year integration programme between 2013 and 2016 is 84 per cent in Laxå. In Sweden overall, 48 per cent of the refugees who were admitted in 2011 were in employment after five years (Swedish government 2018d). This makes Laxå's integration programme even more remarkable. From the interview with the head of the labour and integration unit in Laxå and with the chair of the municipal executive board (a Christian Democrat), it became clear that most of the jobs that refugees get in Laxå are within the private sector.

As noted above, a large amount of the refugee money that Laxå received from the government has been used for purposes other than those directly related to

---

7. Interviews were carried out as part of a research project ("Municipal refugee reception and the conflict over fiscal policy"), awarded by the Centre for Local Government Studies, Linköping University. Project leader: Peo Hansen; co-researcher: Karin Krifors. Interviews were made with the head of the labour and integration unit, the chair of the municipal executive board and the municipal director, and conducted together with Karin Krifors on 29 October 2019.

refugee matters. This could be done despite the fact that Laxå invested much more in the refugees than the regulations stipulated. Consequently, Laxå was able to spend more on the municipality's welfare and beyond. The municipal government defines welfare to include not only daycare, schooling, elderly care and the like, but also infrastructure, the development of businesses, recreation, tourism and culture. Thanks to the refugee money, Laxå has been able to build both a new school and a new elderly care home. In addition, it has expanded one of its daycare centres, and it has also built an extension to a short-term care facility (Laxå kommun 2019a). This is significant for such a small municipality, but also mirrors the rest of Sweden's demographic situation very well. Laxå has also added teaching resources to its schools, beds to its care sectors and new resources to its social services. Moreover, it has invested in road maintenance, playgrounds, tourism, culture and the repair and renovation of buildings, to name just a few areas that have benefited.

When interviewed, the chair of the municipal executive board, the head of the labour and integration unit and the municipal director all concurred in their general assessment of the situation. Although Laxå received many asylum seekers and although there were times when the organization was stretched thin, the municipal leadership refused to refer to the autumn of 2015 in crisis terms. On the contrary, there was a strong political understanding that this was a golden opportunity, and the fact that Laxå already had experience with receiving and integrating refugees certainly helped to make the notion of an *opportunity* realistic. But, as the head of the labour and integration unit is careful to point out, in order to capitalize on this opportunity it was essential to have a strategy, a concept, a comprehensive plan and an organization that was able to implement the plan. Given the many challenges, it also required a great deal of hard work and a high level of ambition. But, with the financing of reception and integration *not* one of the challenges, this was of course crucial, and it created a base that helped make an ambitious plan practical and realistic. It should be kept in mind, however, that many municipalities in Sweden that were given the same auspicious financial conditions by the central government have not been nearly as successful as Laxå, which just goes to prove the obvious fact that, as one author put it, "there is no substitute for good governance in migration management" (Santo Tomas 2005: 247).

Finally, I should also say something about the political implications of the developments in Laxå. In 2014 the Christian Democrats ended six decades of unbroken Social Democratic rule in Laxå, winning 18.4 per cent of the local vote – up from 11.6 per cent in 2010. The Christian Democrats were then in a position to form a coalition government. With the refugee crisis a year later, Laxå consolidated its refugee-led revival. This also meant that the municipal leadership spent four years not simply practising a refugee-welcoming agenda;

it also communicated a welcoming message. At the national level, meanwhile, such an agenda and message soon evaporated, and they have subsequently been replaced by an increasingly hostile approach, as seen in the 2018 election campaign (see Chapter 2). In the 2018 national election, an openly racist and anti-refugee party, the Sweden Democrats, increased its support from 12.9 to 17.5 per cent. In the municipal elections, held at the same time, the Christian Democrats in Laxå boosted their support by more than 20 per cent, winning 39 per cent of the vote. The party thus doubled its vote share on a strong pro-refugee ticket. Meanwhile, the Sweden Democrats in Laxå settled for a meagre increase, growing from 5.2 to 7.4 per cent, coming in ten percentage points below the party's national score of 17.5 per cent.

## Conclusion

The Laxå Christian Democrats' view of refugees is miles from the message peddled by their Stockholm colleagues at the central level, who are vehemently opposed to both refugee reception and the related state spending. In many ways, it is as if we are dealing with two very different political parties. At the central level, the Christian Democrats' migration policy has become almost indistinguishable from the one propagated by the Sweden Democrats, and since the 2018 general election the party has been openly courting the Sweden Democrats in anticipation of what many believe to be a coalition bid for the next election, which would also include the traditional right-wing Moderate party.

But intra-party differences between local and central levels on the migration issue are not unique to the Christian Democrats; they are common within most other political parties in Sweden. We may conceive of this difference as reflective of the sound finance doctrine that is favoured by, more or less, all the parties at the central level and the de facto propensities for functional finance at the local level. As shown in this chapter, many local politicians who for decades have seen their municipalities age, their young people leave and tax revenue drop do not approach refugees as a fiscal burden. Refugee reception is perceived, rather, as a solution to demographic ageing, labour shortages, welfare sustainability and fiscal shortfalls. The realism of this perception was greatly helped by the central government's generous financial aid, which, as shown here, did far more than cover the financing of reception and integration, and so provided a crucial and long-overdue financial boost to local communities.

The admission of refugees – i.e. *real* resources – together with the generous addition of financial resources from the central government proved to be a hugely virtuous combination for scores of depopulating municipalities in Sweden. But, as shown, it also helped the municipal sector as a whole.

Historical surpluses were recorded and the refugee money helped municipalities to invest in welfare, save, improve liquidity and pay down debt. Since this coincided with enormous investment needs in the municipal sector, the central government might have drawn some useful lessons from this unintended experiment in functional finance. But no. With refugee admission reduced to historical lows (starting in 2017), government spending to the municipalities also began to dry up. In the Swedish Association of Local Authorities and Regions' economic report from October 2019, it was estimated that around a third of the municipalities would run deficits that year. Economic hardship has become the norm, and municipalities have been forced to impose austerity measures to balance the books. Besides accounting for the higher costs from the so-called demographic challenge that I discussed above – with simultaneously higher ratios of young and old – the SKR highlights the fact that the central government has slashed spending while also shifting more financial responsibility onto the municipalities (SKR 2019: 7–8).

So, what was the problem? Was the state spending unsustainable in the years 2015 to 2017? Did it jeopardize the solvency of Sweden and force tax hikes? Did it risk overheating the economy, as suggested by the Swedish Fiscal Policy Council in 2017? The answer to all of the above is, of course, no. But, as seen above, rather than identifying the financial aid to the municipalities as a necessary good – as that which helped municipalities to invest in both the newcomers and the municipalities' welfare and infrastructure as a whole – the Swedish government and the centre-right opposition have persisted in describing the spending in negative terms. As detailed above, the spending also boosted growth and tax receipts, to the point at which Sweden started to run surpluses. In fact, the two years, 2016 and 2017, when refugee spending peaked were also the years when the surpluses peaked and met the surplus target. The government and the economic experts were all in agreement that the refugee spending could do nothing but *cause* increasing deficits and worsened economic conditions for the country. Yet what they had ruled out as an impossibility turned out to be the only game in town.

I have also explained why current labour migration policy in the European Union, as described in the previous chapters, cannot, because of its sound finance biases, accommodate refugees as labour who receive social rights and permanent residence. In practice, however, and as seen above, Sweden and its municipalities have been able to accommodate this very well. So well, in fact, that Sweden, thanks to its relatively large refugee admission over the decades, has acquired a uniquely auspicious demographic situation compared to other EU countries. As demonstrated, Sweden is the only country in the EU that has not seen its median age increase during the past decade. Instead of following the EU trend, Sweden is growing its working-age and young population thanks to refugee migration. The labour performed by people with a refugee background, including their offspring, has become indispensable for the Swedish society and economy.

Despite being aware of this, since the autumn of 2015 the Social-Democrat-led government and the right-wing opposition have been competing in churning out sound finance sound bites to back up their claim that refugees pose a fiscal liability and that the large intake of refugees in 2015 partly explains the subsequent fiscal crisis in many municipalities. In February 2018, for instance, the Moderate party put pressure on the government by demanding that it present the real costs of refugee migration in a more transparent fashion while at the same time repeating its position that refugee migration did not benefit Sweden (*Svenska Dagbladet* 2018). As part of this "refugee toughness" competition between the government and the opposition, the asylum insti-tution in Sweden has been externally ring-fenced and internally squeezed of social allowances, permanent residence and family reunification. When the refugee emergency around Greece's border with Turkey erupted in February 2020, the government wasted no time in confirming that Sweden's doors were sealed tight. "2015 will never be repeated" is the mantra regurgitated by the prime minister and the overwhelming majority of politicians in Stockholm. It had all been a waste of money and effort. Elsewhere, however, many ageing municipalities continue to appreciate refugees as vital in making local com-munities liveable again, helping to reverse a decades-long vicious spiral of depopulation, declining tax revenue and welfare service retrenchment. What we have, then, is a central level message of inertia and gloom and a local one of progress and hope. In a nutshell, the difference between sound finance and functional finance.

# 8

# Conclusion

## Now we see it, now we don't

> We will do what is needed or, as has been said elsewhere over the
> years: whatever it takes to handle the situation. [...] Our job [the
> Swedish Riksbank's] is to make sure that we do not run out of
> Swedish kronor. We can provide exactly as many Swedish kronor
> as we see fit.

This statement was made by the governor of the Swedish Riksbank, Stefan
Ingves, in April 2020 (Swedish Television 2020). It was but one in a series
of statements made in response to the Covid-19 pandemic. Prior to this the
Riksbank had announced a smorgasbord of measures to mitigate the financial impact of the pandemic, among them an injection of SEK 500 billion of
interest-free loans into the banks. At the press conference, Ingves described
the SEK 500 billion as follows: "This is basically free money and we expect the
Swedish banks to pass it on to Swedish companies" (Reuters 2020).

From the MMT perspective outlined in this book, Ingves' statements are
interesting in at least two respects. First, Ingves is incorrect in claiming that
banks lend on central bank reserves; they do not. In the Riksbank's (2020) press
release this mistaken conception was reiterated several times: "The Riksbank is
offering the banks up to SEK 500 billion against collateral for onward lending
to non-financial companies operating in Sweden." The statements derive from
the inaccurate "money multiplier" theory. Similar to the "household analogy" and the "budget constraint", the money multiplier makes up yet another
error within orthodox economics that still holds sway among central bank
and finance ministry officials, as well as in macroeconomic textbooks and the

news media.[1] Second, and more important for our purposes here, Ingves is right on the money when he speaks of "free money" and, especially, when clarifying that the Riksbank can provide as many Swedish kronor as it wants. In Chapter 3 I quoted Alan Greenspan saying something very similar about the federal government's money creation ability. In the same context, I also included Ben Bernanke's response when asked by a television host whether he, as the chairman of the Federal Reserve, used tax money to bail out the banks in 2008. "No" was Bernanke's answer: "It's not tax money. [...] The banks have accounts with the Fed, much the same way that you have an account in a commercial bank. So, to lend to a bank, we simply use the computer to mark up the size of the account that they have with the Fed" (CBS 2009).

As with the global financial crisis and the refugee crisis, the Covid-19 crisis offers a fantastic opportunity to learn about economics and the workings of governments' key role in it. By the same token, it offers a golden opportunity to change economic policy. Now we see it! But, as we also know, after the global financial collapse in 2008 it did not take long before the orthodoxy that had been complicit in causing the collapse was able to regroup, with economists at prestigious institutions helping governments to launch austerity, or "expansionary fiscal contraction", as the main response to the crisis – a response that had a devastating impact on many countries and that significantly worsened

---

1. As Ehnts (2017: 133) explains, banks do not lend out their reserves to non-financial firms and households: "Since neither firms nor households have accounts at the central bank and loans are not paid out in cash [there is] no interface between accounts at the central bank and accounts at banks, which is why banks cannot transfer their deposits at the central banks to households and firms." Instead of lending out their deposits at the central bank – or, for that matter, lending out the deposits of the banks' savers (known as the – equally mistaken – loanable funds theory) – banks create new deposits (*ex nihilo*) when they lend to non-financial firms and households. Rather than deposits creating loans, which is what the governor of the Swedish Riksbank is suggesting, it is loans that create deposits. MMT is far from alone in trying to disseminate this correct understanding of credit creation. Neither is the dissemination of the correct view the preserve of academic economists. As the title of a paper written by Standard and Poor's chief economist Paul Sheard (2013) has it: "Repeat after me: banks cannot and do not 'lend out reserves'". Economists with the Bank of England have also weighed in to correct the prevailing view of money creation. As described by Michael McLeay, Amar Radia and Ryland Thomas (2014: 14) of the Bank of England's Monetary Analysis Directorate: "The reality of how money is created today differs from the description found in some economics textbooks." With regard to the money multiplier notion, the authors clarify that "banks cannot directly lend out reserves" (2014: 25). Rather, banks use central bank reserves to settle payments between themselves; therefore, "[w]hen banks make additional loans they are matched by extra deposits – the amount of reserves does not change" (2014: 14). The same applies to the relationship between commercial banks and their savers: "Rather than banks receiving deposits when households save and then lending them out, bank lending creates deposits" (2014: 14).

and prolonged the crisis. It is no wild guess to suggest that EU institutions and governments, not least in the eurozone, will try to hold on to sound finance principles and fiscal rules also in the post-pandemic world.

Nonetheless, in the spring of 2020 governments were churning out new spending programmes and financial guarantees to businesses and households almost daily. "Money will not be a problem," said the Swedish prime minister at a press conference in April; "the government will bear all the extraordinary costs related to the virus outbreak no matter what the final bill ends up being" (Regeringskansliet 2020). At the same time, however, the Swedish finance minister was also very careful to point out that the money spent was taxpayers' money that had accumulated over the "good" surplus years. Without them and without Sweden's minuscule public debt, she assured the public, the massive Covid-19 spending would not be possible. Even if this truly was the case – which it is not – the Swedish surpluses would still be far from enough to "pay for" the Covid-19 spending. So, where did the spring 2020 money come from? The Swedish government said it would have to borrow, but that this would happen later. Meanwhile, no new taxes were being issued and no old ones had been increased; on the contrary, as part of the Covid-19 package, large corporate tax payments were being deferred and, overall, tax revenue was of course plummeting. Clearly, then, what the finance minister was saying could not be accurate. Again, as MMT elucidates, currency-issuing countries, such as Sweden, spend first and tax and borrow later. Just as no tax money "paid for" the extraordinary refugee spending from 2015 and onwards, so no tax money will "pay for" the extraordinary Covid-19 spending.

But what the Swedish finance minister was not denying in the spring of 2020 – and this holds for the eurozone as well – was that, for the time being, the fiscal rules of deficit and debt limits had been mothballed.

But why, we need to ask, did the pandemic make many governments spend without much regard to the otherwise sacrosanct fiscal rules? They did so for the same reason that Sweden decided to suspend temporarily its fiscal rules during the refugee crisis in 2015. In times of severe crisis (e.g. Covid-19; 2008 financial crisis) or when a situation risks spiralling out of control unless powerful measures are swiftly implemented (e.g. refugee situation in 2015), governments, and especially those that can spend freely, often take economic action that they had said beforehand was impossible. At such moments sound finance shows its true colours as an unrealistic and dysfunctional fiscal policy dictate – as something that needs to be swiftly removed in order for society to function and endure. Adhering to sound finance, meaning refusing to spend beyond the stipulated fiscal rules, would mean imminent chaos or catastrophe on a massive scale. Rather than targeting a fiscal balance, in times of sudden crises government spending often starts targeting such things as public welfare, medical needs or the concerns of people fleeing war. Sound finance as it is put to practice in the fiscal rules across the EU and the eurozone has nothing in it that even remotely suggests a public purpose or public interest. Obviously, therefore, had the rules been upheld they would have blocked the fiscal measures needed to manage a crisis – a crisis that sound finance either may have partly caused or, as in the case of Covid-19, has been instrumental in worsening by disarming societies' preparedness to respond.

## The consequences of sound finance

As shown in this book, sound finance's conception of central governments as essentially analogous to households with regard to prudent spending leads policy astray. Public investment is perceived as a fiscal risk, and large cohorts of the population are deemed fiscal costs, even burdens, without any consideration being given to what a *society*, rather than a balanced budget target, needs in order to function. For about three decades the European Union has been governed by fiscal frameworks based on sound finance principles. In their wake, EU societies have seen a steady deterioration and retrenchment of vital social services, welfare functions and infrastructure as well as growing inequality. In 1991, right around the time when Sweden started to abandon full employment in favour of sound finance, the country boasted close to 12 hospital beds per 1,000 inhabitants, a ratio that ranked among the highest in the OECD. In 2017, and several surplus years later, Sweden managed to scrape together only 2.2 beds per 1,000 inhabitants, which ranked close to last in the OECD and was rock bottom in the EU (OECD n.d.). Meanwhile, Sweden went from having 4,300 intensive care beds with respirators in 1993 to having just 574 in 2018 (during which period Sweden grew its population by 1.5 million people). This put Sweden among the very least prepared countries in the EU for Covid-19. When the pandemic hit, even Italy, whose healthcare system has been severely affected by years of eurozone-imposed austerity (e.g. De Falco 2019), retained more than double the intensive care capacity of Sweden (*Svenska Dagbladet* 2020).

In a recent study, Emma Clancy (2019) reveals that between 2011 and 2018 the European Commission, as part of its incessant work to "correct" macroeconomic imbalances in the member states, issued no fewer than "63 demands that governments cut spending on healthcare and/or outsource or privatise health services". In one of its "Country reports" for Italy, the Commission (2017d: 14) thus spoke approvingly of Italy's "restraints on healthcare spending and the public wage bill introduced since 2011". These measures had "helped to contain public expenditure over time". Brussels also appreciated the fact that Italy's "real healthcare expenditure" had been "contained significantly after the excessive deficit procedure in 2005–2008" and that such expenditure had "entered negative territory when the sovereign debt crisis required swift action to restore fiscal sustainability" (2017d: 26). The reader may recall from the discussion in the previous chapter that it was in such a "Country report" that the European Commission in 2016 pointed to Sweden's "higher spending on refugees" as one of "the main negative risks for the budget", something that prompted the Commission to forecast deficits for Sweden in both 2016 and 2017.

The logical sequence of priorities in a fiscal framework built on sound finance lets the economically unnecessary – i.e. a rule of fiscal balance – determine the socially necessary – e.g. healthcare. By heeding the warnings from Brussels about continuous spending cuts to protect the fiscal balance, Italian society, as so many others in the EU, has been thrown off balance. As Thomas Fazi (2016) notes, moreover, if we look at Italy's primary fiscal balance, which accounts for the balance between a country's spending and tax revenue before it has paid the interest on its loans, Italy has been by far the most frugal country in the EU over the past quarter of a century. Germany, the Netherlands and Sweden are nowhere near competing with Italy. "Have Italians been spending irresponsibly?" an article in the *Financial Times* asked in 2018: "One answer is no – at least in terms of the narrow balance between the tax revenues that Italy's government brings in and what it spends on day-to-day running costs, excluding the cost of debt service. On this basis – the country's primary fiscal balance – Italy has been running a fiscal surplus almost continuously since 1992" (*Financial Times* 2018d).

For decades the message peddled by Brussels, governments and scores of economists both inside and outside academia has been that it is precisely such frugality that helps boost growth, prosperity, investment, employment and a sustainable welfare state. Yet, as Fazi (2019) shows, this frugality has actually been instrumental in causing Italy's stagnation:

> Since the financial crisis of 2007–9, Italy's GDP has shrunk by a massive 6 per cent … In terms of per capita GDP, the situation is even more shocking: according to this measure, Italy has regressed back to levels of twenty years ago … Italy and Greece are the only industrialised countries that have yet to see economic activity surpass pre-financial crisis levels. [...] As a result, around 20 per cent of Italy's industrial capacity has been destroyed, and 30 per cent of the country's firms have defaulted. Around 10 per cent of Italy's labour

force – and a shocking 31 per cent of its youth – are out of work. If we include underemployed and discouraged workers ..., we arrive at a staggering effective unemployment rate of 30 per cent, which is the highest in all of Europe. Poverty has also risen dramatically in recent years, with about one Italian in four now at risk of poverty – the highest level since 1989.

This is an apt summary of the effects of three decades of sound finance in Italy. Sweden is, of course, nowhere near the Italian situation. Nevertheless, Sweden's broken healthcare system is certainly not the only victim of the country's fiscal framework. Failing schools, the fastest-growing income inequality in the OECD, one of the most indebted household sectors in the OECD and broken public housing and railway systems are just a few among many other examples. And all the while Sweden has been raking in surpluses and practically reduced its public debt to nothing.

## The fiscal impact of refugee migration

This study does not project into the future. Where the Covid-19 crisis will take us and what its impact will have been once this book hits the shelves are written in the stars. *Will we still see it?* Will we still see that economic policy can be changed to serve the public interest? Or did we fail to spot the fallacy of sound finance in the first place? What is indisputable when I write this, however, is that Covid-19 has proved fiscal frameworks built on sound finance are helpless in responding to the pandemic's economic and social consequences. Otherwise, these fiscal frameworks would not have been immediately abandoned. This much is a fact. Again, however, the extent to which this fact is *understood* is, of course, a different matter. In this book, I have shown that Sweden's decision to (temporarily and reluctantly) suspend sound finance – its surplus target and pay as you go rule – when confronted by the Syrian refugee crisis in 2015 proceeded from the same objective ineptitude on the part of the "sound" fiscal framework.

The book has detailed the effects of this temporary suspension. This means that I have looked carefully at the effects of the increased spending. As we have seen in the preceding: the academic literature, the political establishment, the government, the Finance Ministry, the government's economic expert agencies, the European Commission, the Riksbank as well as the news media *all* agreed that the increased spending on refugee reception and integration would be a very costly affair for Sweden. Hence, it would impact negatively on the Swedish economy and welfare state. It was ruled that the spending was unsustainable and that it would encroach on other spending areas in the budget. The chief reason for the projected misery was the fact that the refugee spending would *cause* fiscal deficits for several years to come, starting in 2015. On this there was total consensus, and the looming deficit was perceived as *the* most detrimental consequence of Sweden's reception of 163,000 asylum seekers.

But the certainties regarding the negative fiscal impact also related to Sweden's long-standing tradition of receiving large numbers of refugees relative to other EU countries. Before 2015 Sweden had been the largest recipient, proportionally speaking, of asylum seekers in the EU for many years. In terms of absolute numbers, Sweden was the second largest recipient also in 2014 (81,000) and the third largest recipient in 2013 (54,000) and 2012 (44,000) (Eurostat 2015). Concerns over the alleged "fiscal burden" posed by refugees had thus been high on the Swedish political agenda for many years. This adds some context as to why the negative fiscal impact has been used so frequently by the government and others when warranting Sweden's decision to break with its long-standing asylum tradition, a break that, since 2015, often gets expressed in terms of "Never again". Let me quote at length how the finance minister, Magdalena Andersson (2019), expresses this to the public:

> Recently I have been talking a lot about the great needs of the welfare sector. In relation to this many people are asking about the rate of employment of the foreign born and about the costs of migration and if these costs are accounted for. Let me explain this. The costs of migration are decreasing steadily. They have been cut in half between 2017, when they totalled almost 60 billion kronor, and this year [2019], when they have been estimated at around 30 billion. Looking ahead, costs will continue to fall to around 15 billion in 2022. [...] We have tightened up migration policy and we shall never go back to the situation in 2015. We have now extended the temporary law whereby the Swedish asylum rules are adapted to the EU's minimum standards and in accordance with international conventions, having, among other things, made temporary residence the main rule.

When the finance minister talks about "the great needs of the welfare sector" she is referring to the *financial* needs of the welfare sector; this is how the central government is approaching and debating the issue. This explains why Andersson goes straight from these financial needs to the fiscal costs of migration. This is the precise causal relation she wants the public to be aware that the government is very concerned about. What the minister is doing is thus to inculcate the notion that there is a trade-off between the financial needs of the welfare sector and the money spent to cover migration costs. By demonstrating the government's successful cuts in migration spending, Andersson also implies that there will be more money for welfare. The alleged trade-off between migration and welfare spending now appears as much less of a problem. By tightening up refugee migration, the government has put the Swedish welfare state back on a more solid footing, which, as we saw in Chapter 2, was one of the Social Democrats' most-rehearsed campaign messages in the 2018 elections.

As I showed in Chapter 7, however, there is a tremendous irony in all this. The irony, simply put, consists in the fact that, whereas there was absolute agreement that the refugee spending would *cause* deficits, it was the absolute opposite that happened. Above, Andersson pointed to 2017 as the year in which the government spent SEK 60 billion on migration. The finance minister perceived of this spending as a necessary evil, and she was therefore certain that 2017 would yield a deficit. From foregone conclusions about refugee spending *causing* deficits, the story soon changed to one of Sweden running surpluses *despite* the large-scale spending on refugee reception and integration. In 2015 the finance minister agonized about having to borrow to finance the refugee spending; in 2017 she boasted about not having borrowed a single krona to finance the refugee spending.

Aside from the embarrassment on the part of all the interested parties of being dead wrong about what they had initially claimed to be dead right about, the most instructive aspect about the deficit panic that swept Sweden in 2015/16 concerns its utterly misplaced focus. Having a large chunk of Sweden's economic expertise preoccupied with helping the government predict the future fiscal impact of its refugee spending was a waste of real resources. It hurts even more in light of the knowledge that such forecasting about everything's future fiscal impact goes on every day because the government is convinced that, if it is not consumed by chasing surpluses and repelling deficits, it is not doing its job. The state of the fiscal balance and public debt has become one of the most important criteria for how to judge the performance of a government and an economy. Hence, if refugees are said to impact negatively on the fiscal balance, they are judged to be an encumbrance on such performance. Economic growth is of course seen as very important too, but, although Sweden's growth in 2015 and 2016 was phenomenal, almost Chinese, this was not enough to beat the gloomy mood brought on by the projected years of refugee-induced deficits. Literally, obituaries were being written for the surplus target while, simultaneously, public consumption was soaring, employment increasing and tax receipts were pouring in.

Apparently, little notice was paid to the impact of the refugee spending on income, investment, employment and growth. Instead, it was the household calculus that ruled supreme, eclipsing much more important economic developments. Money that was spent on refugee reception and integration was an expenditure and a money-losing operation that, according to the government, would force borrowing and diminish the future "fiscal space" for other types of spending. According to some experts, tax increases would also have to form part of the mix of measures to "pay for" the refugee costs.

## Refugee migration and municipal income

From 2015 and onwards Sweden's central government, its economic experts and the media were busy worrying about the expenditure column and the future fiscal balance. Meanwhile, many places away from Stockholm were busy welcoming this expenditure as income. In the interviews conducted in the Laxå municipality, the chair of the municipal executive board referred to this income as "the money rain". Thanks to the refugee spending by the central government, 2016 may have been the best fiscal year ever for Swedish local governments. As MMT helps explain, since municipalities are currency users – as opposed to the central government's status as monopoly issuer of the Swedish krona – they are revenue-constrained, and so surpluses are extremely useful. These surpluses enabled many municipalities to invest, save and pay down debt. Given that a large portion of the financial responsibility for welfare services in Sweden is devolved to the often cash-strapped municipalities – one of sound finance policy's many disciplinary tools – much of the Swedish welfare state can be judged by its performance in the municipalities. And, in order to perform well, Swedish local governments need sufficient financial resources. The central government's refugee spending helped refugee-receiving municipalities with such financial resources and served the often underfunded welfare services very well.

By accounting for the fact that money that is spent will end up *somewhere*, rather than nowhere, we can also appreciate the fallacy of conceiving the refugee spending as simple cost and expenditure. Does this mean that the question concerning the refugee spending's fiscal impact is meaningless? Not at all. But it needs to be radically rethought and devolved. Its *real* meaning, as we have seen in the Swedish case, rests, rather, with the revenue-constrained local level, where the "fiscal space" matters in a very concrete way. *Here*, as opposed to the central government level, it is relevant to ask about the fiscal impact; and, as I have demonstrated, the fiscal impact of the refugee reception and integration at the municipal level was overwhelmingly positive. The central government spending to the municipalities financed the reception and initial integration. In and of itself this boosted economic activity and employment, which added local tax revenue. But, since much more money was transferred than was needed for the immediate refugee concerns, municipalities were able to attend to other things too, such as welfare needs, schools and infrastructure. Finally, the money was also used to pay down debt and to save for the future.

## The *real* impact of refugee migration

The fiscal health of Swedish refugee-receiving municipalities improved remarkably in the aftermath of 2015. This also impacted positively on the health of welfare services in many municipalities. With this we also see the nullification of what scholars and centrally located politicians claim to be an inescapable and indisputable trade-off between refugee spending and welfare spending – between the reception of refugees and strengthened welfare for all. Right before our eyes, then, Sweden had built a real-world model – however reluctantly – that was capable of receiving large numbers of refuges while at the same time investing in welfare. Instead of the misconceived trade-off between migration and welfare, or the alleged choice that has to be made between welfare spending and refugee reception, the Swedish case demonstrated that it is exactly the other way around. Spending on the refugees, the non-citizen newcomers, became a way of rediscovering the viability of welfare for all.

Instead of learning from the refugee-receiving municipalities' sudden fiscal recovery and reversal of depopulation, however, the debate in Sweden was dominated by warnings of the imminent deterioration of Sweden's fiscal health. This served as the main engine driving the government's rationale for closing the door to asylum seekers and for cutting back on refugee spending. Very quickly, asylum seeker numbers were reduced to historical lows and, as a consequence, migration costs were diminished too. The government could claim victory, as it used this as a central plank in its 2018 re-election strategy.

All of this, however, walked hand in hand with a fast deterioration of the municipalities' fiscal health. In the autumn of 2019 (as noted in Chapter 7) the Swedish Association of Local Authorities and Regions (SKR 2019) reported a grim picture: a third of the municipalities were running fiscal deficits and cutting back on welfare services – elderly care, daycare, schools, etc. Not long before Covid-19 struck eight out of ten Swedish municipalities announced that they were planning further cuts in the welfare services. None of these cuts was motivated by the services being over-dimensioned. On the contrary, services continue to be under-dimensioned, in some cases severely so, with services suffering from staff shortages across the board – e.g. nurses, assistant nurses, teachers, pre-school teachers and elderly care staff. With the ratio of both elderly and children growing in Sweden, the staff shortage is worsening and is projected to continue to do so for the foreseeable future. The cuts, then, were motivated solely with reference to shrinking budget margins.

As I pointed out in Chapter 7, because of Sweden's refugee reception in recent decades, the country stands out in the EU context for having seen a significant increase of both children and the working-age population. Like other EU members, Sweden has a growing elderly population, but it is the only country in the Union that has not seen an increase in the median age in the last decade. Even so, the government and most other actors are debating this development not from what should be the obvious perspective of a blessing. For them, the approach is instead one of pessimism – or, to be absolutely precise, one of *fiscal* pessimism. Sweden's demographic blessing has thus been spun into a "demographic challenge", taking aim at the "fiscally burdensome" growth of children and youth. Since refugee migration constitutes the main cause of this growth, the "challenge" can also be framed as a fiscal burden imported by refugees. As a finishing touch to this self-delusion, politicians, researchers and news media are now able to claim that this imported fiscal burden of youth is encroaching on the fiscal space for elderly care.

From a consensus around a general fiscal trade-off between welfare and low-earning and refugee migration, we now also have a consensus around a particular fiscal trade-off between refugee youth and the Swedish elderly. As I have argued and demonstrated in this book, this is an aberration, and it goes to show sound finance's fantastic ability to insulate people and policy from a realistic conception of society. It is not the refugee children who are encroaching on Sweden's fiscal ability to care for its old; it is their parents who are guaranteeing that Sweden's elderly have people to care for them in the first place. A day without the refugees toiling in Swedish elderly care spells a day of collapse for the elderly care. It is the addition of *real* resources by those of refugee background – not their subtraction of financial resources – that is keeping the underfunded and understaffed elderly care sector in Sweden from falling off the cliff. A higher proportion of the foreign-born as compared to the native-born are today working in the Swedish care sector. This is the reality, just as it is a reality that 60 per cent of the cleaners in Sweden are foreign-born, the great majority with a refugee background. Who is cleaning the Swedish hospitals, care homes, daycare centres and schools during the Covid-19 pandemic? Should the cleaners be conceived as the fiscal burdens that Sweden would have been better off without? By implication, this is what the fiscal impact literature and centrally located politicians suggest. Or are these cleaners precisely what they are, namely real resources serving a vital public function?

As part of Germany's lockdown in the spring of 2020, the government banned all entries of seasonal workers. But it took only a week for the ban to be lifted and 80,000 migrants allowed to enter in order to secure food supplies and avoid having harvests go to waste. The interior minister, Horst Seehofer, was happy to announce that "we managed to find a path that allows us to secure the harvest while also protecting the health of the population" (*Financial Times* 2020d). However this was far from enough; an additional 20,000 workers would have to be recruited domestically, targeting, among others, asylum seekers and the unemployed. In Italy the situation was even more dire, with an imminent risk of enormous fruit and vegetable harvests going to waste, which would threaten food supply and result in shortages and price hikes on food. The government therefore scrambled to make up for the loss of seasonal labour by tapping the domestic source of undocumented migrant workers. Rome's plan was to give permits to 200,000 undocumented workers. Italy's agriculture minister, Teresa Bellanova, wanted to go further and regularize all Italy's estimated 600,000 irregular migrant workers. "Today we have to respond to two emergencies," Bellanova stated: "prevent the humanitarian catastrophes that can occur in informal settlements … [where migrants are] at the mercy of the threat from viruses, and tackle the urgent problem of the absence of manpower hitting our farms, jeopardizing work, investments and food" (Roberts 2020).

The lack of seasonal labour from the European Union's poorer members, its eastern and southern neighbours and from Asia was a huge concern across large parts of the EU in the spring of 2020. In Sweden the pandemic-related lack of seasonal labour was threatening the forest industry's planting of some 400 million trees, risking losses of billions of kronor. To mitigate the crisis the government decided to train – surprise! – newly arrived refugees so that they could help save the day.

The latter illustrates yet again the *real* impact of Sweden's relatively large refugee admission over the decades. A sound finance approach, with its preoccupation with fiscal impacts and its failure to understand spending/income dynamics, lacks the tools to appreciate this reality. This also hampers the ability of the central government and its network of economic experts and forecasters to formulate and enact realistic policy. As by default, however, the government's decision to pause its sound fiscal framework and provide (in excess of) the necessary funding to manage the municipalities' refugee reception in 2015 gave us a real opportunity – a natural experiment – to grasp the effects of a more functional approach to fiscal policy. And the municipalities did indeed welcome the new approach. Many of them made use of the opportunity provided by the additional financial resources. Equally importantly, however, municipalities with declining populations understood the blessing of additional real resources in the form of new inhabitants and labour. This is of course crucial, and what distinguishes the situation from one in which financial resources would have been the only addition.

As the Covid-19 pandemic exploded in Sweden, the staff shortages in elderly care worsened, especially in small, depopulating municipalities with a large proportion of elderly inhabitants. The chief economist of the Swedish Association of Local Authorities and Regions, Annika Wallenskog, commented on this, saying that "many of these [small depopulating] municipalities have been very good at employing the resources afforded by the newly arrived refugees". Just previously, Wallenskog had criticized the government for not offering the municipalities enough financial support to compensate for the impact of the pandemic. But in this interview she also took care to emphasize the fundamental point "that money cannot solve everything in these types of [depopulating] municipalities; instead they need support and help with staff, with *finding* staff" (Lunchekot 2020).

Indeed, and as seen above, this is also what many local governments have emphasized about the refugee situation from 2015 and onwards. Just to give one more example of this, we can turn to the depopulating and ageing region of Värmland. In 2018 eight municipalities in this region took a joint initiative to solve their common recruitment problems, foremost in the private sector. A project was thus launched with the aim of matching unemployed newly arrived refugees with employers with recruitment needs. Training programmes in welding, auto mechanics, restaurants, care work and cleaning were started in 2018, admitting 240 people. The result? A year later nine out of ten in the programmes had found employment (*Dagens industri* 2019b). This is but one of several similar initiatives.

## Functional finance in practice

Was the pausing of Sweden's sound fiscal framework unsustainable? Was it inflationary? Meaning, was it unsustainable for the central government to supply sufficient financial resources to the municipalities? Was it unsustainable to provide additional funding to welfare services and infrastructure? Was it bad for municipalities to be able to pay down debt and save? In this context, we should also ask if it was ill-advised of the central government to help municipalities with job creation for the long-term unemployed and the newly arrived refugees. This latter programme, known as "extra jobs", is a state-financed programme that lets municipalities employ the long-term unemployed and newly arrived refugees. As with the central government's financing of refuge reception and integration, the extra jobs programme enables municipalities to substitute state funds for hard-earned municipal taxes. Besides being able to hire new staff for the often understaffed municipal services, the state financing also means that municipalities recover the locally financed social allowances that otherwise would have gone to the unemployed, who now work instead. Local government budgets are also greatly helped by the fact that the new taxes paid by those employed by the extra jobs programme accrue to the municipalities. In Chapter 3 I mentioned the "job guarantee" programme, as designed by MMT scholars, and, although it is not the same, there are important similarities between the extra jobs programme and the job guarantee scheme. At the beginning of 2019 the extra jobs amounted to some 19,000, but the programme has since been scaled down.

What I have just done is to ask a set of questions relating to a functional finance approach. Refugee receiving municipalities of course affirmed this approach. At the central level and in the national debate, however, it was sound finance concerns that prevailed. In that sense, policy-makers and their economic advisers never really had to confront the improvements in the municipalities. Neither were they compelled to explain why it was a necessary evil and not a necessary good to spend to manage the refugee arrival in 2015, and why it was unsustainable to continue to spend for the purpose of making the municipalities function better with regard to welfare services, investment in infrastructure, job creation, schools and other things serving the public interest. They had only to explain why it was fiscally unsustainable to continue the financial support to the municipalities. Consequently, municipalities were returned to the dysfunctional path.

At the same time, however, local governments have continued to insist that the central government will have to shoulder a much greater financial responsibility if Sweden's welfare services, schools and other vital functions are to be sustainable. Here, the debate is growing more and more intense and the lines of conflict are becoming increasingly clear – and the Covid-19 pandemic seems to be accelerating this development further.[2] To no little extent this is a conflict between sound finance, represented by the central political level and the economic expertise, and functional finance, represented by the municipalities. What is also interesting is that much of this debate transcends partisan politics. The "extra jobs" programme, for instance, has been continuously ridiculed as

---

2. Thanks to the big spending increases prompted by the Covid-19 pandemic, Swedish municipalities are now, starting in 2020, expected to run huge surpluses again.

"fake jobs" and "make-believe jobs" by the liberals and the parties of the right in the national parliament. In the municipalities, however, the programme is often supported by local representatives from these same parties.

At the beginning of 2020, just prior to the Covid-19 outbreak, the municipality of Norrköping, which is governed by a coalition led by the Social Democrats, decided to close down an elderly care home and cut the health and care budget by some SEK 40 million, corresponding to 90 nursing staff. These cuts were made in the context of increasing care needs and were thus executed solely to meet the balanced budget requirement for municipalities. Interestingly, however, it was not only the local left party that challenged the cuts. The local right-wing Moderate party also slammed them. Under the headline "Welfare demands more than a balance budget" the Moderate party's local leader wrote in the regional newspaper that "[a] balanced budget has no value if this also means that schools, healthcare and elderly care fail to live up to the laws, guidelines and goals that the municipality has to follow" (Jarl 2020).

Local politicians, especially in small municipalities, form part of the local reality and do not have the same option to look away from the many obvious dysfunctionalities that follow from austerity and a shortage of funds. Because of a lack of tax revenue, municipalities in Sweden are faced with a situation in which they cannot afford to make the necessary investments in, let us say, their decaying water and sewage system unless they make steep cuts in elderly care – both of which are local financial responsibilities in Sweden. If they decide they cannot do the latter, then their water systems break down – as, indeed, they do very often in Swedish municipalities these days. As one typical headline had it: "The municipalities' water systems are like ticking bombs" (Swedish Television 2016). There is no complexity surrounding this issue; this is simply what happens when pipes grow old. Yet, under sound finance, it is a reality that centrally located politicians often decide to ignore. Local politicians, no matter their party colour, do not have this luxury. Under such dire circumstances, therefore, the law of gravity may trump ideology and party colour at the local level.

What the temporary suspension of Sweden's sound fiscal framework demonstrated was the realistic possibility and sustainability of a turn to functional finance. What many municipal representatives also experienced in a very real sense was that refugees do not pose a fiscal burden and they do not threaten the sustainability of welfare services. Rather, they rejuvenate ageing communities and add real resources that support the sustainability of welfare services and the local tax base.

## Understanding the quest for both less and more migration

The misconception of refugees as fiscal burdens forms part of the accounting exercise of ranking migrants according to their tax contributions that has its home in the larger fiscal impact literature (surveyed in Chapter 2). We know how closely aligned research and policy are when it comes to the cost perception of refugees. In Chapters 4 and 5 I showed how this alignment plays itself out in external labour migration policy. I focused on the European Union's labour migration policy and what this policy wants to achieve and what it has accomplished so far. Even if the results in terms of concrete policy are meagre, they nonetheless provide an amazingly clear picture of the strong imprint of sound finance on EU policy. When we distil the combined positions of Brussels and all member states, what emerges as the most conspicuous common denominator is the worry that labour migration will increase welfare costs.

As displayed in Chapter 5, the external labour migration policy regime that member states and Brussels have been able to agree on is built on a sectoral approach. As such it is differential, fragmented and replete with derogations to satisfy member states' discretion in matters of welfare and residence rights. Rules and rights thus apply differently and unequally to different categories of third-country labour migrants. The policy regime's stratified social and residence rights come across as being modelled on the perceived net tax contributions that are to flow from each sectorally defined migrant cohort. If the tax contributions, such as in the case of seasonal migrants, are not expected to exceed a particular, or sectorally defined, migrant group's hypothetical withdrawal of welfare benefits, then such a migrant group will be granted very limited access to the welfare system. By the same token, their residence rights will be extremely ring-fenced and framed as a security concern, given that seasonal migrants' socio-economic vulnerability is seen as incentivizing overstaying. In the EU's Seasonal Workers Directive all these restrictions and safeguards come to the fore, not to speak of the strict ban on bringing family members, over which Brussels proved more rigid in its outlook than some member states.

But, as I also showed, EU directives attending to highly skilled migrants are also subject to many restrictions regarding access to welfare, family and residence rights. Just to point to yet another revealing hedging manoeuvre, we can turn to the Researchers Directive that was discussed in Chapter 5. The directive intends to "make the Union more attractive for third-country nationals wishing to carry out a research activity in the Union". As part of this, researchers' "family members [...] should be allowed to accompany them and benefit from intra-EU mobility provisions" (preamble: 11).[3] Looking further down in the long and detailed preamble, however, the promise of family migration runs into trouble and so has be compromised: "In many Member States," we learn,

> the right to family benefits is conditional upon a certain connection with that Member State since the benefits are designed to support a positive demographic development in order to secure the future work force in that Member State. Therefore, this Directive should not affect the right of a Member State to restrict, under certain conditions, equal treatment in respect of family benefits when the researcher and the accompanying family members are staying temporarily in that Member State. (preamble: 56)

Migrants are supposed to help make up for the current "demographic deficit" and secure an EU member state's workforce today. Should they have children in this same member state, however, they are barred from accessing family benefits that are meant to secure the member state's workforce tomorrow. Again, if we want to know just how strong sound finance's grip is on the design of labour migration policy – including policies designed to attract the world's top talent – then directive details are fantastically informative, and this explains Chapter 5's attention to detail.

In Chapter 1 I addressed the seemingly contradictory objectives of *less* migration, or the EU's current approach to asylum, and *more* migration, which is Brussels' and many member states' current approach to labour migration. Since increasing labour migration is promoted to mitigate labour shortages resulting from demographic ageing, one must ask why refugee migration could not help this purpose too. Taken at face value, this appears as a contradiction. By juxtaposing the aims and logic of the EU's external labour migration policy with the workings of asylum policy, however, we can now discern why this is less of a contradiction and more the result of a mismatch or incompatibility between policy regimes. In other words, labour migration when not applied to the highly skilled – although it can apply somewhat to this category too – is structured around limited access to welfare rights and a temporary stay, so as to be less "burdened" by fiscal commitments. In contrast, asylum policy has a

---

3. Directive (EU) 2016/801 of the European Parliament and of the Council of 11 May 2016 on the conditions of entry and residence of third-country nationals for the purposes of research, studies, training, voluntary service, pupil exchange schemes or educational projects and au pairing (recast).

de facto penchant for permanent residence (or, at least, protracted stays) and delayed labour market participation. The asylum institution, therefore, is much more bound up with fiscal responsibilities, as it provides access to welfare services; it deals with people who cannot immediately join the labour market; and it supports families and children. From the trade-off and sound finance perspective, then, labour migration, if carefully managed, holds out the prospect of being fiscally sustainable and beneficial, whereas asylum migration does not. This provides more than one clue as to why Brussels and member states do not perceive of refugees as part of the solution to their demographic problems. And the fiscal impact literature asserts that "[t]he refugees represent a fiscal burden for the host countries at least short and medium term. Under these conditions refugee migration is unable to help to alleviate the aging related fiscal burden of the host societies, on the contrary, it contributes to its worsening" (Gál 2019: 352). Yet again, we see the literature's misplaced worries. It worries that refugees will subtract from the financial resources going to the elderly, instead of fathoming that they will add real resources to the care of the elderly.

In a more basic sense, EU labour migration policy is the child of the Union's macroeconomic policy objectives. Asylum policy is not – indeed, cannot be – unless it is abrogated altogether. At the same time, it is inevitable that refugees will add real resources, or labour, to the host countries. In that sense, the reception of refugees will be compatible with the needs of ageing EU societies. Currently, however, this is not how centrally placed politicians, their economic experts and researchers look at things. In their view, it is *fiscal* compatibility that matters, not *real* compatibility, and, since the household analogy puts refugees in the fiscal burden column, refugees are deemed to be in conflict with macroeconomic objectives. Refugees are solely a humanitarian matter, and so ultimately a matter of affordability.

From this perspective, refugees can be fiscally compatible with the demographic needs only if they can be treated as the model labour migrant: the one whose residence and welfare access is adapted to his or her tax contributions. But, since refugees do not join the labour market immediately and since many refugees are children, refugees can never assimilate to this model. Indeed, as one headline in the *Financial Times* (2018e) put it: "Germany's push for foreign workers clashes with anxiety over immigration." The article reported on the German government's new plan to increase labour migration while at the same time trying to reassure the public "that the new law must not provide an incentive for more refugees".

To restate: what we are dealing with is a mismatch between two incompatible migration regimes. The labour migration regime is linked up with processes of social disembedding, recommodification and residence and social rights-stratification based on migrants' skills. In contrast, the asylum regime is linked up with processes of social embedding and decommodification. Given the prevailing sound finance rules and neoliberal conjuncture, it is obviously asylum policy – or any migration policy embedded in policies of social incorporation – that gets banged up, with more and more preventive measures put in place and more and more rights and entitlements being stripped away. Few things illustrate this asymmetric process better than the current quest, at both EU and national levels, to abrogate the provisions of permanent residence and family reunification for those granted some form of international protection. These are, namely, the main vehicles to social incorporation and protection from the naked exposure to increasingly disembedded market forces – borrowing from Karl Polanyi (2001 [1944]). Through these changes, the incentives to seek asylum are not simply to be greatly diminished; in the process of adjustment to the rationale of disembedded temporary labour migration, the asylum policy regime also loses its distinctiveness as a regime to ensure protection.

## Implications for EU free movement and EU citizenship

In expanding the understanding of the mismatch between labour migration and asylum policies, we are also spotting a more general mismatch, or tension, between migration policies that tend to provide paths to citizenship and those that do not. Conceptualized as such, around rights and, ultimately, citizenship, the mismatch is also of use in explaining the crisis of the European Union's institution of free movement, a crisis that has been developing since the highly divisive transition rules were imposed to restrict the free movement rights (for work purposes) for the citizens of the new EU members in 2004. The promise of "free movement" to the cousins in the east thus quickly degenerated into a bitter and, by all accounts, mendacious debate about eastern European "welfare tourism" and "immigration problems". Since free movement is positively connoted and migration negatively connoted in the public debate, the fact that politicians almost immediately renamed free movement "EU migration", "benefit tourism" and "poverty migration" speaks to the explosiveness of this crisis – something that was starkly mirrored in the United Kingdom's Brexit referendum.

In Chapter 1 I mentioned Austria, Britain, Germany and the Netherlands' frontal attack on free movement in their joint letter to the Irish presidency and the European Commission in 2013. The letter's main claim was that too many people in the EU exploited free movement for the wrong reasons and that this migration "burdens the host societies with considerable additional costs, in particular caused by the provision of schooling, health care and adequate accommodation" (Mikl-Leitner *et al.* 2013).

The curt response from the then home affairs commissioner, Cecilia Malmström, to the four governments was symptomatic in its desperate attempt to distance free movement from any taint of immigration. As far as Malmström was concerned, the true scandal was that "EU citizens who have the right to travel, live, work and study where ever they want in the Union are put on a par with immigrants from countries outside the EU. For instance, they are being called EU immigrants, a concept that does not exist". "They are mixing apples and oranges like anything," Malmström went on, "they are mixing up internal EU mobility and immigration" (quoted in *Svenska Dagbladet* 2013). Malmström was seconded by her colleague Viviane Reding, then commissioner for justice, fundamental rights and citizenship. In a speech to the Trieste Citizens' Dialogue, Reding (2013) wanted "to make it absolutely clear: free movement is a fundamental right, and it is not up for negotiation. Let language not betray us: European citizens exercising their right to free movement are not 'immigrants'. All European citizens have the same rights."

The European Commission left no room for doubt: it recognized the importance of winning this war of definition and distinction. It knew that the term "immigrants" in the world of politics rarely signifies some long-forgotten dictionary definition of people who move and settle across international borders – in which case it would be perfectly appropriate to refer to EU citizens moving across member state borders as "immigrants". As both Malmström and Reding indicated, the word "immigrants" is for the most part a pejorative term that refers to those who are not "free" and to those who justifiably, in the eyes of member governments and Brussels alike, should be subjected to a number of stringent restrictions and controls. In order to safeguard free movement, therefore, Malmström and Reding had to make sure that the distinction between immigrants and free-moving EU citizens remained intact.

For a long time the European Union's political establishment could place the blame for alleged migration problems exclusively on those coming from outside the EU, mostly the "non-Europeans": the Africans, the Muslims, and so on. Since the eastern enlargements and the onset of the current crisis, many of these problems are now increasingly being projected also onto EU citizens themselves. As a consequence, the European migration drama is now being played out not only between EU members and non-members across the Mediterranean but also between the members themselves, pitting the French against the Poles, Germans against Bulgarians, Dutch against Romanians and everybody against the Roma, in a manner akin to the bigoted articulation of the eurozone crisis (e.g. "diligent" Germans and Dutch against "lazy" Greeks and Spaniards).

For many EU governments, free movement nowadays constitutes an anachronistic and peculiar labour migration policy, in that it bestows numerous social rights and entitlements on those who migrate, independent of their tax contributions. This results from the fact that, formally speaking, the EU's free movement regime is horizontally organized. In contrast to the sectorally organized external labour migration regime, the free movement regime's social and residence rights are not formally stratified. As discussed in Chapter 5, when the European Commission first launched its bid to create an external labour migration policy it proposed a horizontal framework, but immediately had it rejected by the member states.

Obviously, and as touched upon in Chapter 1, many governments and other actors have come to depict the EU's free movement regime as fiscally unsustainable, and they are intent on devaluing its rights catalogue and move it in a more sectoral and stratified direction. In 2014 Karl Lamers, of Germany's CDU, and Germany's finance minister, Wolfgang Schäuble, contributed to this opinion:

> We must uphold the freedom of establishment – the right of people and companies to carry out business wherever they want. But even here, it is essential to set the right incentives in order to prevent "benefit tourism" and a wave of poverty-driven immigration. Levels of economic wellbeing still diverge greatly throughout Europe; for this reason, when it comes to legislation on access to social security systems, we have to find EU-level solutions that take these differences into account. (Lamers & Schäuble 2014)

In recent years this opinion has had some purchase. As many scholars have noted, a "shift has taken place in the Court's [European Court of Justice: ECJ] case law on EU social citizenship … The Court has not only stopped extending cross-border welfare access to further categories of EU citizens, but it has partly reversed its legal doctrine towards a more restrictive approach" (Blauberger et al. 2018: 1424). The ruling by the ECJ that launched this shift was made in 2014 (in the Dano case), and it did not gain the backing only of the then UK prime minister, David Cameron, and other government leaders. The European Commission also applauded the ruling, one of its spokespersons saying that free movement "is not a right to freely access the member states' social assistance systems" (New York Times 2014).

As the asylum institution is being deprived of its mandate to ensure protection, so the EU's free movement regime might be about to lose its distinctiveness as a regime that ensures equal treatment. There is thus a strong political opinion that wants free movement to be more aligned with the EU's external migration policy's sectoral and stratified approach. In such a scenario, some of the features of the external migration policy would be internalized to apply also to EU citizens. As much reporting confirms, this is what a growing number of EU citizens from the Union's expanding periphery are already experiencing (see, further, Amelina *et al.* 2020).

Migration policy's subjection to a sound finance logic is thus visible across the board. Asylum seeking is declining, much to the satisfaction of the European Commission and member state governments; (pre-Covid-19) temporary labour migration and seasonal labour migration are increasing while labour migration for permanent residence is contracting; family reunification migration is decreasing, as well as being hit with several restrictions (OECD 2018a); and, finally, the corpus of social rights that defines the EU's free movement regime and EU citizenship is being challenged. In a nutshell, "Yes" to migration without social incorporation, and, conversely, "No" to fiscally risky migration that demands social incorporation.

## More than a problem of neoliberalism

Some would say that what I am describing is just run-of-the-mill neoliberalism rubbing off on migration policy, or what migration policy inevitably becomes after three decades of sustained neoliberal policy adjustments. That is true, of course, but it is also something else, something more profound, which runs deeper than the simple neoliberal reflection. As shown in this book, sound finance and the state–household analogy are hardwired into both political and scientific approaches to migration policy. From politics to research – independent of political leanings or theoretical perspectives, and whether consciously applied or not – what we see is a basic consensus that treats the cost perception of migration as stemming from economic absolutes rather than from particular ideological and political choices that constrain economic policy and fiscal options.

As noted in Chapter 1, the general character of this hardwiring becomes clear once we spot its assimilation into approaches at odds with neoliberalism. As I noted in the beginning of the book, Branko Milanovic is not your run-of-the-mill neoliberal. In fact, he is very much opposed to neoliberalism and the extreme inequality it has created (e.g. Milanovic 2020). Yet, when speaking of the migration–welfare trade-off and migration's fiscal costs, orthodoxy and tacitly accepted sound finance principles are what drive his reasoning and policy prescriptions. And we should remember that Milanovic advocates migration and has nothing against migration from poorer to richer countries – a sentiment he shares with many other migration scholars who, knowingly or unknowingly, adhere to sound finance orthodoxy. His mission is to adjust migration policies to the migration–welfare trade-off and thus avoid a situation in which migrants become fiscal burdens. If this means that low-earning migrants receive less in the way of rights and become subjected to "discriminatory treatment" (Milanovic 2016b), that is a price worth paying in Milanovic's view. He is ready to go as far as hitting migrants with higher taxes. This not only to make up for low-earning migrant's alleged costs but also to help tame the related popular opposition to such migrants receiving access to the welfare state.

But outright Marxist approaches also suffer from this assimilation of sound finance. The regular contributor to *New Left Review* and director emeritus of the Max Planck Institute for the Study of Societies, Wolfgang Streeck, is a case in point. In contrast to Milanovic, Streeck makes it much easier for himself and simply uses sound finance to argue for less migration, especially refugee migration, since he believes this will make the pie bigger for the native working class. Streeck made a name for himself early on as one of Europe's foremost theorists and critics of neoliberalism. But when it comes to refugee and low-skilled migration he reneges and employs sound finance orthodoxy to make his case against refugee migration.[4] "Costs do matter," he claims, and, although "the fiscal costs of 'integration' may be recovered at a later time once immigrants have jobs and pay taxes", there is still uncertainty "over how long this takes". Initially, "the 'investment' must in any case be significant, and certainly higher than the fiscal costs *per capita* of unemployed citizens". As with the fiscal impact literature, Streeck warns that the spending on refugees – also referred to as a "formidable fiscal burden" – "can give rise to popular resentment, especially if integration takes longer than promised and balanced budget policies cause competition for scarce resources between immigrants and the local population" (Streeck 2018a: 10, emphasis in original). This, moreover, may impact negatively on "the willingness of citizens to be taxed", since "a growing share of the expenditure may be going to newly arriving non-citizens" (Streeck 2019: 135). All of a sudden, balanced budget rules are no longer part

---

4. In her article "The left case against open borders", Angela Nagle (2018) goes one step further than Streeck and makes explicit her orthodox sources, citing economist George Borjas to help her claim that immigration hurts the poor.

of the neoliberal doctrine that Streeck in other contexts has taught us to reject. Instead, he uses them to his own advantage in driving home the point that refugee reception should be resisted by those who profess to be on the left. As Streeck (2018b) argues elsewhere, when he is not addressing the issue of migration: "Economic theories inspired by a mythical 'Swabian housewife' [i.e. sound finance] and assiduously cultivated over decades would have to be abandoned, the fiscal constitution altered or circumvented, and the political-economic austerity coalition that insists on a balanced budget disempowered."

Given the prevalence of sound finance, it should also be rather clear why this perception becomes so much more detrimental when applied to migration and immigrants – the outsiders who want to come in. After all, "they" enter "our" household and "we" are forced to find the money to support "them". It is about how "we" are going to "pay for increased migration", to use Milanovic's telling formulation once more (2016a: 152).

## How to proceed from here?

In confronting migration research with MMT, we are offered the possibility to change the current scientific script on migration. Since the research on migration's fiscal impact is so closely aligned with and consulted by both concrete policy and the political debate, however, changing the scientific script is inseparable from a discussion of what this would do to migration policy and politics. Moreover, such a discussion cannot be confined to migration. Since "Migration now drives Western politics", as one *Financial Times* headline aptly had it (Rachman 2018), changing the script on migration's fiscal and economic impact would also have a significant impact on politics and policy more generally. Just imagine if the academic scholars and the experts within the government's economic advisory agencies no longer ranked migrants according to their tax contributions and conceived of refugee spending as a fiscal risk! And what would happen if governments could no longer rely on researchers for commissioned reports that calculate refugee migration's fiscal costs? I think it would make a huge difference if research stopped confirming the incorrect description of refugee spending as a "cost" that encroaches on other budget items and, instead, explained that government spending is tantamount to income in the non-central government sectors and an investment in new real resources. To be sure, politicians would most likely persist in referring to migrants as fiscal burdens, but the discourse would become destabilized and lose the common-sense status it has today.

In Chapter 1 I quoted a recent article that claimed that, "when the majority thinks that refugees represent a fiscal burden (they 'take out more from the public purse than they pay in'), they are not wrong this time. It is not possible to argue against this with solid empirical evidence" (Gál 2019: 352). This statement is not only representative of the large body of research on migrations' fiscal impact, it also serves to show this research's complicity in fomenting negative public opinion towards refugees – however unpremeditated this may be. As communicated in the quote, "the majority [is] not wrong this time", implying that, although majorities may be wrong most of the time, on the issue of refugees they are not. Here, the majority opinion is in agreement with science. As we all know, the political parties on the extreme right have this piece of "economic science" tattooed into their party programmes and flagship slogans. Here is an instance when the AfD, the Sweden Democrats and the Freedom Party of Austria (FPÖ) cannot be dismissed as populists or as being guilty of simplifying complex issues. As asserted in the quote – which appeared in the International Organization of Migration's prestigious journal *International Migration* – the factuality of refugees constituting a "fiscal burden" "is not possible to argue against […] with solid empirical evidence". And since a fiscal burden, per definition, is synonymous with something bad and undesirable in the public debate, we should not be surprised if politicians and the public take those making up the burden – i.e. the refugees – to be undesirable too.

Needless to say, this is the appalling situation in which countries in the European Union find themselves today, with almost all political parties in agreement – and with all being able to cite science to back up their anti-asylum positions. Showing that the household tale is inaccurate will not change the position of the extreme right. And, even in the unlikely case of this happening, racism will probably make sure it restabilizes the firm belief in non-white migration being invasive, treacherous and evil. But, as already noted, robbing the traditional political establishment and news media of their validation from economic science is a different story. Although the traditional establishment does borrow from the overtly racist vocabulary of the extreme right, the main chunk of their anti-refugee politics is buttressed by the fiscal burden story. For them to be denied the legitimacy and confirmation provided by economics would create real problems. Just think of climate science and its constant criticism and delegitimatization of government policy. Today's governments cannot lean on science when they continue to invest in the fossil economy. A similar scenario would result from a change of the current scientific script on the economics of migration. All of a sudden, EU governments' most common argument against admitting refugees would no longer have economics on its side.

As noted above, there are still a large number of people and organizations, as well as a few voices from within political parties, who think refugee protection is a cause worth fighting for. But, as I have emphasized throughout, this force lacks an alternative narrative to orthodoxy's affordability tale. This makes it vulnerable to constant attacks for being unrealistic and for being insensitive to citizens who think it is unfair that they are footing the refugee bill at the expense of their own social needs. Strands of the left will add that saying "We can afford it" just confirms the refugee movement's out-of-touchness with a reality of growing poverty and working-class hardship.

Debunking sound finance's misleading cost perspective on migration could thus be of great significance for those defending international protection and refugee rights. They would no longer have to think of economics as contradicting their humanism and morals. In the book's opening pages, I argued that the future existence of international protection in the European Union will come to hinge on the resolution of what I termed a *clash of moral and fiscal imperatives*. A proper comprehension of macroeconomics, as outlined by MMT, points to ways in which this clash could be defused. Those advocating that a country or the EU as a whole has a duty to offer protection to refugees would not have to retreat into the defensive "We can afford it" position. With economics as their partner, they could instead explain why real resources can never be an expense and that government spending on reception and integration by definition adds financial resources to municipalities, households and businesses.

A common derogatory reaction to this reasoning that I often get when arguing along these lines in writing or in public talks goes something like this: "OK, since we have all the financial resources in the world to pay for refugee reception, then Sweden could just go ahead and admit all the world's refugees – right?" This is the slightly different version of the knee-jerk response to refugee rights advocates that "We cannot admit the whole world, can we?". Often the refugee rights standpoint is left with little to say here, because, in all likelihood, not everyone could come. In making the distinction between financial and real resources, however, MMT offers an answer, based on a realistic assessment, which says that, of course, not all the world's refugees could come to Sweden, but that is not because of a lack of financial resources; it is because of real resource constraints. There are simply not enough labour, housing, beds, food, schools or medical facilities to go around for Sweden to be able to admit and integrate the world's refugee population in its entirety.

The follow-up question to this may be: "Could the EU host all the refugees in the world?" According to the UNHCR there are some 71 million forcibly displaced people in the world today, of whom 41 million are internally displaced. This leaves us with around 26 million refugees under international protection, as defined by the UNHCR, and 3.5 million asylum seekers. Proportionally speaking, low-income and real-resource-constrained countries host the overwhelming majority (over 80 per cent) of these refugees. Out of the ten largest real number hosts of refugees in the world, only one, Germany, is situated in the EU; the rest are in Africa, Asia, the Middle East and Turkey (UNHCR 2019).

From a real resource perspective, the EU could certainly host the bulk of the world's 26 million refugees, given some time to prepare. But, as I have made painfully clear in this book, the political prospects for this are currently null and void. For the moment, the EU does not even aim for symbolic gestures to international protection. Instead, the president of the European Commission praises violent crackdowns against refugees along the Turkish/Greek border. And, when asked about the rubber bullets and legality of Greece's suspension of asylum law, Brussels' response was that "[i]t is not up to the Commission to offer any opinion or judgement". The comment came from Margaritis Schinas, European Commission vice-president and head of Ursula von der Leyen's newly created Commission group for "Promoting Our European Way of Life", which, among other things, is responsible for migration policy. Originally the Commission group was named "Protecting Our European Way of Life", and, as Nicolaj Nielsen (2020) with EUobserver and many others noted, the name choice was "largely seen as a head nod to right-wing factions" and as providing "clues into what this Commission is prepared to do". So far these assumptions have turned out to be correct. From the perspective of Brussels and the member states, the Common European Asylum System has failed in its purpose every time an asylum seeker slips by the EU's deadly border controls. It is this perspective that is shaping EU asylum policy.

From a realist perspective, therefore, the likelihood of increased capacity being built for refugee reception inside the European Union is less than futile. Such futility has several sources. Racism, xenophobia and anti-Muslim sentiments, in particular, are crucial and absolutely necessary for an understanding of the EU's asylum and human rights crisis. In this context, thankfully, we at least have a growing literature examining and explaining racism's importance. Although they are far from sufficient, Europe's growing racism and extreme right also attract quite a bit of journalistic scrutiny and news media attention. None of this applies to the misconceived economics that feed Europe's asylum crisis. Here, we see no growing literature or journalistic scrutiny. In fact, there is no such literature to begin with. Instead, what we see is a steady growth of the very literature that perpetuates the notion of refugees as fiscal burdens and that feeds and validates policy-making. The only voices of decency within the debate – those saying that we can afford it – are still trapped in the same orthodox affordability paradigm that their opponents thrive on.

My aim here, therefore, has been to begin the work of removing the false economic conceptions that help sustain and lend scientific legitimacy to the EU's and its member states' asylum and labour migration policy – a policy of receiving as few refugees as possible and a policy of stratifying social and residence rights. I have done this using a "three-stage rocket" strategy. For the false conceptions to be invalidated, we first need to rewire our thinking about migration and the economy, and we thus need a new research agenda that studies the impact of sound finance's huge footprint on migration policy and the overall migration debate, both the one taking place within the research community and the general political and public debate. But, as I have shown, we cannot stop here. Describing and critiquing the prevailing order constitute only one-third of the necessary job. Hence, the next third has been devoted to the introduction of an alternative approach to macroeconomics, namely modern monetary theory. Thanks to MMT's descriptive framework, not only is it possible to gain an understanding of the flaws within mainstream macroeconomics; we are also helped with spotting that much of what governments and central banks already do, operationally speaking, *and* what they are capable of doing are perfectly in line with MMT's description. That is the whole point of "Now we see it" or, better, "Now we ought to see it". Because, unless we understand the descriptive points put forth by MMT, it is very likely that we will not see that countries that issue their own currencies are not financially constrained in the ways economists and policy-makers assert. Unless we see it now, a post-pandemic world may just repeat the mistakes made in the post-financial-crisis world, with austerity imposed and progressives complaining that nothing can be done to improve social protection, healthcare, poverty or climate change unless we first manage to increase taxes on the rich. As I showed in Chapter 7, this mistake was repeated also in the aftermath of Sweden's large refugee reception, with the debate focusing exclusively on how and when government spending could be reduced, instead of focusing on the real results of the spending.

For this reason, the third stage of the book launched an examination into these real results, or what happened when Sweden received many refugees while simultaneously suspending its sound-finance-fashioned fiscal framework. I thus applied MMT to migration and let it help us understand the implications of Sweden's large refugee spending. From the perspective of the fiscal impact and trade-off literature, I therefore studied a situation that should make up the absolute worst-case scenario – a scenario in which fiscal health, welfare and the economy should suffer tremendously. None of this materialized. Instead, I have been able to demonstrate that refugees are no fiscal burdens, and neither is there a trade-off between migration and the sustainability of the welfare state. Rather, it was the very opposite that transpired. Most importantly, the central government spending for the municipalities proved perfectly sustainable and also demonstrated that the central government – had it wanted – could have continued to provide the municipal sector with financial resources to help improve welfare services, job creation and other municipal functions. As I showed, the government chose to do the opposite, and so Sweden's municipalities soon (after 2017) became mired in a fiscal crisis, being forced to impose welfare cuts. Another issue I highlighted was that many municipalities also felt robbed of the opportunity to continue to grow their communities with new inhabitants.

This notwithstanding, and no matter how reluctantly the central government approached the idea of spending increases, the management of the refugee situation in Sweden was very successful and sustainable from 2015 to 2017. In these pages I have been able to present only a small selection of the tremendous amount of knowledge and lessons that can be garnered from the Swedish experience. Much work thus remains to be done, and this applies not least to the question as to whether or not Sweden's conduct could serve as a model for the rest of the EU. In principle, I think it could. The eurozone rules are, of course, a huge constraint and obstacle. Even if there had been political support for the Swedish model in the eurozone, its rules would have prevented many eurozone countries from spending the necessary amounts; Germany and Austria were exceptions here. Overall, moreover, the eurozone rules must be said to have provided a huge disincentive to refugee spending. But, as I explained in Chapter 3, these constraints are not of an economic nature but are politically and ideologically driven. Debunking their alleged economic necessity and law-like status is thus always a first step requirement – and, hopefully, Covid-19 will help bring this task to fruition.

At the height of the refugee crisis it was repeatedly said – and several EU leaders warned (e.g. José Manuel Barroso, Juncker, Merkel) – that the refugee crisis could end up being even more devastating for the EU project than the eurozone crisis. Much less thought went into connecting these two crises and gathering that they would have to be dealt with jointly. What I have shown here is that Sweden's big spending increases to manage the refugee crisis spelled a temporary end of austerity. It took managing a "refugee crisis" and a "refugee burden", in other words, to impart a glimpse of how the Swedish welfare state could be renovated, how local communities could be rejuvenated and how citizens could be relieved of the burden of austerity. In demonstrating the realism and sustainability of this model, the Swedish experience has thus already invented the economic wheel for the EU as a whole. But, again, having successfully tested the economic mechanics is no guarantee of a political sequel. The Swedish experience demonstrates this to the full too, with the government reluctantly implementing an economically sustainable model just to discard it at the first opportunity. Even so, this does not take away one iota from the fact that the Swedish model proved perfectly functional and financially sustainable. In doing so, it also proved that the cost perspective, fiscal burden and trade-off approaches to refugee and low-skilled migration are built on flawed economics. The constraints are not economic and financial, as research and politics claim. Again, the recognition of this fact is a necessary first step for grasping why a humanitarian asylum policy and the rebuilding of welfare in the European Union are not mutually exclusive. Conversely, this constitutes the necessary knowledge for grasping that a political solution is not up against any real economic laws of gravity. Rather, it is there for the taking.

But let me be clear: I am not saying that Sweden or the EU as a whole should admit refugees *because* it benefits Sweden and the EU. Sweden and the EU should admit refugees to honour their human rights obligations and commitments. On the economics of it all, there is no argument. In admitting and investing in refugees – that is, *real* resources – societies in Sweden and the EU cannot but benefit.

# Bibliography

Acharya, V. & S. Steffen 2017. "The importance of a banking union and fiscal union for a capital markets union", Discussion Paper 62. Luxembourg: Publications Office of the European Union.

ABC News 2007. "Iraq war refugees turn to Sweden, not US". 15 March.

Adamis-Császár, K. *et al.* 2019. "Labour mobility and recognition in the regulated professions", study for the Committee on Employment and Social Affairs, Policy Department for Economic, Scientific and Quality of Life Policies. Luxembourg: European Parliament.

Afonso A. & C. Devitt 2016. "Comparative political economy and international migration". *Socio-Economic Review* 14 (3): 591–613.

Aldén, L. & M. Hammarstedt 2016. "Flyktinginvandring: sysselsättning, förvärvsinkomster och offentliga finanser", Rapport till Finanspolitiska rådet 2016/1. Stockholm: Finanspolitiska rådet [Fiscal Policy Council].

Alesina, A. & E. Glaeser 2004. *Fighting Poverty in the US and Europe: A World of Difference*. Oxford: Oxford University Press.

Alesina, A., A. Miano & S. Stantcheva 2018. "Immigration and redistribution", Working Paper 24733. Cambridge, MA: National Bureau of Economic Research.

Amelina, A. *et al.* (eds) 2020. *Boundaries of European Social Citizenship: EU Citizens' Transnational Social Security in Regulations, Discourses, and Experiences*. Abingdon: Routledge.

Amnesty International 2017. "EU–Turkey deal: a shameful stain on the collective conscience of Europe". 17 March.

Anderson, B. 2010. "Migration, immigration controls and the fashioning of precarious workers". *Work, Employment and Society* 24 (2): 300–17.

Andersson, M. 2015a. Debatt med anledning av budgetpropositionens avlämnande. *Protokoll* 2015/16:5, Sveriges riksdag, 21 September. Available at: http://data.riksdagen.se/fil/90B3E9ED-4D72-43FC-AD8A-1702C2475677.

Andersson, M. 2015b. "Så klarar vi utgiftstaket 2016". *Dagens industri*, 18 December.

Andersson, M. 2016. "Öppen utfrågning om Finanspolitiska rådets rapport 2016", Rapporter från Riksdagen 2015/16:RFR21. Stockholm: Riksdagstryckeriet. Available at: https://data.riksdagen.se/fil/FAC373A5-8429-4957-93C0-2F587A26F781.

Andersson, M. 2019. Facebook, 25 June. Available at: www.facebook.com/magdalenaeandersson/posts/2090243807751479?comment_id=2090302361078957.

Armellini, A. 2019. "Germans turn to Italy to fill 'catastrophic' medical staff shortage". DPA International, 4 April.

Ascoli, U. 1985. "Migration of workers and the labour market: is Italy becoming a country of immigration?". In *Guests Come to Stay: The Effects of European Labor Migration on Sending and Receiving Countries*, R. Rogers (ed.), 185–206. Boulder, CO: Westview Press.

Banting, K. 2010. "Is there a progressive's dilemma in Canada? Immigration, multiculturalism and the welfare state". *Canadian Journal of Political Science/Revue canadienne de science politique* 43 (4): 797–820.

Banting, K. & W. Kymlicka (eds) 2006. *Multiculturalism and the Welfare State: Recognition and Redistribution in Contemporary Democracies*. Oxford: Oxford University Press.

Barber, T. 2011. "A line to hold". *Financial Times*, 15 June.

Barker, A. 2015. "EU bows deeply to Erdogan in bid to relieve migrant crisis". *Financial Times*, 23 November.

Bauböck, R. & P. Scholten 2016. "Introduction to the special issue 'Solidarity in diverse societies: beyond neoliberal multiculturalism and welfare chauvinism': coping with 'the progressive's dilemma': nationhood, immigration and the welfare state". *Comparative Migration Studies* 3 (4): 1–7.

Bault, O. 2018. "Lacking manpower, Poland relies on Asian immigration besides Ukrainians and Belorussians". *Visegrád Post*, 24 August. Available at: https://visegradpost.com/en/2018/08/24/lacking-manpower-poland-relies-on-asian-immigration-besides-ukrainians-and-belorussians.

BBC 2010. "EU and Libya reach deal on illegal migrants". 16 October.

BBC 2018. "Joking German minister Seehofer urged to quit as Afghan deportee dies". 12 July.

bdnews24.com 2017. "Bangladesh, Poland agree to work on migration and maritime economy sectors". 17 April. Available at: https://bdnews24.com/bangladesh/2017/04/22/bangladesh-poland-agree-to-work-on-migration-and-maritime-economy-sectors.

Bearce, D. & A. Hart 2019. "Labor migration numbers and rights: do they trade off or advance together?". *International Interactions* 45 (1): 28–53.

Bell, D. & N. Piper 2005. "Justice for migrant workers? The case of foreign domestic workers in Hong Kong and Singapore". In *Multiculturalism in Asia*, W. Kymlicka & H. Baogang (eds), 196–222. Oxford: Oxford University Press.

*Berlingske* 2018. "Støjberg om lavt antal asylansøgere: Vi har gjort op med den danske gavebod". 3 January.

Betts, A. *et al.* 2014. *Refugee Economies: Rethinking Popular Assumptions*. Oxford: Refugee Studies Centre, University of Oxford.

Bhambra, G. 2017. "Locating Brexit in the pragmatics of race, citizenship and empire". In *Brexit: Sociological Responses*, W. Outhwaite (ed.), 91–9. London: Anthem Press.

Bi, H. & E. Leeper 2010. "Sovereign debt risk premia and fiscal policy in Sweden", Working Paper 15810. Cambridge, MA: National Bureau of Economic Research.

Billström, T. 2008. "Speech, Euro-African Ministerial Conference on Migration and Development", Paris, 25 November. Available at: www.regeringen.se/sb/d/7621/a/116756.

Blauberger, M. *et al.* 2018. "ECJ judges read the morning papers: explaining the turnaround of European citizenship jurisprudence". *Journal of European Public Policy* 25 (10): 1422–41.

Bloemraad, I. 2015. "Definitional debates, mechanisms and Canada: comment on Will Kymlicka's article: 'Solidarity in diverse societies'". *Comparative Migration Studies* 3 (4): article 16.

Blyth, M. 2015. *Austerity: The History of a Dangerous Idea*. New York, NY: Oxford University Press.

Bodens kommun 2019. "Beskrivning av befolkningen och befolkningsutvecklingen i Bodens kommun". Boden: Bodens kommun. Available at: www.boden.se/kommunen/samhalle-och-infrastruktur/befolkning-och-befolkningsutveckling-prognos.

Boeri, T. 2010. "Immigration to the land of redistribution". *Economica* 77: 651–87.

Boräng, F. 2018. *National Institutions – International Migration: Labour Markets, Welfare States and Immigration Policy*. London: Rowman & Littlefield.

Borjas, G. 1999. "Immigration and welfare magnets". *Journal of Labour Economics* 17 (4): 607–37.

Brieskova, L. 2014. "The new directive on intra-corporate transferees: will it enhance protection of third-country nationals and ensure EU competitiveness?". EU Law Analysis, 17 November. Available at: http://eulawanalysis.blogspot.se/2014/11/the-new-directive-on-intra-corporate.html.

Brinkmann, G. 2012. "Opinion of Germany on the single permit proposal". *European Journal of Migration and Law* 14 (4): 351–66.

Brunila, A., M. Buti & D. Franco 2001. "Introduction". In *The Stability and Growth Pact: The Architecture of Fiscal Policy in EMU*, A. Brunila, M. Buti & D. Franco (eds), 1–20. Basingstoke: Palgrave Macmillan.

Bundesregierung 2015. "Sommerpressekonferenz von Bundeskanzlerin Merkel". 31 August. Available at: www.bundesregierung.de/Content/DE/Mitschrift/ Pressekonferenzen/2015/08/2015-08-31-pk-merkel.html.

Burgoon, B. 2014. "Immigration, integration, and support for redistribution in Europe". *World Politics* 66 (3): 365–405.

Camarota, S. & K. Zeigler 2015. "The high cost of resettling Middle Eastern refugees: given limited funds, relocation to the U.S. may not be the most effective way to help". Washington, DC: Center for Immigration Studies.

Campbell, Z. 2019. "Europe's deadly migration strategy: officials knew EU military operations made Mediterranean crossing more dangerous". *Politico*, 28 February.

Cappelen, C. & T. Midtbø 2016. "Intra-EU labour migration and support for the Norwegian welfare state". *European Sociological Review* 32 (6): 691–703.

Carens, J. 2008a. "Live-in domestics, seasonal workers, and others hard to locate on the map of democracy". *Journal of Political Philosophy* 16 (4): 419–45.

Carens, J. 2008b. "The rights of irregular migrants". *Ethics and International Affairs* 22 (2): 163–86.

Carrera, S. 2018. *An Appraisal of the European Commission of Crisis: Has the Juncker Commission Delivered a New Start for EU Justice and Home Affairs?* Brussels: Centre for European Policy Studies.

Carrera, S. & R. Hernández i Sagrera 2009. "The externalization of the EU's labour immigration policy", Working Document 321. Brussels: Centre for European Policy Studies.

Cassarino, J.-P. 2008. "Patterns of circular migration in the Euro-Mediterranean area: implications for policy-making", CARIM Analytic and Synthetic Note 2008/29. Florence: European University Institute.

Castles, S. 2004. "Why migration policies fail". *Ethnic and Racial Studies* 27 (2): 205–27.

Castles, S. & A. Davidson 2000. *Citizenship and Migration: Globalization and the Politics of Belonging*. Basingstoke: Macmillan.

Castles, S., H. de Haas & M. Miller 2014. *The Age of Migration: International Population Movements in the Modern World*, 5th edn. Basingstoke: Palgrave Macmillan.

CBC/Radio Canada 2007. "Sweden offers safe haven to Iraqi refugees". 14 September.

CBS 2009. "Ben Bernanke's greatest challenge". 12 March. Available at: www. cbsnews.com/news/ben-bernankes-greatest-challenge/2.

Cerna, L. 2014. "The EU Blue Card: preferences, policies, and negotiations between member states". *Migration Studies* 2 (1): 73–96.

Chou, M.-H. 2012. "Constructing an internal market for research through sectoral and lateral strategies: layering, the European Commission and the fifth freedom". *Journal of European Public Policy* 19 (7): 1052–70.

*Christian Science Monitor* 1992. "European divisions persist over Yugoslavia's refugees: Germans criticize other Europeans for not taking in more displaced by war". 31 July.

Cienski, J. 2016a. "Migrants carry 'parasites and protozoa,' warns Polish opposition leader: Law and Justice chief plays on antipathy to foreigners ahead of parliamentary election". *Politico*, 12 February.

Cienski, J. 2016b. "Poland slams door on refugees". *Politico*, 23 March.

Clancy, E. 2019. "Discipline and punish: end of the road for the EU's Stability and Growth Pact?". Brave New Europe, 17 February.

Coda Moscarola, F. 2013. "Long-term care workforce in Italy", Supplement C to NEUJOBS Working Paper D12.2. Luxembourg: Publications Office of the European Union. Available at: www.neujobs.eu/sites/default/files/publication/2014/02/LTCworkforceItalyfinalD12.2.pdf.

Cohen, G. 2012. *In War's Wake: Europe's Displaced Persons in the Postwar Order*. Oxford: Oxford University Press.

Collins, D. 1975. *Social Policy of the European Economic Community*. New York, NY: Wiley.

Collinson, S. 1993. *Beyond Borders: West European Migration Policy towards the 21st Century*. London: Royal Institute of International Affairs.

Connors, L. & W. Mitchell 2017. "Framing modern monetary theory". *Journal of Post Keynesian Economics* 40 (2): 239–59.

Council EU 2001. "Council Directive 2001/55/EC of 20 July 2001 on minimum standards for giving temporary protection in the event of mass influx of displaced persons […]". *Official Journal of the European Communities* L 212, 7. 8.

Council EU 2003. "Council Directive 2003/9/EC of 27 January 2003 laying down minimum standards for the reception of asylum seekers". *Official Journal of the European Union* L 31, 6. 2.

Council EU 2004. "Council Directive 2004/83/EC of 29 April 2004 on minimum standards for the qualification and status of third country nationals or stateless persons as […]". *Official Journal of the European Communities* L 304, 29. 4.

Council EU 2005. "Council Directive 2005/85/EC of 1 December 2005 on minimum standards on procedures in Member States for granting and withdrawing refugee status". *Official Journal of the European Communities* L 326, 13. 12.

Council EU 2008. "European Pact on Immigration and Asylum", 13440/08. Brussels: General Secretariat of the Council.

Council EU 2012. "Draft Council conclusions on the Global Approach to Migration and Mobility", 8361/12. Brussels: General Secretariat of the Council.

Council EU 2015. "Council Decision (CFSP) 2015/972 launching the European Union military operation in the southern central Mediterranean (EUNAVFOR MED)". *Official Journal of the European Union* L 157/51, 23. 6.

Council of Europe 1952. *The Strasbourg Plan*. Strasbourg: Secretariat-General Council of Europe.

Crepaz, M. & R. Damron 2009. "Constructing tolerance: how the welfare state shapes attitudes about immigrants". *Comparative Political Studies* 42 (3): 437–63.

Cummins, M. & F. Rodriguez 2010a. "Is there a numbers vs rights trade-off in immigration policy? What the data say". *Journal of Human Development and Capabilities* 11 (2): 281–303.

Cummins, M. & F. Rodriguez 2010b. "A rejoinder to Ruhs". *Journal of Human Development and Capabilities* 11 (2): 311–14.

*Dagens ETC* 2019. "Jämtland: Ge oss fler flyktingar". 20 November.

*Dagens industri* 2015. "Magdalena Andersson: Flyktingsituationen inte hållbar". 22 October.

*Dagens industri* 2016. "Flyktingvågen ligger bakom Sveriges BNP-tillväxt". 29 February. Available at: www.di.se/artiklar/2016/2/29/flyktingvagen-ligger-bakom-sveriges-bnp-tillvaxt.

*Dagens industri* 2019a. "Andersson: Sverige går mot tuffaste läget på hundra år". 20 March.

*Dagens industri* 2019b. "Transportjättens drömrekrytering: Här får nio av tio jobb". 27 November.

*Dagens Nyheter* 2017. "Kommuner oroade för lågt antal nyanlända". 30 December.

*Dagens Nyheter* 2018. "Finansministern: Barnfattigdom skäl för stramare flyktingpolitik". 28 May.

*Dagens Nyheter* 2020. "Löfven: Antalet asylsökande ska bli rejält många färre". 17 January.

*Dagens Samhälle* 2016. "Sned fördelning av flyktingmiljarder". 29 April.

*Dagens Samhälle* 2019. "SKL: Nyanlända ska rädda äldreomsorgen". 27 August.

*Daily Telegraph* 2015a. "EU chief: close the doors and windows as millions more migrants are coming". 24 September.

*Daily Telegraph* 2015b. "EU should not 'harp on' at Turkey about human rights, says Jean-Claude Juncker". 27 October.

De Falco, R. 2019. "Access to healthcare and the Global Financial Crisis in Italy: a human rights perspective". *e-cadernos CES* 31: 170–93.

Delaney, E. 2013. "Justifying power: federalism, immigration, and foreign affairs". *Duke Journal of Constitutional Law & Public Policy* 8 (1): 153–95.

Deutsche Welle 2017. "Mateusz Morawiecki: EU 'completely misunderstood the situation'". 14 February.

Deutsche Welle 2018. "Germany: New 'Aufstehen' movement of Sahra Wagenknecht is shaking up leftists". 11 August.

*Die Welt* 2015. "Flüchtlingskrise könnte fast eine Billion Euro kosten". 25 November.

*Die Zeit* 2016a. "Sind die Deutschen verrückt? Oder ist es der Rest der Welt, der keine Flüchtlinge aufnimmt". 28 January.

*Die Zeit* 2016b. "Schäuble wirft Gabriel 'erbarmungswürdige Politik' vor". 27 February.

Douglas, R. 2012. *Orderly and Humane: The Expulsion of the Germans after the Second World War*. New Haven, CT: Yale University Press.

Dustmann, C. & T. Frattini 2014. "The fiscal effects of immigration to the UK". *Economic Journal* 124: 593–643.

*Economist* 1952. "The refugees: an unsolved problem". 19 January.

*Economist* 2015. "Let them in and let them earn". 29 August.

*Economist* 2016. "The economic impact of refugees: for good or ill". 23 January.

*Economist* 2018. "Sweden fails to form a government". 17 November.

ECRE 2004. "Broken promises – forgotten principles". London: ECRE Secretariat.

ECRE 2005. "Justice and Home Affairs Council 12–13 October", AD2/10/2005/EXT/RW, 10 October.

ECRE 2007. "Europe must extend solidarity to Iraqi refugees in the EU", Press Release PR2/2/2007/EXT/RW, 15 February.

Ehnts, D. 2017. *Modern Monetary Theory and European Macroeconomics*. Abingdon: Routledge.

Eisele, K. 2013. "Why come here if I can go there? Assessing the 'attractiveness' of the EU's Blue Card Directive for 'highly qualified' immigrants", Paper in Liberty and Security in Europe 60. Brussels: Centre for European Policy Studies.

Ekberg, J. 2009. "Invandringen och de offentliga finanserna", Rapport till expertgruppen för studier i offentlig ekonomi 2009:3. Stockholm: Finansdepartementet, Regeringskansliet.

Emmeneggar, P. & R. Klemmensen 2013. "Immigration and redistribution revisited: how different motivations can offset each other". *Journal of European Social Policy* 23 (4): 406–22.

ESV 2015. *Prognos: Statens budget och de offentliga finanserna: November 2015.* Stockholm: ESV.

ESV 2016. *Prognos: Statens budget och de offentliga finanserna: April 2016.* Stockholm: ESV.

ESV 2017. *Prognos: Statens budget och de offentliga finanserna: November 2017.* Stockholm: ESV.

ESV 2019. *Prognos: Statens budget och de offentliga finanserna: November 2019.* Stockholm: ESV.

EC 1994. "On immigration and asylum policies", COM(94) 23 final, 23 February. Brussels: European Commission.

EC 1996. *Europe ... Questions and Answers: The European Union – What's in it for Me?* Luxembourg: Office for Official Publications of the EC.

EC 1999. "Proposal for a Council Directive on the right to family reunification", COM(1999) 638 final, 1 December. Brussels: European Commission.

EC 2000. "On a Community immigration policy", COM(2000) 757 final, 22 November. Brussels: European Commission.

EC 2001a. "Proposal for a Council Directive concerning the status of third-country nationals who are long-term residents", COM(2001) 127 final, 16 March. Brussels: European Commission.

EC 2001b. "Proposal for a Council Directive on the conditions of entry and residence of third-country nationals for the purpose of paid employment and self-employed economic activities", COM(2001) 386 final, 11 July. Brussels: European Commission.

EC 2002. "Green Paper on a community return policy on illegal residents", COM(2002) 175 final, 10 April. Brussels: European Commission.

EC 2003. "Towards more accessible, equitable and managed asylum systems", COM(2003) 315 final, 3 June. Brussels: European Commission.

EC 2005. "Policy plan on legal migration", COM(2005) 669 final, 21 December. Brussels: European Commission.

EC 2007a. "Attractive conditions for the admission and residence of highly qualified immigrants", MEMO/07/423, 23 October. Brussels: European Commission.

EC 2007b. "Proposal for a Council Directive on the conditions of entry and residence of third-country nationals for the purposes of highly qualified employment", COM(2007) 637 final, 23 October. Brussels: European Commission.

EC 2007c. "On circular migration and mobility partnerships between the European Union and third countries", COM(2007) 248 final, 16 May. Brussels: European Commission.

EC 2010a. "EUROPE 2020: A strategy for smart, sustainable and inclusive growth", COM(2010) 2020 final, 3 March. Brussels: European Commission.

EC 2010b. "Proposal for a directive [...] on the conditions of entry and residence of third-country nationals for the purpose of seasonal employment", COM(2010) 379 final, 13 July. Brussels: European Commission.

EC 2011a. "Communication on migration", COM(2011) 248 final, 4 May. Brussels: European Commission.

EC 2011b. "The Global Approach to Migration and Mobility", COM(2011) 743 final, 18 November. Brussels: European Commission.

EC 2011c. "A dialogue for migration, mobility and security with the southern Mediterranean countries", COM(2011) 292 final, 24 May. Brussels: European Commission.

EC 2011d. "Report from the Commission to the European Parliament and the Council on the application of Directive 2004/114/EC on the conditions of admission of third-country nationals for the purposes of studies, pupil exchange, unremunerated training or voluntary service", COM(2011) 587 final, 28 September. Brussels: European Commission.

EC 2011e. "Report from the Commission to the Council and the European Parliament on the application of Directive 2005/71/EC on a specific procedure for admitting third-country nationals for the purposes of scientific research", COM(2011) 901 final, 20 December. Brussels: European Commission.

EC 2012a. "Treaty on Stability, Coordination and Governance in the Economic and Monetary Union", press release. 1 February. Available at: https://europa.eu/rapid/press-release_DOC-12-2_en.htm.

EC 2012b. *The 2012 Ageing Report: Economic and Budgetary Projections for the 27 EU Member States (2010–2060)*. Luxembourg: Publications Office of the European Union.

EC 2012c. "3rd Annual report on immigration and asylum", COM(2012) 250 final, 30 May. Brussels: European Commission.

EC 2013a. "Maximising the development impact of migration: the EU contribution for the UN High-level Dialogue", COM(2013) 292 final, 21 May. Brussels: European Commission.

EC 2013b. "Proposal for a directive of the European Parliament and of the Council on the conditions of entry and residence of third-country nationals for the purposes of research, studies, pupil exchange, remunerated and unremunerated training, voluntary service and au pairing", COM(2013) 151 final, 25 March. Brussels: European Commission.

EC 2013c. "On the work of the Task Force Mediterranean", COM(2013) 869 final, 4 December. Brussels: European Commission.

EC 2014a. "On EU return policy", COM(2014) 199 final, 28 March. Brussels: European Commission.

EC 2014b. "5th annual report on immigration and asylum (2013)", COM(2014) 288 final, 22 May. Brussels: European Commission.

EC 2014c. "On the implementation of Directive 2009/50/EC on the conditions of entry and residence of third-country nationals for the purpose of highly qualified employment", COM(2014) 287 final, 22 May. Brussels: European Commission.

EC 2014d. "Report on the implementation of the Global Approach to Migration and Mobility 2012–2013", COM(2014) 96 final, 21 February. Brussels: European Commission.

EC 2014e. "An open and secure Europe: making it happen", COM(2014) 154 final, 11 March. Brussels: European Commission.

EC 2014f. "Commissioner Malmström welcomes the European Parliament vote on intra-corporate temporary transferees", statement. 15 April.

EC 2015a. *The 2015 Ageing Report: Economic and Budgetary Projections for the 28 EU Member States (2013–2060)*. Luxembourg: Publications Office of the European Union.

EC 2015b. "EU action plan on return", COM(2015) 453 final, 9 September. Brussels: European Commission.

EC 2015c. "Macroeconomic imbalances: Country Report – Sweden 2015", Occasional Paper 226. Brussels: Directorate-General for Economic and Financial Affairs, European Commission.

EC 2016a. "An economic take on the refugee crisis: a macroeconomic assessment for the EU", European Economy Institutional Paper 33. Brussels: Directorate-General for Economic and Financial Affairs, European Commission.

EC 2016b. "Proposal for a Directive of the European Parliament and of the Council on the conditions of entry and residence of third-country nationals for the purposes of highly skilled employment", COM(2016) 378, 7 June. Brussels: European Commission.

EC 2016c. "The EU and the refugee crisis". July. Available at: https://op.europa.eu/en/publication-detail/-/publication/1aa55791-3875-4612-9b40-a73a593065a3.

EC 2016d. "Proposal for a Regulation amending Council Directive 2003/109/EC of 25 November 2003 concerning the status of third-country nationals who are long-term residents", COM(2016) 466 final 2016/0223 (COD), 13 July. Brussels: European Commission.

EC 2016e. "European Economic Forecast: Winter 2016", Institutional Paper 20. Brussels: Directorate-General for Economic and Financial Affairs, European Commission.

EC 2017a. "Country report Sweden 2017: including an in-depth review on the prevention and correction of macroeconomic imbalances", SWD(2017) 92 final, 22 February. Brussels: European Commission.

EC 2017b. "The Fiscal Compact: taking stock". 22 February. Available at: https://
ec.europa.eu/info/publications/fiscal-compact-taking-stock_en.

EC 2017c. "The EU and the migration crisis". July. Available at: http://
publications.europa.eu/webpub/com/factsheets/migration-crisis/en.

EC 2017d. "Country report Italy 2017: including an in-depth review on the
prevention and correction of macroeconomic imbalances", SWD(2017) 77
final, 22 February. Brussels: European Commission.

EC 2018a. "Enhancing legal pathways to Europe: an indispensable part of a
balanced and comprehensive migration policy: a contribution from the
European Commission to the Leaders' meeting in Salzburg on 19–20
September 2018", COM(2018) 635 final, 12 September. Brussels: European
Commission.

EC 2018b. *The 2018 Ageing Report: Economic and Budgetary Projections for the
28 EU Member States (2016–2060)*. Luxembourg: Publications Office of the
European Union.

EC 2018c. "Communication on a new Africa–Europe Alliance for sustainable investment and jobs", COM(2018) 643 final, 12 September. Brussels:
European Commission.

EC 2018d. "Proposal for a Directive on common standards and procedures
in Member States for returning illegally staying third-country nationals
(recast)", COM(2018) 634 final, 20 September. Brussels: European
Commission.

EC 2018e. "European Economic Forecast: Autumn 2018", Institutional Paper
89. Brussels: Directorate-General for Economic and Financial Affairs,
European Commission.

EC 2019a. "Country report Sweden 2019: including an in-depth review on
the prevention and correction of macroeconomic imbalances", SWD(2019)
1026 final, 27 February. Brussels: European Commission.

EC 2019b. "Progress report on the Implementation of the European Agenda
on Migration", COM(2019) 481 final, 16 October. Brussels: European
Commission.

EC 2019c. *Cyclical Adjustment of Budget Balances: Autumn 2019*. Brussels:
Directorate-General for Economic and Financial Affairs, European
Commission.

EC n.d.–a. "The European Semester: why and how". Available at: https://
ec.europa.eu/info/business-economy-euro/economic-and-fiscal-policy-
coordination/eu-economic-governance-monitoring-prevention-correction/
european-semester/framework/european-semester-why-and-how_en.

EC n.d.–b. "Global Approach to Migration and Mobility". Available at: https://
ec.europa.eu/home-affairs/what-we-do/policies/international-affairs/
global-approach-to-migration_en.

EC n.d.–c. "Integration, migration and home affairs". Available at: https://ec.europa.eu/home-affairs/what-we-do/policies/legal-migration/integration_en.

Euractiv 2010. "EU to ease restrictions on seasonal workers". 16 July.

Euractiv 2019. "Austrian far-right leader urges fight against 'population exchange'". 29 April.

Euronews 2016. "Tusk tells migrants 'Do not come to Europe'". 3 March.

Euronews 2020. "Frontex border operation in Greece 'lacks legal basis' after Greece suspends asylum law". 11 March.

European Council 1999. "Presidency conclusions: Tampere European Council, 15 and 16 October 1999".

European Council 2014. "Conclusions", EUCO 79/14, CO EUR 4, CONCL 2. 27 June.

European Council 2016. "EU–Turkey statement 18 March 2016", Press Release 144/16. 18 March.

European Economic and Social Committee 2005. "Opinion of the European Economic and Social Committee on the Green Paper on an EU approach to managing economic migration", SOC/199. Brussels: European Economic and Social Committee.

European Economic and Social Committee 2016. "Towards a coherent EU labour immigration policy with regard to the EU Blue Card", opinion, SOC/539 – EESC-2016-02508-00-00-AC-TRA. Brussels: European Economic and Social Committee.

European Migration Network 2015. "Attracting and retaining talent in Europe: conclusions and summary". Riga: National Contact Point for Latvia, European Migration Network. Available at: https://emnbelgium.be/sites/default/files/attachments/emn_conference_2015_conclusions_final_24_april_2015.pdf.

European Parliament 1990. "Report drawn up on behalf of the Committee of Inquiry into Racism and Xenophobia on the findings of the Committee of Inquiry", Session Document A3–195/90. Brussels: European Parliament.

European Parliament 2005. "European Parliament resolution on an EU approach to managing economic migration (COM(2004)0811 – 2005/2059(INI))", P6 TA(2005)0408. 26 October.

European Parliament 2014. "More rights and better working conditions for non-EU seasonal workers", press release. 5 February.

European Parliament 2019a. "European Parliament resolution on search and rescue in the Mediterranean", B9-0000/2019. 21 October.

European Parliament 2019b. "Immigration policy", factsheet on the European Union. December. Available at: www.europarl.europa.eu/factsheets/en/sheet/152/immigration-policy.

European Union External Action 2015. "European Union Naval Force – Mediterranean Operation Sophia", update November. Rome: EU Naval Force Mediterranean, Media and Public Information Office.

Eurostat 2007. "Asylum applications in the European Union", Statistics in Focus: Population and Social Conditions 110/2007. Luxembourg: Publications Office of the European Union.

Eurostat 2013. "Migration and migrant population statistics". March. Available at: http://eeurostat.ec.europa.eu/statistics_explained/index.php/Migration_and_migrant_population_statistics.

Eurostat 2014. "Residence permits statistics". October. Available at: http://ec.europa.eu/eurostat/statistics-explained/index.php/Residence_permits_statistics.

Eurostat 2015. "Number of (non-EU) asylum applicants in the EU and EFTA Member States, by age distribution, 2014". Available at: https://ec.europa.eu/eurostat/statistics-explained/index.php?title=File:Number_of_(non-EU)_asylum_applicants_in_the_EU_and_EFTA_Member_States,_by_age_distribution,_2014_($^{1}$)_YB15_III.png.

Eurostat 2018. "Asylum applicants 2017". 29 June. Available at: https://ec.europa.eu/eurostat/news/themes-in-the-spotlight/asylum2017.

Eurostat 2019a. "Intra-corporate transferee permits issued, renewed and withdrawn by type of permit, length of validity and citizenship". 28 February. Available at: http://appsso.eurostat.ec.europa.eu/nui/show.do?dataset=migr_resict1_1&lang=en.

Eurostat 2019b. "Residence permits – statistics on first permits issued during the year". October. Available at: https://ec.europa.eu/eurostat/statistics-explained/index.php?title=Residence_permits_–_statistics_on_first_permits_issued_during_the_year#First_residence_permits_by_reason.

Eurostat 2019c. "Employment statistics". May. Available at: https://ec.europa.eu/eurostat/statistics-explained/index.php/Employment_statistics.

Eurostat 2019d. "Migration and migrant population statistics". March. Available at: https://ec.europa.eu/eurostat/statistics-explained/index.php/Migration_and_migrant_population_statistics.

Eurostat n.d.–a. "Population on 1 January by sex, age and country of birth". Available at: http://ec.europa.eu/eurostat/web/products-datasets/-/migr_pop3ctb.

Eurostat n.d.–b. "EU Blue Cards by type of decision, occupation and citizenship". Available at: https://ec.europa.eu/eurostat/web/asylum-and-managed-migration/data/database.

Evans, W. & D. Fitzgerald 2017. "The economic and social outcomes of refugees in the United States: evidence from the ACS", Working Paper 23498. Cambridge, MA: National Bureau of Economic Research.

Facchini, G. & A. Mayda 2009. "Does the welfare state affect individual attitudes toward immigrants? Evidence across countries". *Review of Economics and Statistics* 91 (2): 295–314.

Fawley, B. & L. Juvenal 2011. "Why health care matters and the current debt does not". *Regional Economist*, October: 4–5.

Fazi, T. 2016. "Renzi's 'anti-austerity' charade and the truth about Italy's deficit". Social Europe, 6 October.

Fazi, T. 2019. "Thomas Fazi – lessons from the Italian budget crisis". Brave New Europe, 31 January.

Fehr, H., S. Jokisch & L. Kotlikoff 2004. "The role of immigration in dealing with the developed world's demographic transition", Working Paper 10512. Cambridge, MA: National Bureau of Economic Research.

Feldman, G. 2012. *The Migration Apparatus: Security, Labour, and Policymaking in the European Union*. Stanford, CA: Stanford University Press.

*Financial Times* 2015. "War victims feel warmth of 'Generation Merkel'". 10 September.

*Financial Times* 2016a. "Surging Swedish economy raises questions over negative rates". 29 February.

*Financial Times* 2016b. "Apparent affluence distracts from underlying strains and weaknesses". 3 November.

*Financial Times* 2017. "German growth boosts Merkel poll hopes". 13 January.

*Financial Times* 2018a. "Polish companies target Ukrainian workers as consumers: telecoms, banking and property groups take advantage of growing number of immigrants". 10 July.

*Financial Times* 2018b. "Polish boundaries challenged by cricket-playing Indians". 15 September.

*Financial Times* 2018c. "Romania minister calls for curbs on EU free movement". 28 November.

*Financial Times* 2018d. "Italy's ambitious budget proposals in charts". 17 October.

*Financial Times* 2018e. "Germany's push for foreign workers clashes with anxiety over immigration". 28 August.

*Financial Times* 2019a. "Croatia warns on EU population drop". 31 January.

*Financial Times* 2019b. "Mittelstand feels strain from ageing workforce". 7 January.

*Financial Times* 2019c. "Italy birth rate falls to lowest since at least 1861". 4 July.

*Financial Times* 2020a. "Greek guards fire tear gas as migrants mass on Turkish border". 2 March.

*Financial Times* 2020b. "Resurgent Marine Le Pen revels in Macron's woes". 30 January.

*Financial Times* 2020c. "Austria renews illegal immigration battle". 14 January.

*Financial Times* 2020d. "Germany performs U-turn on seasonal farmworker ban". 3 April.

Finseraas, H. 2008. "Immigration and preferences for redistribution: an empirical analysis of European survey data". *Comparative European Politics* 6 (3): 407–31.

*Fokus* 2018. "Samarbetet som blev en twitterfejd". 26 May. Available at: www. fokus.se/2018/05/samarbetet-som-blev-en-twitterfejd.

Folkerts-Landau, D. 2016. "Immigration: making work pay". *Konzept* 8: 24–35.

Fondapol 2017. "What next for our democracy: an international survey by the Foundation Pour l'Innovation Politique". Available at: www.fondapol.org/ en/whatnextfordemocracy.

Frank Hansen, M., M. Schultz-Nielsen & T. Tranæs 2017. "The fiscal impact of immigration to welfare states of the Scandinavian type". *Journal of Population Economics* 30: 925–52.

Frattini, F. 2007. "Enhanced mobility, vigorous integration strategy and zero tolerance on illegal employment", Speech 07/526, High-Level Conference on Legal Immigration, Lisbon, 13 September.

Freeman, G. 1986. "Migration and the political economy of the welfare state". *Annals of the American Academy of Political and Social Science* 485: 51–63.

Freeman, G. 2011. "Comparative analysis of immigration politics: a retrospective". *American Behavioral Scientist* 55 (12): 1541–60.

Friðriksdóttir, B. 2017. *What Happened to Equality? The Construction of the Right to Equal Treatment of Third-Country Nationals in European Union Law on Labour Migration.* Leiden: Brill.

Fudge, J. & P. Herzfeld Olsson 2014. "The EU Seasonal Workers Directive: when immigration controls meet labour rights". *European Journal of Migration and Law* 16: 439–66.

Gál, Z. 2019. "Fiscal consequences of the refugee crisis". *International Migration* 57 (5): 341–54.

Garand, J., P. Xu & B. Davis 2015. "Immigration attitudes and support for the welfare state in the American mass public". *American Journal of Political Science* 61 (1): 146–62.

Geddes, A. 2000. "Lobbying for migrant inclusion in the European Union". *Journal of European Public Policy* 7 (4): 632–49.

Gesthuizen M., T. van der Meer & P. Scheepers 2009. "Ethnic diversity and social capital in Europe: tests of Putnam's thesis in European countries". *Scandinavian Political Studies* 32 (2): 121–42.

Giertz, A. & H. Jönsson 2018. "Har invandrare som arbetar inom äldreomsorgen en besvärligare arbetssituation än sina svenskfödda kollegor?". *Socialvetenskaplig tidskrift* 1: 1–22.

Godin, R. 2015. "Why Angela Merkel is so generous to the refugees". Euractiv, 9 September.

Goldirova, R. 2007a. "EU proposes 'blue card' to attract skilled immigrants". EUobserver, 23 October.

Goldirova, R. 2007b. "'Blue card' to attract top talent from outside EU". EUobserver, 27 July.

Goodhart, D. 2004. "Too diverse?". *Prospect* 95: 30–7.

Greenspan, A. 1997. "Remarks by Chairman Alan Greenspan, at the Catholic University Leuven". Federal Reserve Board, 14 January. Available at: www.federalreserve.gov/boarddocs/speeches/1997/19970114.htm.

Grütters, C. & T. Strik (eds) 2013. *The Blue Card Directive: Central Themes, Problem Issues, and Implementation in Selected Member States.* Oisterwijk: Wolf Legal Publishers.

*Guardian* 2015a. "Poles don't want immigrants: they don't understand them, don't like them". 2 July.

*Guardian* 2015b. "Europe needs many more babies to avert a population disaster". 23 August.

*Guardian* 2018a. "What is the current state of the migration crisis in Europe?". 21 November.

*Guardian* 2018b. "Sweden election: political uncertainty looms after deadlock". 10 September.

Guild, E. *et al.* 2015. "Enhancing the common European asylum system and alternative to Dublin", Paper in Liberty and Security in Europe 83. Brussels: Centre for European Policy Studies.

Guiraudon, V. 1998. "Citizenship rights for non-citizens: France, Germany, and the Netherlands". In *Challenge to the Nation-State: Immigration in Western Europe and the United States,* C. Joppke (ed.), 272–318. Oxford: Oxford University Press.

Guiraudon, V. 2000. "The Marshallian triptych reordered: the role of courts and bureaucracies in furthering migrants' social rights". In *Immigration and Welfare: Challenging the Borders of the Welfare State,* M. Bommes & A. Geddes (eds), 72–89. London: Routledge.

Gümüs, Y. 2010. "EU Blue Card scheme: the right step in the right direction?". *European Journal of Migration and Law* 12: 435–53.

Gustafsson, A., L. Hultkrantz & P. Österholm 2020. "De stora kostnaderna för äldre ligger framför oss". *Svenska Dagbladet,* 23 January.

Hailbronner, K. 1994. "Asylum law reform in the German constitution". *American University International Law Review* 9 (4): 159–79.

Hailbronner, K. 1998. "European immigration and asylum law under the Amsterdam Treaty". *Common Market Law Review* 35 (5): 1047–67.

Hall, R. 2019. "EU 'letting refugees die' at sea after cancelling Mediterranean rescue missions". *Independent*, 28 March.

*Handelsblatt* 2016. "Asylum costs: Germany's budgetary burden". 19 February.

Hansen, P. & S. Hager 2012. *The Politics of European Citizenship: Deepening Contradictions in Social Rights and Migration Policy*. New York, NY: Berghahn.

Hansen, P. & S. Jonsson 2011. "Demographic colonialism: EU–African migration management and the legacy of Eurafrica". *Globalizations* 8 (3): 261–76.

Hansen, P. & S. Jonsson 2014. *Eurafrica: The Untold History of European Integration and Colonialism*. London: Bloomsbury.

Hanson, G. 2010. "The governance of migration policy". *Journal of Human Development and Capabilities* 11 (2): 185–207.

Hashimzade, N., G. Myles & J. Black 2017. *A Dictionary of Economics*, 5th edn. Oxford: Oxford University Press.

Holler, J. & P. Schuster 2018. "Long-run fiscal consequences of refugee migration: the case of Austria", staff paper. Vienna: Fiskalrat [Austrian Fiscal Advisory Council].

Horn, H. 2016. "Can the welfare state survive the refugee crisis?". *The Atlantic*, 18 February.

Human Rights Watch 2008. "EU–Libya relations: human rights conditions required". 3 January.

Human Rights Watch 2019. "No escape from hell: EU policies contribute to abuse of migrants in Libya". 21 January.

IMF 2016. "The refugee surge in Europe: economic challenges", Staff Discussion Note 16/02. Washington, DC: IMF.

*Independent* 2004. "Sharp fall in number of asylum seekers". 24 February.

*Independent* 2015. "Refugee crisis: the map that shows why some European countries love asylum seekers". 16 September.

*Independent* 2018. "Growing number of refugees and asylum seekers falling into poverty in Britain". 5 February.

*International Herald Tribune* 1998a. "Bonn lists steps to close Europe's borders to Kurds". 6 January.

*International Herald Tribune* 1998b. "Bonn hails 8-nation European pact to slow flood of Kurdish refugees". 10–11 January.

International Refugee Organization 1951. *Migration from Europe 1946–1951*. Geneva: International Refugee Organization.

IOM 2018. "Mediterranean migrant arrivals reached 171,635 in 2017; deaths reach 3,116". 5 January. Available at: www.iom.int/news/mediterranean-migrant-arrivals-reached-171635-2017-deaths-reach-3116.

IOM 2019. "Mediterranean migrant arrivals reach 72,263 in 2019; deaths reach 1,041". 4 October. Available at: www.iom.int/news/mediterranean-migrant-arrivals-reach-72263-2019-deaths-reach-1041.

*Irish Times* 2016. "Wolfgang Schäuble warns German budget surplus must go to refugees". 25 February.

Jarl, S. 2020. "Välfärden kräver mer än en budget i balans". *Norköpings Tidningar*, 14 February.

Jonjić, T. & G. Mavrodi 2012. "Immigration in the EU: policies and politics in times of crisis 2007–2012", Report 2012/5. Florence: European Union Democracy Observatory, Robert Schuman Centre for Advanced Studies.

Joppke, C. 1998. "Immigration challenges the nation-state". In *Challenge to the Nation-State: Immigration in Western Europe and the United States*, C. Joppke (ed.), 5–45. Oxford: Oxford University Press.

Joppke, C. 1999. *Immigration and the Nation-State: The United States, Germany, and Great Britain*. Oxford: Oxford University Press.

Juncker, J.-C. 2016. *State of the Union 2016*. Luxembourg: Publications Office of the European Union. Available at: https://ec.europa.eu/priorities/state-union-2016_en.

Kaczmarczyk, P. 2015. "Burden or relief? Fiscal impacts of recent Ukrainian migration to Poland", Discussion Paper 8779. Bonn: Forschungsinstitut zur Zukunft der Arbeit [Institute of Labor Economics]. Available at: http://ftp.iza.org/dp8779.pdf.

Kancs, d'A. & P. Lecca 2017. "Long-term social, economic and fiscal effects of immigration into the EU: the role of integration policy", JRC Working Paper in Economics and Finance 4. Luxembourg: Publications Office of the European Union.

Kelton, S. 2018. "Republicans want to make entitlements the next caravan". Bloomberg, 19 November.

Kelton, S. 2020. *The Deficit Myth: Modern Monetary Theory and How to Build a Better Economy*. London: John Murray.

Kelton, S., A. Bernal & G. Carlock 2018. "We can pay for a Green New Deal". HuffPost, 30 November.

Kerr, S. & W. Kerr 2011. "Economic impacts of immigration: a survey", Working Paper 16736. Cambridge, MA: National Bureau of Economic Research.

Kolbe, M. & E. Kayran 2019. "The limits of skill selective immigration policies: welfare states and the commodification of labour migrants". *Journal of European Social Policy* 29 (4): 478–97.

Koopmans, R. 2010. "Trade-offs between equality and difference: immigrant integration, multiculturalism and the welfare state in cross-national perspective." *Journal of Ethnic and Migration Studies* 36 (1): 1–26.

Koser, K. 2015. "A migration agenda for the private sector". Project Syndicate, 27 October.

Kostakopoulou, T., D. Acosta Arcarazo & T. Munk 2014. "EU migration law: the opportunities and challenges ahead". In *EU Security and Justice*

*Law: After Lisbon and Stockholm*, T. Kostakopoulou, D. Acosta Arcarazo & T. Munk (eds), 129–45. Oxford: Hart Publishing.

Kubosova, L. 2006. "EU has limits in respecting Muslim traditions, says Frattini". EUobserver, 9 October.

Kulin, J., M. Eger & M. Hjerm 2016. "Immigration or welfare? The progressive's dilemma revisited". *Socius* 2: 1–15.

Kymlicka, W. 2015. "Solidarity in diverse societies: beyond neoliberal multiculturalism and welfare chauvinism". *Comparative Migration Studies* 3 (4): article 17.

La Strada International *et al.* 2011. "EU Seasonal Migrant Workers' Directive: full respect of equal treatment necessary", joint NGO statement. Amsterdam: La Strada International. Available at: http://lastradainternational.org/lsidocs/joint%20ngo%20statement.pdf.

Lamers, K. & W. Schäuble 2014. "More integration is still the right goal for Europe". *Financial Times*, 31 August.

Larsson, E. 2013. "'Om du har ett jobb borde du få komma in i EU'" [interview with Cecilia Malmström]. *Arbetet*, 15 March.

Laxå kommun 2019a. "Budget 2019: Verksamhetsplan 2019–2022". Laxå: Laxå kommun.

Laxå kommun 2019b. "Överskott i Laxå kommun" ["Surplus in Laxå Municipality"] [document received by the municipality].

Laxå kommun 2019c. "Utredning: Plan för flyktingmottagandet, integration och arbetsmarknad 2019–2022". Laxå: Laxå kommun.

Lazarowicz, A. 2014. "A success for the EU and seasonal workers' rights without reinventing the wheel", policy brief. Brussels: European Policy Centre.

Lerner, A. 1946. *The Economics of Control: Principles of Welfare Economics*. New York, NY: Macmillan.

Lévy-Vroelant, C. 2016. "The 'immigrant' through the prism of hospitality 'à la française'". In *Migration and Integration: New Models for Mobility and Coexistence*, R. Hsu & C. Reinprecht (eds), 215–28. Vienna: Vienna University Press.

Leyen, U. von der 2020. "Remarks by President von der Leyen at the joint press conference […]". European Commission, 3 March. Available at: https://ec.europa.eu/commission/presscorner/detail/en/statement_20_380.

Liebig, T. & J. Mo 2013. "The fiscal impact of immigration in OECD countries". In *International Migration Outlook 2013*, 125–90. Paris: OECD Publishing.

Liebsch, B. 2015. "Flüchtlingshilfe: Unser Land überrascht sich selbst". Zeit Online, 18 September.

Lietzmann, J. & B. Böök 2019. "Labour mobility and recognition in the regulated professions: annex C1 – Germany: case study", study for the Committee on Employment and Social Affairs, Policy Department for

Economic, Scientific and Quality of Life Policies. Luxembourg: European Parliament.

Lindsay, F. 2018. "Ukrainian immigrants give the Polish government an out on refugees". Forbes, 19 September.

Los Angeles Times 2015. "For Germany, refugees are a demographic blessing as well as a burden". 10 September.

Lunchekot 2020. Swedish Radio, 16 April.

Lutz, H. 2018. "Care migration: the connectivity between care chains, care circulation and transnational social inequality". Current Sociology 66 (4): 577–89.

McLeay, M., A. Radia & R. Thomas 2014. "Money creation in the modern economy". Quarterly Bulletin Q1: 14–27.

Malmström, C. 2010. "Malmström proposes EU coordination of labour migration". 13 July. Available at: http://ec.europa.eu/commission_2010-2014/malmstrom/news/archives_2010_en.htm.

Malmström, C. 2011. "Hope for democracy in Libya". Blog, 22 August. Available at: https://gadaffi3.rssing.com/chan-14400043/latest-article1.php.

Malmström, C. 2012. "Statement by EU Commissioner Cecilia Malmström on International Migrants Day", MEMO/12/1003. Brussels: European Commission.

Manthei, G. & B. Raffelhüschen 2018. "Migration and long-term fiscal sustainability in welfare Europe: a case study". FinanzArchiv 74: 446–61.

Martin, M. 2018. "Facing far-right challenge, minister says Islam 'doesn't belong' to Germany". Reuters, 16 March.

Maurice, E. 2018. "Migration is 'mother of all problems', says German interior minister". EUobserver, 6 September.

Mayblin, L. 2020. Impoverishment and Asylum: Social Policy as Slow Violence. Abingdon: Routledge.

Menz, G. 2009. The Political Economy of Managed Migration: Nonstate Actors, Europeanization, and the Politics of Designing Migration Policies. Oxford: Oxford University Press.

Middle East Online 2007. "Billstrom interviewed on Iraq refugees in Sweden". 26 September.

Mikl-Leitner, J. et al. 2013. Letter to Mr Alan Shatter, president of the European Council for Justice and Home Affairs. 15 April. Available at: http://docs.dpaq.de/3604-130415_letter_to_presidency_final_1_2.pdf.

Milanovic, B. 2016a. Global Inequality: A New Approach for the Age of Globalization. Cambridge, MA: Harvard University Press.

Milanovic, B. 2016b. "There is a trade-off between citizenship and migration". Financial Times, 20 April.

Milanovic, B. 2019. "Dutiful dirges of Davos". Brave New Europe, 24 January.

Milanovic, B. 2020. "Trump as the ultimate triumph of neoliberalism". Brave New Europe, 9 April.

Milne, S. 2008. "The persecution of Gypsies is now the shame of Europe". *Guardian*, 10 July.

Ministry of Finance 2016. "The direction of fiscal policy – September 2016". 20 September. Available at: www.government.se/articles/2016/09/the-direction-of-fiscal-policy–september.

Mitchell, W. 2020. "The coronavirus will redefine what currency-issuing governments can do – finally". 16 March. Available at: http://bilbo.economicoutlook.net/blog/?p=44507.

Mitchell, W. & T. Fazi 2017. *Reclaiming the State: A Progressive Vision of Sovereignty for a Post-Neoliberal World*. London: Pluto Press.

Mitchell, W., R. Wray & M. Watts 2019. *Macroeconomics: A Modern Money Theory Approach*. London: Red Globe Press.

Monar, J. 2013. "Justice and home affairs". *Journal of Common Market Studies* 51 (S1): 124–38.

Moses, J. 2017. *Eurobondage: The Political Costs of European Monetary Union*. Colchester: ECPR Press.

Mosler, W. 2010. *The 7 Deadly Innocent Frauds of Economic Policy*. US Virgin Islands: Valence Economics.

Münz, R. & R. Ulrich 1997. "Changing patterns of German immigration, 1945–1994". In *Migration Past, Migration Future: Germany and the United States*, K. Bade & M. Weiner (eds), 65–119. New York, NY: Berghahn.

Münz, R. *et al.* 2006. "The costs and benefits of European immigration", Policy Report 3. Hamburg: Hamburg Institute of International Economics.

Nagle, A. 2018. "The left case against open borders". *American Affairs* 2 (4): 17–30.

Nannestad, P. 2007. "Immigration and welfare states: a survey of 15 years of research". *European Journal of Political Economy* 23 (2): 512–32.

National Research Council 1997. *The New Americans: Economic, Demographic, and Fiscal Effects of Immigration*. Washington, DC: National Academies Press.

Nauman, E. & L. Stoetzer 2018. "Immigration and support for redistribution: survey experiments in three European countries". *Western European Politics* 41 (1): 80–101.

Neo, J. 2015. "Riots and rights: law and exclusion in Singapore's migrant worker regime". *Asian Journal of Law and Society* 2 (1): 137–68.

Neuman, G. 1993. "Buffer zones against refugees: Dublin, Schengen, and the German Asylum Amendment". *Virginia Journal of International Law* 33: 503–26.

*New York Times* 1992. "Yugoslav refugee crisis: Europe's worst since 40's". 24 July.

*New York Times* 2007. "Iraqi refugees find sanctuary, and fellow Iraqis, in Sweden". 16 January.

*New York Times* 2014. "Court lets EU nations curb immigrant welfare". 11 November.

*New York Times* 2017. "In Denmark, passage of rules on immigration called for cake". 15 March.

Nielsen, N. 2020. "Migrants: EU commission not fit to guard treaties". EUobserver, 6 March.

NIER 2015. *The Swedish Economy: December 2015*. Stockholm: NIER.

NIER 2016. *The Swedish Economy: August 2016*. Stockholm: NIER.

Nilsson, A. & Ö. Nyström 2016. *Flyktingkrisen och den svenska modellen* [*The Refugee Crisis and the Swedish Model*]. Lund: Celanders förlag.

Nilsson, K. 2018. "Trendbrott: Fler nyanlända i arbete". *Arbetet*, 18 June.

Nyman, P. & R. Ahlskog 2018. "Fiscal effects of intra-EEA migration", REMINDER Working Paper. Uppsala: Uppsala University. Available at: www.reminder-project.eu/wp-content/uploads/2018/03/March-2018-FINAL-Deliverable-4.1_with-cover.pdf.

OECD 2013. *OECD International Migration Outlook 2013*. Paris: OECD Publishing.

OECD 2014. "Is migration good for the economy?", Migration Policy Debate 2. Paris: OECD Publishing.

OECD 2015a. "How will the refugee surge affect the European economy?", Migration Policy Debate 8. Paris: OECD Publishing.

OECD 2015b. *OECD Economic Outlook: November*. Paris: OECD Publishing.

OECD 2016a. *OECD Economic Outlook: June*. Paris: OECD Publishing.

OECD 2016b. *OECD Economic Outlook: November*. Paris: OECD Publishing.

OECD 2017a. *OECD Economic Surveys: Sweden: February 2017*. Paris: OECD Publishing.

OECD 2017b. *OECD Economic Outlook: June*. Paris: OECD Publishing.

OECD 2017c. *Health at a Glance 2017: OECD Indicators*. Paris: OECD Publishing.

OECD 2018a. *International Migration Outlook 2018*. Paris: OECD Publishing.

OECD 2018b. "Migration: using migration to meet skills shortages", Germany policy brief. Paris: OECD Publishing.

OECD 2019. *Recent Trends in International Migration of Doctors, Nurses, and Medical Students*. Paris: OECD Publishing.

OECD n.d. "Hospital beds" [indicator]. Available at: doi: 10.1787/0191328e-en.

*Östgöta Correspondenten* 2015. "Utan invandring rasar äldreomsorgen". 3 January.

Pascouau, Y. & S. McLoughlin 2012. "EU Single Permit Directive: a small step forward in EU migration policy", policy brief. Brussels: European Policy Centre.

Paul, R. 2015. *The Political Economy of Border Drawing: Arranging Legality in European Labour Migration Policy*. New York, NY: Berghahn.

Pearce, N. 2004. "Diversity versus solidarity: a new progressive dilemma". *Renewal: A Journal of Labour Politics* 12 (3): 79–87.

Peers, S. 2009. "Legislative update: EC immigration and asylum law attracting and deterring labour migration: the Blue Card and Employer Sanctions Directives". *European Journal of Migration and Law* 11: 387–426.

Peers, S. 2016. "The final EU/Turkey refugee deal: a legal assessment". EU Law Analysis, 18 March. Available at: http://eulawanalysis.blogspot.com/2016/03/the-final-euturkey-refugee-deal-legal.html.

Peers, S. *et al.* 2012a. "Single permits and workers' rights". In *EU Immigration and Asylum Law (Text and Commentary)*, vol. 2, *EU Immigration Law*, 2nd rev. edn, S. Peers *et al.* (eds), 223–45. Leiden: Martinus Nijhoff.

Peers, S. *et al.* 2012b. "Intra-corporate transferees". In *EU Immigration and Asylum Law (Text and Commentary)*, vol. 2, *EU Immigration Law*, 2nd rev. edn, S. Peers *et al.* (eds), 95–128. Leiden: Martinus Nijhoff.

Pillai, P. 2019. "The EU and migrant detention in Libya: complicity under the microscope finally?". Opinio Juris, 5 July. Available at: http://opiniojuris.org/2019/07/05/the-eu-and-migrant-detention-in-libya-complicity-under-the-microscope-finally.

Poland In 2018. "Poland needs immigrants for its labor market: PM Morawiecki". 2 July. Available at: https://polandin.com/37906502/poland-needs-immigrants-for-its-labor-market-pm-morawiecki.

Polanyi, K. 2001 [1944]. *The Great Transformation: The Political and Economic Origins of Our Time*. Boston: Beacon Press.

Preston, I. 2014. "The effect of immigration on public finances". *Economic Journal* 124: 569–92.

Putnam, R. 2007. "*E pluribus unum*: diversity and community in the twenty-first century: the 2006 Johan Skytte Prize Lecture". *Scandinavian Political Studies* 30 (2): 137–74.

Rachman, G. 2018. "Migration now drives Western politics". *Financial Times*, 18 May.

Ratna, N. 2016. "Are migrants good for the host country's economy?". In *Routledge Handbook of Immigration and Refugee Studies*, A. Triandafyllidou (ed.), 75–81. Abingdon: Routledge.

Razin, A. & E. Sadka 2005. *The Decline of the Welfare State: Demography and Globalization*. Cambridge, MA: MIT Press.

Reding, V. 2013. "Main message: Trieste Citizens' Dialogue", Speech 13/706, 16 September. Brussels: European Commission.

Refugees International 2017. "'Hell on Earth': Abuses against Refugees and Migrants Trying to Reach Europe from Libya", field report. Washington, DC: Refugees International.

Regeringskansliet 2015. "Tal av statsminister Stefan Löfven vid manifestationen för flyktingar". 6 September.

Regeringskansliet 2020. Pressträff med statsministern. 17 April.

Reuters 2015a. "France's Sarkozy disowns ally over 'white race' comments". 30 September.

Reuters 2015b. "Angela Merkel wants to 'drastically reduce' refugee arrivals in Germany". 14 December.

Reuters 2015c. "Ballooning refugee costs threaten Germany's cherished budget goals". 17 September.

Reuters 2016a. "Ukrainian ambassador rejects Polish premier's 'million refugees' claim". 20 January.

Reuters 2016b. "Spending on refugees helps support German fourth quarter growth". 23 February.

Reuters 2017. "Italy's Renzi urges end to 'do gooder' mentality on migrant influx". 7 July.

Reuters 2018. "More refugees find jobs in Germany, integration going 'pretty well'". 21 August.

Reuters 2020. "Swedish c. bank urges banks to supply credit to companies". 13 March.

Riding, A. 1991. "Immigrants unrest alarming French". *New York Times*, 23 June.

Riksbank 2015. *Monetary Policy Report: September 2015*. Stockholm: Riksbank.

Riksbank 2016a. *Monetary Policy Report: April 2016*. Stockholm: Riksbank.

Riksbank 2016b. *Monetary Policy Report: September 2016*. Stockholm: Riksbank.

Riksbank 2019. *Financial Stability Report 2019: 1*. Stockholm: Riksbank.

Riksbank 2020. "Riksbank lends up to SEK 500 billion to safeguard credit supply", press release. 13 March.

Roberts, H. 2020. "Italy's coronavirus farmworker shortage fuels debate on illegal migration". *Politico*, 15 April.

Romer, D. 2012. *Advanced Macroeconomics*, 4th edn. New York, NY: McGraw-Hill/Irwin.

Roodenburg, H., R. Euwals & H. ter Rele 2003. *Immigration and the Dutch Economy*. The Hague: Centraal Planbureau [Netherlands Bureau for Economic Policy Analysis].

Rowthorn, R. 2008. "The fiscal impact of immigration on the advanced economies". *Oxford Review of Economic Policy* 24 (3): 560–80.

Rowthorn, R. 2015. *The Costs and Benefits of Large-Scale Immigration: Exploring the Economic and Demographic Consequences for the UK*. London: Civitas.

Ruhs, M. 2013. *The Price of Rights: Regulating International Labour Migration*. Princeton, NJ: Princeton University Press.

Ruhs, M. 2015. "Is unrestricted immigration compatible with inclusive welfare states? The (un)sustainability of EU exceptionalism", Working Paper 125. Oxford: Centre on Migration, Policy and Society, University of Oxford.

Ruhs, M. 2016. "Is unrestricted immigration compatible with inclusive welfare states? National institutions, citizenship norms and the politics of free movement in the European Union". Paper presented at the 23rd International Conference of Europeanists, Philadelphia, 16 April. Available at: https://papers.ssrn.com/sol3/papers.cfm?abstractid=2625486.

Ruhs, M. & P. Martin 2008. "Numbers vs rights: trade-offs and guest worker programs". *International Migration Review* 42 (1): 249–65.

Ruist, J. 2015. "The fiscal cost of refugee immigration: the example of Sweden". *Population and Development Review* 41 (4): 567–81.

Ruist, J. 2018. "Tid för integration: en ESO-rapport om flyktingars bakgrund och arbetsmarknadsetablering", rapport till expertgruppen för studier i offentlig ekonomi 2018:3. Stockholm: Finansdepartementet, Regeringskansliet.

Sainsbury, D. 2012. *Welfare States and Immigration Rights: The Politics of Inclusion and Exclusion*. Oxford: Oxford University Press.

Samers, M. 2010. "Strange castle walls and courtyards: explaining the political economy of undocumented immigration and undeclared employment". In *Labour Migration in Europe*, G. Menz & A. Caviedes (eds), 209–31. Basingstoke: Palgrave Macmillan.

Santo Tomas, P. 2005. "Filipinos working overseas: opportunity and challenge". In *World Migration 2005: Costs and Benefits of International Migration*, I. Omelaniuk (ed.), 239–50. Geneva: International Organization for Migration.

Schierup, C.-U., P. Hansen & S. Castles 2006. *Migration, Citizenship, and the European Welfare State: A European Dilemma*. Oxford: Oxford University Press.

Schierup, C.-U. *et al.* (eds) 2015. *Migration, Precarity, and Global Governance: Challenges and Opportunities for Labour*. Oxford: Oxford University Press.

Scocco, S. 2019. *Och några antar jag är OK!* [*And Some I Guess Are OK!*]. Stockholm: Atlas.

SFPC 2015. *Swedish Fiscal Policy: Fiscal Policy Council Report 2015*. Stockholm: SFPC.

SFPC 2016. *Swedish Fiscal Policy: Fiscal Policy Council Report 2016*. Stockholm: SFPC.

SFPC 2017. *Swedish Fiscal Policy: Fiscal Policy Council Report 2017*. Stockholm: SFPC.

SFPC 2018. *Swedish Fiscal Policy: Fiscal Policy Council Report 2018*. Stockholm: SFPC.

Sheard, P. 2013. "Repeat after me: banks cannot and do not 'lend out reserves'". Standard and Poor's RatingsDirect, 13 August. Available at: www.hks.harvard.edu/sites/default/files/centers/mrcbg/programs/senior.fellows/2019–20%20fellows/BanksCannotLendOutReservesAug2013_%20(002).pdf.

Siyam, A. & M. Dal Poz (eds) 2014. *Migration of Health Workers: WHO Code of Practice and the Global Economic Crisis*. Geneva: World Health Organization.

Skodo, A. 2018. "Sweden: by turns welcoming and restrictive in its immigration policy". Migration Policy Institute, 6 December. Available at: www.migrationpolicy.org/article/sweden-turns-welcoming-and-restrictive-its-immigration-policy.

Skolverket 2019. "Lärarprognos 2019". 5 December. Available at: www.skolverket.se/getFile?file=5394.

SKR 2017. "Ekonomirapporten, maj 2017". Stockholm: SKR.

SKR 2018. *Sveriges viktigaste jobb finns i välfärden: Rekryteringsrapport 2018* [*Sweden's Most Important Jobs are in Welfare: Recruitment Report 2018*]. Stockholm: SKR.

SKR 2019. "Ekonomirapporten, oktober 2019". Stockholm: SKR.

Socialstyrelsen 2019. *Vård och omsorg om äldre: Lägesrapport 2019* [*Care and Nursing for the Elderly: Status Report 2019*]. Stockholm: Socialstyrelsen. Available at: www.socialstyrelsen.se/globalassets/sharepoint-dokument/artikelkatalog/ovrigt/2019-3-18.pdf.

*Södermanlands Nyheter* 2015. "Utan invandrare kollapsar vården". 24 April.

Soroka, S. *et al.* 2016. "Migration and welfare state spending". *European Political Science Review* 8 (2): 173–94.

Spahn, J. 2016. "Germany needs cool heads and a swift cut in migrant numbers". *Financial Times*, 17 February.

SPES 2018. *Arbetsmarknadsutsikterna hösten 2018: Prognos för arbetsmarknaden 2018–2020* [*Labour Market Outlook Autumn 2018: Forecast for the Labour Market 2018–2020*]. Stockholm: SPES.

Spiegel Online 2007. "Iraqi refugees in Sweden: 'anything is better than Baghdad'". 18 April.

Spiegel Online 2018. "Arbeitgeberpräsident Ingo Kramer: 'Die Integration der Flüchtlinge läuft besser als erwartet'". 14 December.

Spies, D. 2018. *Immigration and Welfare State Retrenchment: Why the US Experience Is Not Reflected in Western Europe*. Oxford: Oxford University Press.

Statistics Sweden 2016. *Sveriges ekonomi: Statistiskt perspektiv*, 1.

Statistics Sweden 2019a. "Pizza makers have largest share of foreign born persons". 7 March. Available at: www.scb.se/en/finding-statistics/statistics-by-subject-area/labour-market/employment-and-working-hours/the-swedish-occupational-register-with-statistics/pong/statistical-news/the-swedish-occupational-register.

Statistics Sweden 2019b. "Summary of population statistics 1960–2018". 21 March. Available at: www.scb.se/en/finding-statistics/statistics-by-subject-area/population/population-composition/population-statistics/pong/tables-and-graphs/yearly-statistics–the-whole-country/summary-of-population-statistics.

Statistics Sweden 2019c. "Utrikes födda i Sverige". 2 February. Available at: www.scb.se/hitta-statistik/sverige-i-siffror/manniskorna-i-sverige/utrikes-fodda.

Statistics Sweden 2019d. "Asylsökande i Sverige". 22 March. Available at: www.scb.se/hitta-statistik/sverige-i-siffror/manniskorna-i-sverige/asylsokande-i-sverige.

Statistics Sweden 2020. "Yrkesregistret med yrkesstatistik 2018" ["Swedish occupational register with statistics 2018"]. March. Available at: www.scb.se/contentassets/b49d7efc2653457f8179f18461d2bf38/am0208_2018a01_sm_am33sm2001.pdf.

Stichnoth, H. & K. Van der Straeten 2013. "Ethnic diversity, public spending, and individual support for the welfare state: a review of the empirical literature". *Journal of Economic Surveys* 27 (2): 364–89.

Storesletten, K. 2000. "Sustaining fiscal policy through immigration". *Journal of Political Economy* 108 (2): 300–23.

Storesletten, K. 2003. "Fiscal implications of immigration: a net present value calculation". *Scandinavian Journal of Economics* 105 (3): 487–506.

Streeck, W. 2018a. "Between charity and justice: remarks on the social construction of immigration policy in rich democracies". *Culture, Practice & Europeanization* 3 (2): 3–22.

Streeck, W. 2018b. "Germany: a renewed left as the imperative of political reason". Brave New Europe, 27 September.

Streeck, W. 2019. "Progressive regression: metamorphoses of European social policy". *New Left Review* 118: 117–39.

*Süddeutsche Zeitung* 2016. "'Rückkehr sollte der Normalfall sein'". 16/17 January.

*Svenska Dagbladet* 2013. "Hot om bidragsturism får fart igen". 3 June.

*Svenska Dagbladet* 2015a. "Underskottet i statens finanser växer". 23 November.

*Svenska Dagbladet* 2015b. "Andersson: Flyktingvågen skapar tillväxt". 2 November.

*Svenska Dagbladet* 2017a. "'Inte lånat en enda krona för flyktingkrisen'". 20 September.

*Svenska Dagbladet* 2017b. "Jämtland rundar lag för att ta emot fler flyktingar". 23 February.

*Svenska Dagbladet* 2018. "M: Invandringen är inte lönsam". 8 February.

*Svenska Dagbladet* 2020. "Tusentals respiratorer borta sedan 90-talet". 19 March.

Swedenmark, E. 2019. "Salvinis lag skruvar åt villkoren för migranter". *Norrköpings Tidningar*, 10 June.

Swedish government 2015. Budgetproposition för 2016. *Regeringens proposition* 2015/16: 1, 15 September.

Swedish government 2016. Budgetproposition för 2017. *Regeringens proposition* 2016/17: 1, 14 September.

Swedish government 2017a. Årsredovisning för staten 2016. *Regeringens skrivelse* 2016/17: 101, 6 April.

Swedish government 2017b. Budgetproposition för 2018. *Regeringens proposition* 2017/18: 1, 14 September.

Swedish government 2018a. Årsredovisning för staten 2016. *Regeringens skrivelse* 2017/18: 101, 11 April.

Swedish government 2018b. "Framtidens äldreomsorg – en nationell kvalitetsplan". *Regeringens skrivelse*, 2017/18: 280, 20 June.

Swedish government 2018c. "About the Swedish fiscal policy framework". Ministry of Finance, 11 July. Available at: www.government.se/ government-of-sweden/ministry-of-finance/central-government-budget/ the-fiscal-policy-framework.

Swedish government 2018d. "Nyanländas etablering går snabbare". Ministry of Employment, 31 January. Available at: www.regeringen.se/ pressmeddelanden/2018/01/nyanlandas-etablering-gar-snabbare.

Swedish government 2019. Budgetproposition för 2020. *Regeringens proposition* 2019/20: 1, 13 September.

Swedish Migration Agency 2020. "Statlig ersättning till kommuner" ["State compensation to municipalities"]. 5 February. Available at: www. migrationsverket.se/Andra-aktorer/Kommuner/Statlig-ersattning.html.

Swedish Radio 2014. "Borg: more refugees will affect the budget". 20 August. Available at: https://sverigesradio.se/sida/artikel.aspx?programid=2054&ar tikel=5942999.

Swedish Radio 2015a. "Regeringen lovar satsning på ensamkommande". 20 August. Available at: https://sverigesradio.se/sida/artikel.aspx?programid= 3993&artikel=6236652.

Swedish Radio 2015b. "Finansministern släpper krona för krona-principen". 12 December. Available at: https://sverigesradio.se/sida/artikel.aspx?progr amid=83&artikel=6324584.

Swedish Radio 2018. "Färre sökte asyl i Sverige 2017". 7 January.

Swedish Radio 2019a. Ekot, 12 August.

Swedish Radio 2019b. Ekot, 16 September.

Swedish Radio 2019c. Ekot, 3 September.

Swedish Television 2016. "Kommunernas vattennät är som tickande bomber". 21 November. Available at: www.svt.se/nyheter/lokalt/smaland/manga-kommuners-vattennat-ar-som-en-tidsinstalld-bomb.

Swedish Television 2020. Rapport. 2 April.

Taylor-Gooby, P. 2005. "Is the future American? Or, can left politics preserve European welfare states from erosion through 'racial diversity'?". *Journal of Social Policy* 34 (4): 661–72.

Tcherneva, P. 2018. "The job guarantee: design, jobs, and implementation", Working Paper 902. Annandale-on-Hudson, NY: Levy Economics Institute, Bard College.

Tcherneva, P. 2020. *The Case for a Job Guarantee*. Cambridge: Polity Press.

Therborn, G. 2018a. "Twilight of Swedish social democracy". *New Left Review* 113: 5–26.

Therborn, G. 2018b. *Kapitalet, överheten och alla vi andra: Klassamhället i Sverige – det rådande och det kommande* [*Capital, the Government and All the Rest of Us: Class Society in Sweden – Now and in the Future*]. Lund: Arkiv förlag.

Thielemann, E. & M. Hobolth 2016. "Trading numbers vs rights? Accounting for liberal and restrictive dynamics in the evolution of asylum and refugee policies". *Journal of Ethnic and Migration Studies* 42 (4): 643–64.

Thyssen, M. 2017. "Speech at the second European dialogue on skills and migration". Brussels, 23 May. European Commission.

Tidholm, P. 2016. "Resten av Sverige" (episode 3) [documentary broadcast on Swedish Television].

Tilles, D. 2018. "Poland's 'anti-immigration' government is overseeing one of Europe's biggest waves of immigration – but doesn't want to admit it". Notes from Poland, 3 October. Available at: https://notesfrompoland.com/2018/10/03/polands-anti-immigration-government-is-overseeing-one-of-europes-biggest-waves-of-immigration-but-doesnt-want-to-admit-it.

Tomkiw, L. 2015. "EU refugee crisis: how will European countries pay for the influx of thousands of people?". *International Business Times*, 23 September.

Triandafyllidou, A. (ed.) 2013. *Circular Migration between Europe and Its Neighbourhood: Choice or Necessity?* Oxford: Oxford University Press.

UNHCR 2018. "Forced displacement at record 68.5 million". 19 June. Available at: www.unhcr.org/news/stories/2018/6/5b222c494/forced-displacement-record-685-million.html.

UNHCR 2019. "Worldwide displacement tops 70 million, UN Refugee Chief urges greater solidarity in response". 19 June. Available at: www.unhcr.org/news/press/2019/6/5d03b22b4/worldwide-displacement-tops-70-million-un-refugee-chief-urges-greater-solidarity.html.

United Nations 2016. *International Migration Report 2015: Highlights*. New York, NY: United Nations.

United Nations 2017. *World Population Prospects: The 2017 Revision: Key Findings and Advance Tables*. New York, NY: United Nations.

United Nations 2018. "Desperate and dangerous: report on the human rights situation of migrants and refugees in Libya". Geneva: Office of the High Commissioner for Human Rights. Available at: www.ohchr.org/Documents/Countries/LY/LibyaMigrationReport.pdf.

Uslander, E. 2012. *Segregation and Mistrust: Diversity, Isolation, and Social Cohesion*. Cambridge: Cambridge University Press.

Van Oorschot, W. & W. Uunk 2007. "Welfare spending and the public's concern for immigrants: multilevel evidence for eighteen European countries". *Comparative Politics* 40 (1): 63–82.

Vargas-Silva, C. 2015. "The fiscal impact of immigrants: taxes and benefits". In *Handbook of the Economics of International Migration*, vol. 1B: *The Impact and Regional Studies*, B. Chiswick & P. Miller (eds), 845–76. Oxford: Elsevier.

Vargas-Silva, C. & M. Sumption 2019. "The fiscal impact of immigration in the UK", briefing. Oxford: Migration Observatory, University of Oxford. Available at: https://migrationobservatory.ox.ac.uk/wp-content/uploads/2016/04/Briefing-The-Fiscal-Impact-of-Immigration-in-the-UK-2.pdf.

*Värnamo Nyheter* 2017. "Statsbidrag räddar Gnosjö". 28 April.

Venturini, A. 2008. "Circular migration as an employment strategy for Mediterranean countries", CARIM Analytic and Synthetic Note 2008/39. Florence: European University Institute.

*Washington Post* 2007. "Iraqi refugees: our problem or Sweden's?". 18 June.

*Washington Post* 2015. "Denmark wants to seize jewelry and cash from refugees". 18 December.

*Washington Post* 2018. "Denmark plans to send some migrants to an island once reserved for experiments on animals". 5 December.

Willis, R. 1971. *Italy Chooses Europe*. New York, NY: Oxford University Press.

Wray, R. 2002. "State money". *International Journal of Political Economy* 32 (3): 23–40.

Wray, R. 2007. "Minsky's approach to employment policy and poverty: employer of last resort and the war on poverty", Working Paper 515. Annandale-on-Hudson, NY: Levy Economics Institute, Bard College.

Wray, R. 2015. *Modern Money Theory: A Primer on Macroeconomics for Sovereign Monetary Systems*, 2nd edn. New York, NY: Palgrave.

Wray, R. 2016. *Why Minsky Matters: An Introduction to the Work of a Maverick Economist*. Princeton, NJ: Princeton University Press.

Wray, R. 2019. "Alternative paths to modern money theory". *Real-World Economics Review* 89: 5–22.

Zahra, T. 2016. *The Great Departure: Mass Migration from Eastern Europe and the Making of the Free World*. New York, NY: W. W. Norton.

Zoeteweij-Turhan, M. 2017. "The Seasonal Workers Directive: '… but some are more equal than others'". *European Labour Law Journal* 8 (1): 28–44.

# Index

Page references in **bold** refer to tables.

ABC News 121
Afghanistan 137
Africa–Europe Alliance for Sustainable Investment and Jobs 90
Alemanno, A. 8
Alesina, A. 38
Alternative für Deutschland (AFD) 10, 16, 195
Amnesty International 129
Amsterdam Treaty 87–8, 118, 126, 136
Andersson, M. 27, 133, 141, 152, 173, 177–8
Åre 162–3, 165
*Atlantic, The* 24
Aufstehen movement 6
austerity 94, 140, 144–5, 151–3, 168, 185, 198–9
  eurozone 64, 67, 69, 174
Austria 9, 155, 199
  postwar Austria as "overcrowded" 82
Avranopoulos, D. 99

Bangladesh 128
Bank of England 172n1
Barker, A. 119
Bartley, J. 5
Bauböck, R. & P. Scholten 45–6, 49–50
Bearce, D. & A. Hart 40n1
Bellanova, T. 182
Bellis, M. de 129
Bengtsson, F. 128
Bernanke, B. 53, 172
Billström, T. 121

Blue Card, EU *see* EU external labour migration policy
Blunkett, D. 125
Blyth, M. 64n5
Boden 163
border control *see* security and migration control
Borjas, G. 37, 38, 42
Boräng, F. 40n1
Bosnian refugee crisis 124
"brain drain" 14
Brexit 189
British Office of Budget Responsibility 36
Bulgaria 13, 77

Carens, J. 46–7
Carrera, S. & R. Hernández i Sagrera 114
Castels, S. 85
CBC/Radio Canada 120–1
central and eastern European EU member states
  emigration 13–17
  migration policy 9–17
central banks
  "independence" of 57n2
Chirac, J. 9
Chou, M.-H. 99
Christian Social Union (CSU)
  support of Victor Orbán 10
circular migration 89–90, 106, 114, 122
Clancy, E. 174
Common European Asylum System (CEAS) *see* EU asylum policy

Council of Europe
  emigration policy for postwar Western
    Europe  81–2
  *Strasbourg Plan* (1952)  81
Covid-19  62, 69, 139, 171–4, 176,
    180–5, 198
  role of migrants during  181–2
Croatia  14, 15–16
Cummins, M. & F. Rodriguez  40n1

demand gap  64
demographic ageing
  EU  13, 16, 17–18, 74, 88, 93, 103, 110,
    130, 132–3, 138
Denmark  9, 131–2
  "jewellery law"  131
*Die Zeit*  115, 117
Draghi, M.  68
Dublin Convention/System  123
Dustmann, C. & T. Frattini  23

*Economist, The*  24, 26, 82, 132, 148
Edlund, J.  162
Egypt  137
Ehnts, D.  55, 66, 172n1
Emergency Relocation Mechanism, EU  12
Employers Sanctions Directive  106
Ethiopia  137
EU–Africa Strategic Partnership
  on Migration, Mobility and
  Employment  90
EU asylum policy
  burden sharing  124
  carrier sanctions  118
  Common European Asylum System
    (CEAS)  126–7, 131, 197
  directives on minimum standards  126
  externalization/"external
    solution"  126–7
  historical development of  116, 118
  "more Europe"  122, 135–6
  Qualification Directive  104
  refugee reception capacity-building in
    the EU  126
  return policy  92, 128, 136–8
  visa policy  118
EU external labour migration policy  20,
    76, 130, 168, 186
  Blue Card  18, 100–5, 109–10, 111, 138
  demographic ageing  86, 187

EU competence  74, 95–6
  family reunification  111–12
  horizontal approach to  96
  Intra-Corporate Transferees
    Directive  108–9, 112
  Long-Term Residence
    Directive  97–8, 102
  permanent residence  76–7, 111–12,
    130–2, 188
  Researchers Directive  98–100,
    102, 186–7
  seasonal  76–7
  Seasonal Workers Directive  105–8,
    112–13, 186
  sectoral approach to  96, 186
  Student Directive  98–9
  temporary residence  76–7, 192
  towards Africa  90, 137
  towards north Africa  89, 106
  "volume of admission"  102
  "zero" external labour migration
    policy  7, 84–6, 93
"EU migration" *see* free movement, EU
EU-Turkey Statement  7, 119, 128–9
EUobserver  197
"Europe 2020"  87, 99
European Agenda on Migration  103
European Central Bank (ECB)  66–9
  Outright Monetary Transactions (OMT)
    programme  68, 69
  Securities Market Programme  68
European Coal and Steel Community  82
European Commission  63, 68, 69,
    109–10, 113, 118, 127
  fiscal impact of refugees in
    Sweden  146, **147**
  healthcare expenditure cuts  174–5
  spending on refugees in
    Sweden  159–60
European Council  118
European Council on Refugees and Exiles
    (ECRE)  121, 136
European Court of Justice  191
European Economic and Social
  Committee  96
European Migration Network  75
European Neighbour Policy  90
European Parliament
  "resolution on search and rescue in the
    Mediterranean"  129

European semester  67
European Union External Action
    Service  120
eurozone  66–9, 173, 199
external labour migration policy *see* EU
    external labour migration policy

Fazi, T.  175
Federal Reserve Bank of St Louis  53
Fehr, H., S. Jokisch & L. Kotlikoff  34
fiat currency *see* floating exchange rate
*Financial Times*  119, 148, 175, 188, 194
Fiscal Compact  67, 69
fiscal impact of migration
    political salience of  1–6, 23–8, 194–6
    research findings  33–5, 48, 188, 195
    static and dynamic research approaches
        to  30, 35
fiscal rules  57–8, 63–4, 173–6, 199
    Sweden  141, 143–5, 151–3, 159, 173
fixed exchange rate  53–4, 66
Fladvad, J.  163
floating exchange rate  53–4, 68
Frattini, F.  8, 101
Freeman, G.  44
free movement EU  15, 74, 82, 189–92
    as fiscally unsustainable  189–91
    EU citizenship  15, 20, 190–2
    third country nationals
        (TCNs)  88–9, 112
Friðriksdóttir, B.  103, 112
Folkerts-Landau, D.  4–5
Fondapol  1, 23
"Fortress Europe"  17–18, 130
Fuele, S.  119
functional finance  65, 139, 162,
    167–9, 183–5

Gabriel, S.  141
Germany
    article 16, Basic Law  122–3
    asylum debate in early 1990s  25, 122–4
    Blue Card  103
    demographic ageing  133
    "European Germany"/"German
        Europe"  123
    fiscal impact of refugee spending  149
    fiscal spending, refugees  139–41
    Iraqi refugee reception
        2006–2008  121, 125
    Italian labour migration, postwar West
        Germany  82–3
    labour demand, postwar West
        Germany  82
    labour migration to  11, 111, 188
    neo-Nazi violence  123
    postwar West Germany as
        "overcrowded"  82
    refugees in the labour market  17
    refugees, postwar  78–82, 83–4
    refugee reception 2015  115–17, 132–5,
        139, 199
    Republicaner party  9
    Social Democrats (SPD)  123, 140
Global Approach to Migration and Mobility
    (GAMM), EU  89–90, 99, 106
Global South
    refugee reception in  117, 197
Gnosjö  160
Godley, W.  60
Greece  8
    emigration  14
    postwar Greece as "overcrowded"  82
    public debt  67–8
Greenspan, A.  51–2, 172
*Guardian, The*  24–5
Guiraudon, V.  93–4

Hailbronner  124
*Handelsblatt*  140
Holler, J. & P. Schuster  37
human rights  200
Hungary  9

"illegal migration" *see* irregular migration
India  14
inflation  53, 56, 65, 67
integration of migrants  16
    EU policy on  107
    municipalities in Sweden  162–3, 165–6
*International Business Times*  24
International Monetary Fund (IMF)  68
International Organization for Migration
    (IOM)  129, 195
International Refugee Organization
    (IRO), UN
    emigration policy for postwar Western
        Europe  81
irregular migration
    EU  84–5, 106, 125

Italy 9
  emigration 14, 25
  fiscal policy 175–6
  healthcare 174–5
  irregular migrant 182
  migrants and refugees working in health
    and elderly care 25–6, 77
  population decline in 25
  postwar Italy as "overpopulated" 82
  public debt 67–8
  stagnation 175–6
Ireland
  emigration 14

Japan
  public debt 67
Johansson, M. 27, 133
Joppke, C. 94
Juncker, J.-C. 7, 119
Jämtland 162

Kanther, M. 125–6
Kohl, H. 123
Koser, K. 134
Kramer, I. 17
Kurz, S. 10
Kymlicka, W. 45

labour migrants
  precarious situation of 4
labour migration
  conceptualized 73–8
  member state policy versus
    EU policy 110–11
  sound finance 74–5, 138, 186–7, 192
Lamers, K. & W. Schäuble 191
Lampedusa 89
Latvia 14
Laxå 164–7, 179
"left behind" working class 6
Le Pen, Marine 10
Lerner, A. 65
Libya 89
  EU migration cooperation with 7,
    91, 119–20
  Gaddafi, M. 91, 119–20
Lisbon High-Level Conference on Legal
  Immigration 8
Lisbon Strategy 87

Lisbon Treaty 102
Lithuania 14
Los Angeles Times 133
low-skilled labour migrants
  as costs, "fiscal burdens" 2–3, 34, 37,
    39, 42, 48
Löfven, S. 27, 116, 133, 158

Maizière, T. de 132–3
Malmström, C. 13, 87–8, 108–9, 112, 113,
  119, 132, 190
Mare Nostrum, Operation 129
Mediterranean
  migrant deaths 124–5, 129
Merkel, A. 17, 116, 134, 141
Milanovic, B. 3–5, 38, 42, 43, 44, 192–4
Mitchell, W. 68
Mitchell, W., R. Wray & M. Watts 58
Mitchell, W. & T. Fazi 58, 69
Moback, H. 163
Mobility Partnerships 90
modern monetary theory (MMT) 19,
  196, 198
  borrowing by governments 57–9,
    66, 173
  currency/monetary sovereignty 53–7
  deficit and surplus explained 59–64
  job guarantee 54, 184
  money issuer and money user, distinction
    between 55–7, 59, 64, 66–7
  real and financial resources, distinction
    between 43, 50–2, 70
  role of money in orthodox
    economics 55
  solvency requirement and budget
    constraint explained 52–6, 68
  taxation, currency sovereign central
    governments 56, 173
money multiplier 172n1
Morawiecki, M. 12–14
Morocco 137
Moses, J. 66n6
Muslims
  anti-Muslim racism 9, 11, 17, 135, 197

National Institute of Economic
  Research (Konjunkturinstitutet)
  NIER 146, **147**
neoliberalism 192–4

Netherlands, the   15
Neuman, G.   26, 123
*New York Times*   121
Nielsen, N.   197
Norrköping   185

OECD   23, 25, 77
  fiscal impact of refugees in Sweden   **147**
  refugee spending, impact on growth in
    Sweden   149, 150–1
Operation Sophia, European Union Naval
    Force Mediterranean (EUNAVFOR
    MED)   120
Orbán, V.   16, 117
orthodox economics   2, 5–6, 19, 31,
    172–3, 175–6, 192–6
  budget constraint   31–2, 46–7
  household-government
    analogy   31, 55, 61
  solvency requirement   31
Östersund   163
"overpopulation" in postwar Europe   78, 81

Pawłowicz, K.   12
Peers, S.   96, 109
permanent residence   45, 74–5, 189
Poland   9
  Asian and Muslim labour migration
    to   12, 17
  labour migration to   111
  Law and Justice party and
    government   11–13, 17
  Ukrainian labour migration to   11–17
Polanyi, K.   138, 189
"population exchange"   10, 13
Portugal
  emigration   14
Preston, I.   32, 36
"progressive's dilemma"   44, 46
Putnam, R.   44

racism   16, 195, 197
Reding, V.   190
refugees
  "affordability" of   6, 196
  costs, "fiscal burdens"   1–3, 16, 34–6,
    47, 48, 130, 133, 186, 188, 195
  postwar Europe   78–82
"refugees welcome"   115–16

REMINDER   61
Renzi, M.   118
Riksbank (Sweden's central
    bank)   **147**, 171
Rohingya   128
Roma   10, 191
Romania
  emigration   14, 15
  emigration of medical doctors and
    healthcare workers   77
Romer, D.   31
Rowthorn, R.   30, 33, 35
Ruhs, M.   38, 40
Ruhs, M. & P. Martin   39, 40, 42, 46
Ryan, P.   51

Salvini, M.   25–6
Schengen   7, 123
Schinas, M.   197
Schäuble, W.   117, 122–4, 140–1
Schönhuber, F.   9
Scocco, S.   154n5
seasonal labour migration   182
sectoral balances   60–2
  Spain   61–2
security and migration control   73
  security logic in EU migration
    policy   91–3, 124–8
Seehofer, H.   7, 10, 16, 182
Six Pack   67
Slovakia   9
Söderström, M.   162–3
sound finance *see* orthodox economics
Spahn, J.   134, 140
Spain
  emigration   14
  labour migration to   111
  public debt   68
Spiegel Online   121
Stability and Growth Pact (SGP)   67
Storesletten, K.   32, 27
Streeck, W.   193–4
Støjberg, I.   131–2
Sweden
  cleaners, foreign-born   154, 181–2
  demographic impact of refugees   49,
    155, 157, 168, 181
  economic growth, refugee
    spending   148–50

employment rate 156
fiscal impact of refugee
    spending 141–53, 176–7
fiscal spending, refugees 139,
    141–53, 179–80
healthcare 174
health and elderly care, migrants and
    refugees working in 25, 154, 181, 183
household debt 62–3
Iraqi refugee reception
    2006–2008 120–2
job creation ("extra jobs") 184–5
labour market, foreign-born 154–5
labour recruitment needs 154, 156,
    181, 183
median age, impact of
    migration 156, 181
municipalities, refugees 151–2,
    159–69, 179–80, 183–4
postwar welfare state's relation with
    migration 83
refugees, as fiscal burden 26–8, 157–8,
    169, 181
refugee migration in international
    press 24, 120–2
refugee model 21, 180, 200
refugee reception 2015 115–17, 132–5,
    139, 177
seasonal migration 182
Social Democrats on refugee
    migration 26–8, 158–9, 169
unaccompanied minors,
    refugees 133, 160
unemployment gap between foreign-
    and Swedish-born 156
working-age population, impact of
    migration 155–7, 181
Swedish Association of Local Authorities
    and Regions, SKR 154, 160, 162,
    168, 180
Sweden Democrats 24, 28, 167, 195
Swedish Fiscal Policy Council
    (Finanspolitiska rådet) SFPC 150,
    152–3, 168
    fiscal impact of refugees 144–6, 151, 157
Swedish Government
    central government budget 143–4,
    **147**, 150
Swedish Migration Agency 128

Swedish National Financial Management
    Authority (Ekonomistyrningsverket)
    ESV **147**
    fiscal impact of refugees 141–3
Syria
    refugee crisis 1, 14, 119, 125, 126, 128
Szydło, B. 12

Tampere European Council 87–8, 118,
    126, 136
Task Force Mediterranean, EU 89
temporary residence 122
Teodorovici, E. 14
Therborn, G. 5
Thyssen, M. 87
trade-off between migration and the
    welfare state 3, 6, 26, 38–42, 46–7,
    50, 54–5, 93–4, 188
    postwar Western Europe 83
    Sweden 83, 180
trade-off between recognition and
    redistribution 43–7, 54–5
Treaty of Paris 82
Treaty of Rome 82
Turkey 8, 119, 197
Tusk, D. 7, 118
Two Pack 67

UNHCR (UN Refugee Agency) 196–7
United Kingdom
    asylum policy 125

von der Leyen, U.
    European ασπίδα [English: shield] 7,
    135, 197
Värmland 183

Wallenskog, A. 183
*Washington Post* 121
welfare state in Western Europe
    historical relation with migration 45, 83
West Germany *see* Germany
Winnicki, R. 13
Wray, R. 53, 63–4, 67, 70

Yugoslavia
    refugee crisis 123–4

Zetsche, D. 133